EARLY CHILDHOOD EDUCATION SERIES

NANCY FILE & CHRISTOPHER P. BROWN, EDITORS

ADVISORY BOARD: Jie-Qi Chen, Cristina Gillanders, Jacqueline Jones,
Kristen M. Kemple, Candace R. Kuby, John Nimmo,
Amy Noelle Parks, Michelle Salazar Pérez, Andrew J. Stremmel, Valora Washington

To look for other titles in this series, visit www.tcpress.com

continued

D1519841

Leading Anti-Bias Early Childhood Programs

A Guide to Change, for Change

SECOND EDITION

Louise Derman-Sparks, Debbie LeeKeenan, and John Nimmo

Foreword by Iheoma U. Iruka

TEACHERS COLLEGE PRESS

TEACHERS COLLEGE | COLUMBIA UNIVERSITY
NEW YORK AND LONDON

Published by Teachers College Press,® 1234 Amsterdam Avenue, New York, NY 10027

Excerpts and adaptations from *Anti-Bias Education for Young Children and Ourselves* by Louise Derman-Sparks and Julie Olsen Edwards with Catherine M. Goins, 2020, are used with permission conveyed through Copyright Clearning Center, Inc.
Excerpts in Chapter 4 are used with permission of NAEYC and are from "Being an Equity Leader," John Nimmo, Debbie LeeKeenan, and Louise Derman-Sparks, *Young Children*, Volume 76, Issue 3, 2021, permission conveyed through Copyright Clearning Center, Inc.
Excerpts in Chapter 6 from "Moving Beyond the Anti-Bias Activities: Supporting the Development of Anti-Bias Practice" by L. Kuh, M. Beneke, D. LeeKeenan, and H. Given in Young Children are copyright ©2016 NAEYC®. Reprinted with permission.

Library of Congress Cataloging-in-Publication Data

Names: Derman-Sparks, Louise, author. | LeeKeenan, Debbie, author. |
   Nimmo, John, 1956– author.
Title: Leading anti-bias early childhood programs : a guide to change, for change /
   Louise Derman-Sparks, Debbie LeeKeenan, and John Nimmo ; Foreword by
   Iheoma U. Iruka.
Description: Second edition. | New York, NY : Teachers College Press, [2023] |
   Series: Early childhood education series | Includes bibliographical references and index.
Identifiers: LCCN 2023017179 (print) | LCCN 2023017180 (ebook) | ISBN 9780807768532
   (hardcover) | ISBN 9780807768525 (paperback) | ISBN 9780807781814 (ebook)
Subjects: LCSH: Multicultural education—United States. | Toleration—Study and teaching
   (Early childhood)—United States. | Race discrimination—United States—Prevention.
Classification: LCC LC1099.3 .D465 2024 (print) | LCC LC1099.3 (ebook) |
   DDC 370.117—dc23/eng/20230705
LC record available at https://lccn.loc.gov/2023017179
LC ebook record available at https://lccn.loc.gov/2023017180

ISBN 978-0-8077-6852-5 (paper)
ISBN 978-0-8077-6853-2 (hardcover)
ISBN 978-0-8077-8181-4 (ebook)

Printed on acid-free paper
Manufactured in the United States of America

With my love and profound gratitude to the many anti-bias education activist leaders in the United States and internationally who have inspired me, taught me, thought critically with me,
and were there when I needed help and support. You have been my village.
—Louise

In memory of my mom, Mabel G. Lee, an inspiring public school teacher, and my first teacher and role model.
—Debbie

To Ella and Jack, who continue to teach me about being a dad and who inspire me with their own journeys through life.
—John

To young children everywhere—for the brilliance, joy, and hope they bring to realizing our vision of social justice.
—Louise, Debbie, and John

Contents

Foreword

First the line of progress is never straight. For a period, a movement may follow a straight line and then it encounters obstacles and the path bends. . . . Often it feels as though you are moving backwards and you lose sight of your goal; but in fact you are moving ahead, and soon you will see the city again, closer by.

—Martin Luther King Jr., (1967/2010)

The summer of 2020 will be anchored as one of the lynchpins in America's pernicious fight against systemic racism as the world dealt with the first year of a global pandemic. This dual pandemic of racism and COVID-19 set the stage for Americans and the world to confront the harmful nature of racism and other systems of oppression by protesting the violation of Black persons and other persons of color's rights and civil liberties, which have largely been ignored until now. Many corporations, organizations, agencies, and policymakers moved to confront systemic racism, bias, and other oppressive systems and processes from which early care and education was not immune. It was no longer acceptable to ignore that the systems of education, including early care and education, are rife with racial, gender, and economic inequities.

As is often the case with any racial or economic progress, it is always challenged by those in power with (unearned) privileges, as seen with the conjured-up "anti-CRT movement" and the fight against diversity, equity, and inclusion initiatives, and "not making white children cry in the classroom." However, it is up to us to continue moving the ball up the mountain despite fear tactics, banning diverse books, disinformation and misinformation, and attempting to remove factual histories such as Black History from American books and courses. This fight can't happen without vision and tools.

Leading Anti-Bias Early Childhood Programs: A Guide to Change, for Change is both the vision and the tool we need to continue to fight for progress and justice. It is often easy to dissect and complain about a problem, but finding and leaning into a solution is frequently hard. This book provides us with the tool that we need to move beyond the apathy of slow progress by ensuring that our brain builders—our early childhood administrators, leaders, educators, and advocates—know how they can armor themselves, their programs, and their children with the ability to see injustice and actively challenge and demand equity, justice, and fairness.

The authors remind us that part of creating humanizing early childhood environments is not just about pictures and books, but also about how adults interrogate their beliefs, identity, and privileges. That is, to ensure high-quality early childhood programming, one must commit to unlearning biased ideas of who is superior and intelligent and relearn what it means to value the perspectives, knowledge, and experiences of those who have been systematically silenced and denied.

The reboot of this book comes at the right time when leaders, administrators, families, and advocates are seeking answers on how the summer of 2020 fight for racial justice can move from the streets to the board room, classroom, state houses, and Capitol Hill. It provides a common language, real-life examples for practitioners to engage and lean in, and, most importantly, addresses the tension of anti-bias education as the path forward to ensuring that children experience high-quality early education.

This book is especially critical for our leaders, who are seeking to advance the 3Ps: protection, promotion, and preservation. The text ensures that we can *protect* our children from adversity, trauma, and discrimination; *promote* their mental and social health and access to educational excellence; and *preserve* the culture, language, and positive racial, ethnic, and self-identity of children. This requires all of us to lean into justice-centered education.

Leading Anti-Bias Early Childhood Programs is a must in our treasure trove of tools to ensure that our journey for progress and humanity goes beyond good intentions to "good trouble."

Iheoma U. Iruka

REFERENCE

King, M. L. Jr. (2010). *Where do we go from here: Chaos or community?* Beacon Press. (Original published 1967)

Acknowledgments

Anti-bias education (ABE) is a journey. So, too, is writing collaboratively. As with anti-bias work, it involves hard work, learning from and with one another, sometimes needing to find the third space to resolve different perspectives on an issue, and, always, moving forward. We brought our critical love for each other and our sense of urgency about social justice to this latest revision.

We are mindful that we conceptualized and wrote this second edition of our book on the unceded lands of Native Peoples. We show respect for the First Peoples, past, present, and future, and offer gratitude for the ancestral land we inhabit. John, who lives in Portland, Oregon, acknowledges the land of the Multnomah, Kathlamet, Tumwater, Clackamas, Watlala Band of the Chinook, the Tualatin Kalapuya, and other Indigenous Peoples of the Columbia River. Debbie, who lives in Seattle, Washington, acknowledges the traditional lands of the Coastal Salish Peoples, specifically the Duwamish, Suquamish, Stillaguamish, and Muckleshoot Peoples. And Louise, who lives in Pasadena, California, acknowledges the homelands of the Gabrielieño Band of Mission Indians of the Sisitcanongna Village and Kizh Nation, and the ancestral lands of the Hahamog'na Tongva people. Together, we embrace our responsibility to move beyond recognition to meaningful action in support of Indigenous Peoples' rights and sovereignty.

Much of the first edition of this book was drawn from the experiences of Debbie, as director of the Eliot–Pearson Children's School at Tufts University from 1996 to 2013, and of John, as executive director of the Child Study and Development Center at the University of New Hampshire from 2003 to 2013. We recognize and extend our immense gratitude to all the staff, teachers, faculty, families, and children who attended the programs during that time. Thank you for all the questions, insights, learning, and love. Over the past 7 years, we have been engaged in sharing these ideas through film, publications, and presentations with thousands of leaders and educators across the United States and internationally. This work includes our conversations with teachers, directors, and families for our film *Reflecting on Anti-Bias Education in Action: The Early Years* (LeeKeenan, Nimmo, & McKinney, 2021) and our forthcoming film focused on how families engage with ABE. In this second edition, we bring that collective learning to bear, along with the stories we collected recently from talking with diverse ECCE leaders, including our colleagues Julie Bisson, Tashon McKeithan, Rukia Rogers, Karina Rojas Rodriguez, Ellen Wolpert, and Miriam Zmiewski-Angelova.

Together, we thank Mary Ellen Larcarda and Sarah Jubar, our editors at Teachers College Press, who showed us much-appreciated support and encouragement. We also are indebted to the helpful suggestions and efforts of the publications and marketing staff at the Press. We are deeply grateful to Iheoma Iruka for her foreword to our book. Her research and writing both compliment and stretch our thinking and practice.

We send heartfelt thanks to the many colleagues in the United States and internationally with whom we have worked over so many years. We are indebted to all of you for deepening and expanding our understanding of what equity and social justice mean—what differs contextually and what we hold in common. A special shout-out to Julie Olsen Edwards, who is Louise's steadfast soul sister and colleague of many, many years.

Our families supported us in big and small ways. I (Debbie) thank my husband, Chris, for taking this journey of being my life partner in the joys and challenges of being a multiracial family. Thank you for your love and support. To my children, Jason and Kira, and my granddaughters, Tabatha, Maya, and Raya, I send my love and thank you for being my inspiration and motivation to do this work. I (John) send admiration to my wife, Shelly, who was with me on the anti-bias journey at our alma mater, Pacific Oaks College, 35 years ago and continues to share insights from her work with children, students, and families. To our children, Ella and Jack, I send my love for the optimism and hope they give me for the coming generations. I (Louise), as always, thank Bill, Doug, and Sean for their lifetime support.

Finally, we, Debbie and John, extend our deep appreciation to our mentor and friend, Louise. Her vision and wisdom inspired us to lead anti-bias efforts in our programs and to embark on and continue this journey of documentation.

Leading Anti-Bias Early Childhood Programs

Introduction

Our hope for creative living in this world house that we have inherited lies in our ability to reestablish the moral ends of our lives in personal character and social justice.

—Martin Luther King Jr. (in C. S. King, 1983, p. 58)

In preparing this second edition, we have been conscious of how the illusion of a post-racial society has clearly evaporated, even as there have been significant advances in affirming the rights of those who have been historically oppressed. Much has happened in the past 7 years that has changed the landscape of our social justice efforts in early education. In the light of resounding protests against racial injustice, the urgency of anti-bias education (ABE) is doubly clear. We see a greater willingness by leaders and educators in the early childhood care and education (ECCE) field to learn, to take risks, and to do more to seek social justice for children, families, and communities—even in the face of escalating pushback and opposition at all levels of society. As we emerge from the COVID-19 pandemic and the spotlight it shone on inequity, disability justice activist Alice Wong (2022) offers hopeful wisdom for us as ECCE leaders, declaring, "[Now is] our chance to re-envision the world, a world centered on justice, liberation, interdependence, mutual care, and mutual respect" (p. 335).

In this second edition we offer an expanded conceptual framework, along with additional strategies and practical tools for leaders who are initiating and growing anti-bias early childhood programs. The book builds upon the solid foundation laid by current thinking about best early childhood leader practices, while extending them to incorporate the specific elements of anti-bias education work. Our own experiences in building and leading successful anti-bias education programs and in working with diverse leaders and teachers in the United States and other countries ground our writing. In this second edition, we are joined by program leaders of diverse early childhood programs across the United States who generously shared their collective wisdom and practice with us.

Although we are aware of the many resources available for early childhood teachers seeking to introduce ABE in their classrooms, there continues to be much less on the complex work of the leaders who set the stage for this approach. Together, we updated this second edition for anyone who is already familiar with anti-bias education and wants to learn about what it takes to be an anti-bias leader of ECCE programs. This includes directors, managers, administrators, principals, and administrators of agencies—everyone who supervises early

1

childhood programs. It will also be useful to the people who educate teachers and school leaders, including college faculty, teacher trainers, and coaches/mentors, as well as individual teachers who want to understand what creating an anti-bias program involves.

What our book does *not* directly address is how to implement anti-bias education with young children. Leading an ABE program requires having a solid knowledge base about its classroom implementation and the strategies to share this information with teachers and families. To expand your understanding of what it means to integrate an anti-bias approach into the children's learning environment and curriculum, we refer you to several resources that directly explore that subject as part of the professional development strategies described in Chapter 4. In addition, our online appendices at www.tcpress.com include recommended book and website resources on ABE (see Appendix A), as well as additional tools that are referenced in this second edition and can be downloaded for your use.

ORGANIZATION OF THIS BOOK

We have found that developing programs based on anti-bias education principles is a multifaceted undertaking requiring both organizational and educational change. It is doable—but only with persistence, time, and strategic thinking. Those realities are reflected in the content of this book. Many of the stories and examples are based on Debbie's and John's experiences over the course of their long careers as teachers and directors in various ECCE settings, as well as those of the directors we interviewed. The details of stories have been changed or stories made into composites to protect anonymity and to help illustrate particular concepts and ideas. In addition, we have interspersed comments collected from teachers and parents at ECCE centers throughout the chapters to bring their voices into our exploration of anti-bias change.

Chapter 1 lays out key concepts that underlie the building of anti-bias ECCE programs. Chapter 2 reviews current research and thinking about the best practices for early childhood program leaders. It also notes how these practices set a foundation for effective anti-bias leadership. Chapter 3 explores the work of "reading the program" as an essential prelude to commencing strategic anti-bias education leadership. It describes relevant information to collect, provides tools for making sense of what you find, and suggests some basic preparatory steps. Chapters 4 and 5 discuss specific issues and strategies for program leaders working with staff and families. Chapter 6 builds on the themes of these two chapters, with professional development strategies for integrating, deepening, and sustaining anti-bias work after staff have come to understand and practice its fundamentals. This chapter also considers what program leaders can do to strengthen teachers' skills for working with families on anti-bias issues.

We then turn in Chapter 7 to the issue of productively managing the inevitable disequilibrium and conflicts that arise in anti-bias work as part of the dynamics of change. This chapter also addresses dealing with opposition from outside an ECCE program that leaders may encounter as they seek greater equity and inclusion. In Chapter 8 we discuss strategies for documenting and assessing progress in a program and staff's anti-bias transformation. We also relate strategies that leaders in diversity and equity work draw on to meet the challenges of standards. Finally, in our epilogue, we consider how to sustain our journey toward a vision of social justice in ECCE. We offer reflections from each of us and from the program leaders who shared their own ABE journeys throughout this new edition of our book.

We recognize that the terms people use in diversity, equity, and inclusion (DEI) work vary, depending on their analysis of issues and strategies for addressing the issues. In addition, the same term may have different meanings that reflect people's diverse viewpoints, identities and contexts. In Figure I.1 we provide our updated definitions of the main terms found throughout the chapters with the understanding that language is a dynamic and evolving medium.

Figure I.1. Definitions of Terms

Anti-bias education (ABE). An approach that includes addressing children's development of intersecting social identities, social–emotional relationships with people different from oneself, prejudice, discrimination, critical thinking, and taking action for fairness with and by children. This educational approach includes an emphasis on adult anti-bias growth and understanding of the systemic dynamics of oppression (e.g., racism, classism, etc.), and alignment with other approaches to seeking social justice such as anti-racism and disability justice. Throughout this book we also incorporate *culturally sustaining care and education* (defined below) within the ABE concept.

BIPoC (Black, Indigenous, and People of Color). This recent acronym and term are intended to include the range of groups targeted by systemic racism in the United States. In addition to Black and Indigenous peoples, the term also includes Asian American, Native Hawaiian, Pacific Islanders (AANHPI), Middle Eastern, and Latinx peoples. The BIPoC term also highlights the core position of Black and Indigenous peoples in discussions about race and racism. In the text, we also use the original meaning of the term People of Color (PoC), which refers to all the groups included under the new term BIPoC, when it is referenced in our interviews or cited sources.

Culturally sustaining care and education. A framework and approach in which the program's pedagogy, curriculum, and environment are not only *responsive* and *relevant* to differences in the culture of all individuals and groups, but also *sustain* diverse communities and cultures that have faced marginalization (Paris & Alim, 2017). Historically, schools have only reflected the dominant culture (see below under "Privileged culture" definition) and have expected other groups to assimilate.

Disability. There is current debate about whether to use language that is "people-first" (person with a disability; child who is deaf) or "identity-first" (disabled person; Deaf child) (C.W. Morgan et al., 2022). While it is always important to be guided by what the person or community involved prefers, we have intentionally used identity-first language in this book to honor the person or community's embrace of disability as integral to their identity.

(continued)

Figure I.1. (*continued*)

Diversity. We use this term in its broadest sense—inclusive of all people's intersecting racial, ethnic, familial, cultural, gendered, linguistic, class, sexual, religious, and ability identities. Diversity exists in the differences *among* people and groups. It is not a term that refers to some people and not to others.

Diversity, equity, and inclusion (DEI) education. An umbrella term for a range of educational approaches, all of which address various facets of diversity, inclusion, and equity. Anti-bias education is one such approach included under this umbrella. We include the necessity of equity in the power relationships and dynamics between people of different backgrounds. This means that everyone gets an equivalent place at the table and opportunities to use their voice.

Early childhood care and education (ECCE). While often used interchangeably with *early childhood education (ECE)*, we believe that ECCE is a more inclusive term because it encompasses child care, family child care, preschools, and other education and care institutions serving young children. The acronym is used throughout the book.

Family. We primarily use this term instead of *parents and/or guardians.* It is a more inclusive way to describe the realities of the diversity of children's primary caregivers and relationships within the home.

Leader/leadership. In this book we specifically focus on the role of *positional* leaders in ECCE programs, that is, those responsible for the supervision and development of staff, policy development, and broad oversight of the program mission and vision. We also recognize the importance of supporting and developing the *leadership* capacity of staff and family members when seeking to create deep and enduring change in values, structures, and practice (i.e., *distributed/democratic* leadership).

Marginalized (subordinate, minoritized, target) culture. In U.S. society, peoples from specific social identity groups are pushed to the "margins" of society by systemic rules, structures, languages, and worldviews that deny access to economic and political power, opportunity, and outcome. The term "minoritized" indicates that these power inequities are not the result of simply being in the minority.

Privileged (dominant, mainstream, majority, agent) culture. The term used to refer to the rules, values, language, and worldview of the groups with economic and political power in a society. In the United States, the privileged or dominant group has historically been White, Christian, affluent, heterosexual, cisgender, able-bodied, and male. This privileged group defines its way of life as the "normal" and the right way to live, and judges others who differ from this standard.

Program(s). An inclusive term for the range of group care and education programs serving young children, including preschools, schools, after-school programs, and child care centers. While the approach and strategies described in this book can be adapted for use in family child care and other home-based settings, they are most relevant to institutions with a number of staff and serving larger groups of children and families.

Program leader. We use this term to be inclusive of a wide range of specific terms for this professional role (as noted above under the term *Leader*), including *director, center manager*, and *principal*. This terminology reflects the diverse organizational forms that early childhood care and education takes. In some programs this executive role may be shared by more than one person.

Figure I.1. (*continued*)

Social justice. We view social justice as the *aspirational* goal of anti-bias education; it is a vision of society in which all peoples are fully visible, able to participate and contribute to society, and have equitable access to power and resources. In early childhood care and education, social justice means that all children will have access to and experience equitable education and the resources that sustain it.

Staff. All the employees in the ECCE program—teachers as well as the business manager, administrative assistant, cook, nurse, and so on. We use *teachers* to refer to staff members who have some form of classroom teaching responsibility, including assistant teachers, aides, and interns. *Educators* is used as a broader term that includes teachers and other personnel with educational responsibilities, such as educational coordinators, assistant directors, and special education leaders.

MEET THE AUTHORS AND CONTRIBUTORS

This book comes out of our personal and professional journeys pursuing the vision of anti-bias education. As leaders of early childhood centers, Debbie (she/her) and John (he/him) were engaged in the work of initiating, growing, and sustaining anti-bias education programs for many years. Louise (she/her) has been writing, teaching, and speaking about anti-bias education with early childhood teachers throughout the United States and internationally since 1989. The following mini-biographies describe the life and work influences that shaped who we are and informed our professional journeys. Our stories are followed by brief biographical notes to introduce the six remarkable program leaders whose thinking and practice appear throughout this second edition of the book.

Debbie's Story (she/her)

I come to social justice work from my professional experience as an educator, but also my personal experiences as a Chinese American born in New York City, of an immigrant working-class family, who opened a Chinese restaurant and Chinese laundry. Growing up in predominately White communities during the 1950s and 1960s, I experienced discrimination and prejudice, but also the power of activism through the civil rights movement. I still remember on the first day of 3rd grade on a new school playground. A child came up to me and said, "Last year we had a Mexican. What do we got this year?" No one said anything—not the teachers, the other children, or the playground monitors. Everyone just stared. I knew then that I would be a teacher. I won't let anyone be treated or feel so bad. I met my husband, an Irish American, in college; we have two adult children and three multiracial granddaughters. Finding communities to raise our children that were accepting of differences was important to us. After 65 years on the East Coast, I moved with my husband to Seattle to be part of the "village" caring for our granddaughters.

My personal experiences led me to work in diverse communities from Bolivia to Taiwan, Hong Kong, and New Mexico and to the inner cities of Philadelphia,

New York, and Boston. Diversity and anti-bias work was the framework I lived and brought to the classroom, whether my students were children, families, teenagers, or college students.

As director of the Eliot–Pearson Children's School (EPCS) at Tufts University in Medford, Massachusetts, for 17 years, I had the opportunity to think strategically about shifting the whole program to an anti-bias perspective. As a BIPoC leader, I did not want my staff to just "do" anti-bias work because it was important to me, but because it was the right thing to do. The leader provides the vision and direction, but the motivation for change needs to bubble up, not just trickle down. When I first came to the school, it was known for its inclusion model of integrating disabled children with typically developing children. One of the first strategic shifts I did was to expand the definition of inclusion to include all kinds of differences. Ability differences became another kind of difference at the school.

I have learned that conflict is inevitable; it is not to be avoided or feared. While my Chinese culture emphasized not rocking the boat, and keeping peace and harmony, my professional experience taught me that conflict and tension are when growth happens. We may have different viewpoints, but when we struggle together, and really listen, we are often surprised. Now I guide leaders to create communities that not only support differences but also support a climate that allows discomfort around conflict and risk-taking. Writing this book with Louise and John, and producing the film *Reflecting on Anti-Bias Education in Action: The Early Years* (LeeKeenan, Nimmo, & McKinney, 2021), has been a capstone of my work life.

John's Story (he/him)

As a White Australian with European heritage, my beginnings in the 1950s and 1960s were marked by middle- and upper-class (unearned) privileges and hearing stories of family trees proudly rooted in the nobility of Scotland and Germany. As the son of a small-town doctor, I recall the status afforded to my family and the entitlement of attending a Christian boarding school for boys in the city. My economic class provided opportunities to travel and interact with cultures different from my own. I vividly remember the silence I received from those around me when I, as a young child, made naive observations and raised questions about human difference. It was during my adolescence and teacher education that I began to question injustice; I marched with the student union and rallied for gay rights.

As a cisgender, bisexual male in the early childhood field (one of only a few men at that time in Australia), I became focused passionately on issues of sexism and homophobia in my profession and the broader society. My decade as a preschool teacher and director in Australia included contact with families from differing backgrounds. Looking back, my assumptions, experience, and knowledge meant that these differences often remained invisible in my classroom and consciousness. I recall now with disbelief that I dressed up each year as Santa Claus for Christmas celebrations at my Australian preschool—oblivious to the message of exclusion.

While I was at home with liberal views, my sojourn to Pacific Oaks College in California for graduate work brought me into contact with the U.S. cultural milieu. The strong women mentors there (including Louise Derman-Sparks) challenged me to examine my identity, and introduced me to the work of Paulo Freire. Later, my education continued as a faculty member at the Pacific Oaks campus in Seattle for a decade, where I had the confronting experience of being the only White male on a multicultural staff. During this time, I was a member of the Culturally Relevant Anti-Bias Education Leadership group and performed in the Seattle Theater of Liberation troupe. Most significantly, I embarked with my partner on the journey of raising two children with social justice values.

From 2003 to 2013, I made the leap between theory and practice as the executive director of the Child Study and Development Center at the University of New Hampshire. While explicit about my intentions, I soon realized that I would face many challenges in a setting where diversity was often hidden or nonexistent. This situation drove home the importance of identifying allies who could help me in initiating change. In the last decade, now a professor at Portland State University, I have found film to be a powerful medium to engage the minds and hearts of educators and families. In collaboration with Debbie, I have had the opportunity to produce films that bring anti-bias education to life in all its glorious messiness.

Louise's Story (she/her)

I have been an educator and activist for social justice for much of my 83 years. I grew up in a White, Jewish American, working-class family in Brooklyn and Manhattan, New York City. I learned about activism from an early age, by observing and listening and by accompanying my parents on some of their community activism work. I went to public schools from kindergarten through college. In elementary and junior high school, a few very good teachers illuminated the possibilities of caring and meaningful education. I was fortunate to attend a high school more diverse than most in New York City at that time, and with the civil rights and anti-nuclear-bomb movements blossoming, I began becoming an activist in my own right.

Over the many years of doing social justice and anti-bias work, I have had to come to a critical understanding of the multiple parts of my identity—especially my racial, class, and gender identities. While the anti-racism movement challenged me to critically examine my role on the *privileged* side of societal power, the women's movement challenged me, as a woman, to comprehend the *marginalized* side of societal power. On the other hand, being heterosexual gave me societal legitimacy and important legal rights. In my family of origin, I was working-class. As a college professor—a different socioeconomic status—I continued to identify with my working-class and activist roots.

I come to this book with a perspective honed by my scores of years working in early childhood education. I began as a teacher of 3- and 4-year-olds in the Perry Preschool Project in Ypsilanti, Michigan. My one experience as an early childhood program director was brief, when I led a small cooperative child care center for 3 years. It was there that I first began exploring children's thinking about diversity and fairness—seeds that ultimately grew into the anti-bias curriculum approach. Then my many years as a faculty member at Pacific Oaks College enabled me to study, collaborate, teach, and write about the interwoven issues of identity and attitude development and change in both children and adults. Since the 1989 publication of *Anti-Bias Curriculum: Tools for Empowering Young Children* (Derman-Sparks & The Anti-Bias Taskforce, 1989), which we developed at Pacific Oaks College and Children's School, I have had the very informative and exhilarating opportunity to talk with thousands of early childhood educators and observe outstanding anti-bias education in the United States and several other countries. These learning encounters convinced me of the pivotal role of the program leader in growing anti-bias education in their particular settings.

Contributors From the Field

Julie Bisson

I am a White, second-generation Italian American woman. I grew up in rural Connecticut, where my peers looked like me. Moving to Los Angeles and later Seattle broadened my experiences with human diversity and cemented my commitment to anti-bias education. I have been in the field of ECCE for 35+ years. My 20 years leading programs includes being director since 2011 of Epiphany Early Learning Preschool in Seattle, Washington. We have a diverse community of 60 children (toddlers to 5 years) and 22 staff in our full-day, year-round program.

Tashon McKeithan

I have worked in public and private education for almost 30 years and have dedicated my life to teaching for equity. I identify as an African American cisgender woman and mother of a biracial, pansexual, special-needs woman king. Since 2020, I have served as the executive director of the Child Educational Center, an educational nonprofit with seven sites located across La Canada and Pasadena in California.

Rukia Rogers

My story is part of the ongoing journey of my ancestors. Born in the Midwest, I hold Southern and African roots. I have worked with young children and their families for over 25 years, including work as a preschool and toddler teacher, a studio teacher, and a curriculum coordinator. I am inspired by the educators of Reggio Emilia, bell hooks, Bettina Love, Dr. Martin Luther King Jr., and many others who saw education as a fundamental right, as well as a catalyst for social change. I founded The Highlander School in Atlanta in 2013, a nature-centered program committed to anti-bias work and cultivating a community full of love.

Karina Rojas Rodriguez

I was born in Aguascalientes, Mexico, and grew up in Tukwila, Washington. I work in a diverse community of culturally and linguistic learners in West Seattle. My school, Southwest Early Learning Bilingual Preschool, where I have been since 2009, is 100% city-funded by the Seattle Preschool Program, serving a dual-language Spanish/English model. As a center director my goal is for children, families, and educators to know where they stand with their language, culture, and identity and to feel validated in our learning community. Our center serves 66 families with 14 exceptional educators.

Ellen Wolpert

My career in early childhood education spanned 45 years. As a white Jewish woman, I grew into being an activist for equity. During 13 years as the director of the Washington-Beech Community Preschool in a racially mixed public housing development in Boston, together with a diverse staff, we worked to create an anti-bias, anti-racist environment and educational program for children, families, and ourselves.

Miriam Zmiewski-Angelova

Originally from Chicago, I am an Afro-Indigenous mother of two, educational consultant, activist, and Early Learning Coach for the City of Seattle Department of Education and Early Learning. I formerly served as the director of Daybreak Star Preschool. I am currently a co-founder of a parent-led cooperative called the Native Family Learning Lodge. For nearly 25 years, I have dedicated my life to creating nurturing, inclusive, and culturally affirming spaces for young children, and their families, as well as birthing people.

*   *   *

Now, together we embark on the lessons we have learned about the journey of leading and building an anti-bias ECCE program. Join us—and through your own endeavors, add further knowledge and insights about the leader's role in this essential work of seeking social justice alongside children, families, and all those committed to this vision.

CHAPTER 1

Pursuing the Anti-Bias Vision
The Conceptual Framework

> Dominator culture has tried to keep us all afraid, to make us choose safety instead of risk, sameness instead of diversity. Moving through that fear, finding out what connects us, reveling in our differences; this is the process that brings us closer, that gives us a world of shared values, of meaningful community.
>
> —bell hooks (2004, p.197)

Literally millions of children in the United States from diverse heritage and backgrounds live a significant part of their childhoods in early childhood programs (Cui & Natzke, 2021). While the COVID-19 pandemic disrupted child care attendance and has highlighted inequities in access and resources, the diversity among children attending these programs, particularly in public settings, continues to reflect the nation's changing demographic realities (Paschall et al., 2020). The children's abilities, cultures, religions, languages, and family structures bring both vibrancy and complexities to our communities. Ensuring that ECCE programs are places where all children and families are visible and thrive requires educators to pursue an unyielding commitment to equity, inclusion, and social justice. Anti-bias education (ABE) (see our definition in Figure I.1 in the Introduction) can play a significant role in this pursuit. Program leaders are central to building the ABE programs that can make this commitment to social justice a reality for all young children and their families.

In this first chapter we discuss ideas and issues underlying and impacting the philosophy and practice of anti-bias education. These include: (1) what is at the heart of anti-bias education, (2) what it takes organizationally to become an anti-bias program, (3) what adults need to know in order to pursue an ABE approach, (4) the phases of the anti-bias journey, and (5) how issues that are contested ground in ECCE impact ABE.

REVISITING ANTI-BIAS EDUCATION

The heart of anti-bias education is a vision of a world in which all children and families can become successful, contributing members of their society. To achieve this goal, they need to experience affirmation of all their identities and cultural ways of being, and learn how to live and work together in diverse and inclusive environments (Derman-Sparks et al., 2020). The anti-bias vision incorporates the basic human rights described in the United Nations Convention on the Rights of the Child (UNICEF, 1990), which embrace the right to an identity, to be free from discrimination, to express opinions, and to participate actively in the community. In their *Advancing Equity in Early Childhood Education Position Statement*, the National Association for the Education of Young Children (NAEYC) (2019b) affirms that "all children have the right to equitable learning opportunities that enable them to achieve their full potential as engaged learners and valued members of society" (p. 5).

However, this vision for children that is at the heart of ABE is grounded in the reality that institutions in U.S. society, such as housing, health, law, and schooling, are structured by the dominant culture. Access to power and resources is defined by race, ability, language, and other social identities (Meek et al., 2020). NAEYC (2019b) argues that "advancing the right to equitable learning opportunities requires recognizing and dismantling the systems of bias that accord privilege to some and are unjust to others" (p. 5). ECCE program leaders' commitment to social justice values extends beyond the classroom and into their interactions with adults, including staff, parents, and community members.

Anti-bias education supports children in developing a fuller, truer understanding of themselves and the world, and strengthens their sense of themselves as capable, empowered people. They have a better opportunity to develop curiosity, openness to multiple perspectives, and critical-thinking skills. They can also develop their ability to resist and reject the harm that prejudice, misinformation, and discrimination can do to their sense of competence and efficacy. ABE rejects a deficit view of children (and families) and instead centers their strengths (Wright & Counsell, 2018). These social-emotional and cognitive abilities increase the likelihood that children of all backgrounds will be able to navigate the larger worlds of school and community more constructively and effectively.

The core goals of anti-bias education form a framework for guiding practice in a program's learning environment, curriculum, child–teacher interactions, and family relationships. These goals take into account the body of research about how children construct their identities and attitudes and about the impact of "isms," particularly racism, on these developmental processes. Such research about children has been accumulating for more than 70 years (e.g., Aboud et al., 2012; Beneke, 2021; Clark, 1963; Clark & Clark, 1947; Goodman, 1952; Hirschfeld, 2012; Katz, 1976; Kaufman & Wiese, 2012; Park, 2011; Raabe & Beelmann, 2011; Tatum, 2017; Williams & Steele, 2019; Yu, 2020).

While embracing the critical role of anti-racist approaches given the endemic nature of racism in U.S. society (Escayg, 2018; Iruka et al., 2020; Iruka et al., 2023; Nash et al., 2018; White & Wanless, 2019), ABE considers the early childhood years as a time when children are also examining and making sense of multiple intersecting social identities and the biases they encounter in the world.

The following four anti-bias education goals, adopted by NAEYC (2019b, p.5), are for children of all identities, family backgrounds, and communities, and each goal interacts with and builds on the others:

> *Goal 1*: Identity. Children will demonstrate self-awareness, confidence, family pride, and positive social identities.
> *Goal 2*: Diversity. Children will express comfort and joy with human diversity, use accurate language for human differences, and form deep, caring human connections across all dimensions of human diversity.
> *Goal 3*: Justice. Children will increasingly recognize unfairness (injustice), have language to describe unfairness, and understand that unfairness hurts.
> *Goal 4*: Activism. Children will demonstrate a sense of empowerment and the skills to act, with others or alone, against prejudice and/or discriminatory actions. (Derman-Sparks et al., 2020, p. 5)

These ABE goals for children are accompanied by the four parallel goals teachers need to pursue to support children's learning and development (Derman-Sparks et al., 2020, p. 5).

BECOMING AN ANTI-BIAS PROGRAM

An anti-bias program puts diversity, equity, and inclusion goals at the center of all aspects of its organization and daily life. It involves much more than adding new materials and activities into the already existing learning environment. Rather, broad systemic changes are necessary. The learning environment and curriculum, as well as program policies, structures, procedures, and processes, all come into play. Change also includes the perspectives and attitudes of all the program stakeholders. Rather than a series of events, the program undertakes a journey.

Significant organizational change requires shared commitments, a collaborative process, and facilitation. Change also calls for program leader/s and staff to pursue their own consciousness-raising (Souto-Manning, 2013). While the urgency to implement anti-bias education is great from the perspective of the children's needs, the process of change happens over time; an anti-bias education leader must plan for the long haul. Successful anti-bias education change needs an intentional and thoughtful strategic approach.

Two central dynamics of organizational change come into play. One is shifting the cultural core of the program; the second is recognizing the impact of the process of change on the stakeholders. As the program leader, you have a primary role in facilitating both dynamics.

Shifting the Culture of the ECCE Program

While the importance of culturally sustaining ECCE programs is a major theme in the field, too many early childhood programs continue to ground their environment, curriculum, teaching styles, and language in the dominant culture (defined in Figure I.1 in the Introduction). Staff and families may act out societal power relationships of advantage and disadvantage and socially prevalent biases, even if they are not aware of what is happening. Research has documented the implicit racial and gender biases of ECCE teachers that lead to disproportionate disciplining and expulsion of BIPoC children (Blackson et al., 2022; Gilliam et al., 2016).

The dynamics of dominant-culture–centered early childhood programs push other viewpoints to the margins—even when the majority of families at the program come from other cultural backgrounds. This means that many young children experience two differing cultural contexts every day. Worse, children may experience their home or heritage culture as invisible or inferior. When teachers use child development norms and criteria based on dominant group culture to judge the ability of children from other cultural groups, the teachers are hindered in seeing the actual developmental abilities and growth of many children (Long et al., 2015). This dynamic automatically privileges children from the dominant culture group and marginalizes children from nondominant groups.

The more discontinuity young children face, the more likely they are to find that what they are learning in their family about how to be in the world, including their heritage language, does not work for them outside their family. The lack of familiarity with a program's practices makes it harder for them to adjust, to build strong relationships, to act and feel competent, and to feel secure. Conversely, the more continuity between home and school a child experiences, the better able they are to be active, competent participants, and to feel respected for who they are.

Minimizing cultural discontinuity between home and school programs and eliminating indicators of discounting or prejudice against a child's home and heritage culture foster an equitable playing field for all the children (Gay, 2018). Young children thrive when their early childhood program integrates their home languages and cultures into all of its operations. Developmentally and culturally appropriate programs pay attention to the social and cultural contexts in which each child lives, and not just to a child's individual characteristics (NAEYC, 2019a, 2022).

Building an anti-bias ECCE program requires shifting the dominant-culture core of a program's thinking, organizational structures, and practice. It means intentionally moving to a many-cultures, anti-bias approach. Shifting the culture of a program brings groups at the margin of ECCE theory and practice into the center of all that happens (Anderson, 2006). This process of change also requires deconstructing the dominant and traditional approaches to ECCE to incorporate other stories and ways of thinking and doing.

Shifting the culture of a program calls for a broad vision of equity and inclusion and an intentional effort to create change. It demands attention to the seemingly small and everyday details of a program's life, as well as to the broader structures, relationships, and teaching practices. An anti-bias program continually evolves as the composition and structure of the program changes. Doing all of this requires strong leadership and engagement from the various stakeholders in the program or organization.

Recognizing the Responses to Change

Change inevitably brings disequilibrium, dissonance, and conflicts—until specific changes become part of everyday life. There will likely be differences about what to change and how to carry out agreed-upon changes, or even whether to change at all.

Some program stakeholders (e.g., staff, families, administration) may fear that creating a program where the dominant culture shares space with other perspectives is a threat to their own rights, even though the goal is for *everyone* to have a voice and place. Similarly, some may fear that a shift away from the dominant culture approach requires abandoning all they have previously learned about creating quality early childhood programs. Staff or family members who fear loss of their own way of life or of program quality may try to push back against change. The discomforts of disequilibrium challenge people to search for solutions that will bring equilibrium again—either retreating to the safety of familiar ways or, hopefully, searching for fresh perspectives. Finding ways to move the organization and its individual members closer to anti-bias education goals is a crucial part of the anti-bias education leadership role.

Even when everyone wants change, people will still experience disequilibrium. Inevitably, disagreements will arise about which aspects of the policy, structures, and curriculum to work on and with what strategies. The organization's stakeholders may want different timetables. Some may want to shift the culture of the program faster than the rest of the staff are willing to take on. Some may want it to take longer or have a different sequence.

Even in the midst of change, the pull to keep things as they are (the status quo) will arise. We compare this dynamic to the function of the default mode on a computer. If the font of a computer is changed from its default mode to another font, the computer reverts to the default the next time it is used. Making change rarely follows a clean, linear course of action. A program may make progress in one arena, but hit pushback to change in another. From time to time, everyone needs a brief respite before taking up the challenge once again. External events, such as changing demographics in the neighborhood, may open up and support changes on a specific aspect of diversity, or they may create bumps in the road.

CHANGING ADULT CONSCIOUSNESS AND BEHAVIOR

Realistically, ECCE practitioners who have been absorbing their families' and societal assumptions, stereotypes, and prejudices about human identity since childhood cannot be expected to suddenly teach children not to absorb these same beliefs and attitudes (Matias, 2016). And yet that is exactly what a program leader may expect.

The learning goals for adults reflect current thinking about identity as a combination of social group memberships and individual life experiences. Exploring and deepening an individual's understanding of one's own and others' social identities and their influence on perspectives and behaviors are important components of becoming effective anti-bias educators.

Social Identities

William Cross's (1991) pioneering analysis of the studies of Black identity development compellingly argued for a societal component to self-concept. Calling it "reference group orientation," in contrast to "personal identity," Cross used these two categories to reconceptualize thinking about the impact of racism on Black Americans' identities. His work remains central to anti-bias education. In this book, we use the term *social identity* instead of *reference group orientation*.

Everyone has many social identities in addition to (and connected to) an individual personal identity. Social identities connect individuals to larger groups beyond their family. They comprise characteristics such as people's racial and ethnic identity, gender, culture, religion, language, economic class, family structure, sexual orientation, and abilities, as these characteristics are defined by the society in which people live. Social identities play a significant role in how an individual is seen and treated by others, and they affect access to the society's institutions, such as education, health, and the legal system (Derman-Sparks et al., 2020). For all of us, these social identities intersect with one another, creating more complexity in how we experience society (Crenshaw, 1991). For instance, being Indigenous *and* being an autistic person could mean that culturally appropriate accommodations are even more difficult to access. For John, as an immigrant to the United States *and* an English-speaking White man, he was very aware of the preferential treatment he received at the immigration office compared to people who spoke a language other than English and had brown skin.

How an individual feels about and experiences their various social identities may stand in opposition to the societal realities of privilege and marginalization connected to them. For example, social discrimination and negative messages about being working-class do not necessarily stop people from being personally proud of their family story. We have found it helpful to differentiate between two dimensions of group identity. One key dimension is society's imposition of how identities are defined and the rules that govern access to institutional power and privilege. At the same time, another dimension is how we think and feel about our membership in the families and communities that we grew up in. We may hold these groups close to our hearts and important to who we are in the world. We do not necessarily get the same messages about ourselves from these two dimensions. For many people, the same group membership might be viewed through *both* the lens of positive self and community definition (how I and my community see me) *and* through society's biases and oppressive construction of one's identities.

The definitions and ideas about various social identities are not a static situation. Because of movements for social justice, as well as specific social-political-economic dynamics, the definition, criteria, and specific privileges or inequities connected to social identities have legally changed throughout U.S. history. One example is the changes in women's rights to property, education, the vote, and jobs. Another is the changing status and rights of people who are gay, lesbian, transgender, or bisexual to marry and receive partner benefits. We also recognize that these advances can be followed by backsliding, such as the recent limits on reproductive health and transgender rights. These changes in human rights transform how individuals think about themselves and how others view them.

Adult Learning Goals

While children are always at the heart of ABE, adults' growth on anti-bias issues is vital to children's learning. The ABE goals for adults affect our conversations, interactions, and activism with colleagues, parents, and other caregivers, and necessarily extend into our lives outside the ECCE classroom, out into the broader community. Adults bear great responsibility for seeking social justice in society; these discussions and actions with other adults will also inform our work with young children and families. For instance, a program director might join a book club in an intensive discussion with colleagues of Imani Perry's (2019) book *Breathe: A Letter to My Son* and then take those insights into how they interact with BIPoC families at their program.

Four anti-bias learning goals for adults parallel the goals for children:

1. *Identity:* Increase your awareness and understanding of your own social identity in its many facets (race, ethnicity, gender, ability, sexual orientation, family structure, economic class) and your own cultural contexts, both in your childhood and currently.
2. *Diversity.* Examine what you have learned about differences, connection, and what you enjoy or fear across all aspects of human diversity.
3. *Justice.* Identify how you have been advantaged or disadvantaged by the "isms" (ableism, classism, heterosexism, racism, sexism) and the stereotypes or prejudices you have absorbed about yourself or others.
4. *Activism.* Explore your ideas, feelings, and experiences of social justice activism. Open up dialogue with colleagues and families about all these goals. Develop the courage and commitment to model for young children that you stand for fairness and to be an active voice for children. (Derman-Sparks et al., 2020, p. 19)

Too few ECCE teacher preparation programs adequately engage students in serious learning about culturally sustaining and anti-bias education or in the self-reflection and growth that these approaches require (Durden & Curenton, 2021; Flores et al., 2021; Greene et al., 2022; Matias, 2016). Indeed, teacher certification standards and assessments often reinforce dominant cultural "ways of being and behaving" (Souto-Manning et al., 2020, p. 54). Similarly, many already practicing teachers have not had sufficient inservice professional development framed by an equity lens. They may have gone to a conference presentation or workshop in their school or center, but these quick-fix approaches do not provide more than surface learning without sustained engagement over time (Dunst & Trivette, 2012).

Program leaders need to shoulder a large part of the task of facilitating their staff's growth toward achieving the adult anti-bias goals. This means starting to work on the four adult goals themselves before facilitating staff anti-bias development, and then continuing to learn along with the staff.

UNDERSTANDING THE PHASES OF ADULT ANTI-BIAS DEVELOPMENT

Several anti-racism educators and psychologists (Cross, 1991; Derman-Sparks & Phillips, 1997; Helms, 1993, 1995; Tatum, 1992; Wijeyesinghe & Jackson, 2012) write about the developmental patterns or phases in the racial identity journey among BIPoC and White adults. These models offer a useful perspective for understanding the changes that staff experience as they go on their journey of developing anti-bias education understanding and skills. You may recognize some of the characteristics of these phases as similar to what you have and are experiencing on your own anti-bias journey. In this section, we adapt these anti-racism stages to the journey in ABE consciousness and behaviors we have documented among staff (and ourselves) over many years as ECCE leaders.

Staff in any given ECCE program will likely be at different phases in their awareness, curiosity, and knowledge of the anti-bias approach. Some will express enthusiasm, readiness, and engagement. They may show some of the characteristics of the second or third phases of the anti-bias developmental path. Others will need encouragement to begin, showing the characteristics of people in the beginning phases of the anti-bias journey. Karina Rojas Rodriguez, the director of Southwest Early Learning Bilingual Preschool, a city-funded bilingual preschool program in Seattle, relates how she takes into account a prospective teacher's alignment with ABE values:

> I hire teachers who are on point, but we also hire teachers who show potential, and teachers that are willing to say, "You know what, yes, I'm not an anti-bias educator, I've never even heard about it. But I'm willing to learn, I'm willing to look at the values and the vision and the mission of your program. And really, that aligns with who I am."

Each individual's anti-bias growth also may look different in relation to the various areas of their intersecting social identities. This includes people's attitudes and behavior, as well as their understanding of the privileges or inequities that society connects to the various kinds of identities (Nieto et al., 2010). For example, an individual may be farther on their anti-bias journey in regard to gender and sexism than in comprehension of racism. Additionally, while someone might be conscious of the impact of sexism in their life, they may not understand how race or ability might intersect with gender to create differing dynamics. Each person's social identities portrait influences their anti-bias journey.

We urge you to refer to this discussion of the five phases of the anti-bias journey outlined in this section as you create an initial portrait of your program (see Chapter 3), work with your staff and families (Chapters 4, 5 and 6), and document their growth (Chapter 8). It can be a helpful framework for scaffolding your anti-bias efforts with individual staff members and with the program as a whole. It suggests when to challenge people to move ahead on their anti-bias journey, and when not to push people too fast, so that they stop expressing their ideas and feelings, and growth stops. Understanding the journey of staff also enables the program leader to appreciate both the common dynamics and the individual differences in the anti-bias journey.

Before the Journey Begins

Denial of the significance of diversity and bias, either explicitly or unconsciously, indicates that a staff member is not yet on the anti-bias education journey. It is expressed in comments such as "I have no prejudices so I don't need to do this;" "Children do not care about differences among people"; and "I do not see any awareness or interest from them."

Teachers in programs primarily serving White children often use the rationale that "it isn't that we are not interested in diversity, but we are not a diverse school" to deny the need for anti-bias education. They usually refer to a lack of racial or ethnic diversity, ignoring the fact that children absorb misinformation and biases whether or not they have direct contact with people different from themselves. Moreover, diversity comes in multiple forms (e.g., economic class, ethnic/cultural groups, religion, gender roles, abilities), so all groups of children (even when all come from the same racial or ethnic background) represent some diversity.

Denial of the need for anti-bias education may also come from teachers in programs only serving BIPoC children. Their reasons tend to take the form of "we have to focus on fostering our children's positive identity; we do not have time to concern ourselves with other groups." In the first edition of *Anti-Bias Education for Young Children and Ourselves* (Derman-Sparks & Edwards, 2010), Carol Brunson Day offers her insights about this issue:

> People of Color often have the feeling that anti-bias education is work that Whites need to do, because the sources of racism come from White history and culture. They question its relevancy for children of color, for whom they believe empowerment is

the key issue. White children definitely need anti-bias education. So, too, do children of color, although the specific work differs from that with White children. Educational efforts that prevent internalized oppression by fostering strong personal and social identities and counter prejudices about *other* groups of color are two essential tasks that are part of the larger anti-bias work. We also need to create alliances to achieve our shared ultimate goal of a more equitable society. (p. 7)

Pushback from members of the dominant social identity groups may also come from their anxiety that anti-bias education will leave them out (a reversal of the current dominant-culture–centered approach, where many groups are invisible in the curriculum and learning environment). Comments include "My family is White and I don't see myself in the center as much as I did before. There are photos of diverse families, but I'm not there," or "I do not want my children to be prejudiced, but where do White people fit in an anti-bias curriculum?" While an anti-bias approach includes everyone—including White people—it is true that dominant-culture groups have to share space and attention with others. When an ECCE program shifts toward an anti-bias culture, it can feel to some members of the dominant culture as if these changes have taken their world away from them.

When you have staff in the pre-journey phase, the challenge is to identify what aspects of diversity and bias connect with their lives and to tap into their feelings. It is important to ascertain if those staff members are really separating themselves from issues of diversity and bias or are just being silent about their thoughts and feelings. Many of them will not have experienced talking openly about social differences and biases (Bonilla-Silva, 2017) Another key is to help staff in this phase discover the realities of diversity and bias in children's lives, through sharing both research and personal stories that challenge their assumptions.

Beginning to Face the Issues

People embarking on their first steps on the anti-bias journey begin to look critically at their identities and attitudes. Signs include openness, honesty, and taking risks in storytelling about who they are. As staff members become more open about their experiences and feelings about diversity, they also discover how much anti-bias issues are a part of their lives. You also discover how much complexity exists in their lives and how easy it is to see a staff member through a narrow lens.

Another indicator of this phase is an individual's realization that everyone has a culture and their openness to exploring its characteristics (Souto-Manning, 2013). This is often more difficult for White people, since their European ancestors, as immigrants and settler colonists, "melted" (assimilated) their heritage to form the dominant society of the United States. Even though White privilege was affirmed through this assimilation, some White people feel a sense of loss, wondering where they go to learn about their families' heritage. They may even express envy of marginalized cultural groups who know their cultural history and identity.

A third indicator is a teacher being aware that children are noticing and have ideas about differences, and taking some initial steps in the classroom to address these through conversations with the children and by making environmental changes. At this point teachers may become open to sharing uncertainties about how to respond to children's questions and negative comments about various aspects of diversity and express interest in enhancing their skills.

Another indicator of movement in anti-bias development is openness to learning about the various ways families raise their children and seeing the need to learn *from* families. Teachers also show willingness to interact with families about childrearing, even if they feel uncomfortable because they are not sure of what to say or worry that their questions will offend a family.

As individuals begin to uncover their own issues and understand how bias harms children's development, they may show signs of emotional and intellectual disequilibrium. People express pain, guilt, or anger, or try to divert the conversation to a more familiar and comfortable topic. In some cases, an individual may respond to disequilibrium by wanting to go back to denial: "I'm all for diversity, but aren't we talking too much about it?" or abdicating responsibility for issues that arise by referring to a colleague as the "diversity person."

Committing to the Work of the Anti-Bias Education Journey

By this phase, staff members demonstrate continuing reflection about themselves and their work, and engagement with ongoing learning. As a college student in a class about racism and human development declared, "It feels like I had this big closet to clean out . . . and was now trying to decide what stayed, what needed fixing, and what to throw out. It's a big job, but it feels great" (Derman-Sparks & Phillips, 1997, p. 112).

In this phase, it is important to ensure that staff members do not view anti-bias ideas as only applicable to children, but also engage in critical self-reflection. One marker is evidence of growth in staff members' understanding of their social identities and appreciating the relationship between identity and their actions as a teacher. For example, a teacher who only speaks English might share in a newsletter how they view this as a limitation in their capacity as a teacher. This openness indicates that they realize that knowing who they are strengthens the work they do with the children and families. Families whose backgrounds are similar to or different from theirs will benefit by their greater self-insight.

Ownership of anti-bias education work is another key indicator. This includes staff implementing anti-bias education because it is what they want to do, rather than something they are doing to please the program leader. Evidence of ownership includes teachers regularly sharing anecdotes about children's interest in diversity and signs of discomfort or early prejudice, and wanting to problem-solve ways to address what they are observing. They actively raise conversations about differences in the classroom with children and initiate activities. Although they may still not be comfortable with pursuing the fourth anti-bias goal of taking *action* against injustice, teachers do begin to take the initiative in moving the anti-bias mission forward.

Anti-Bias Education as a Way of Being in the Classroom

Not only do staff members routinely integrate anti-bias values and concepts into the various experiences in their daily curriculum, they also set goals for themselves that reflect their commitment to ongoing anti-bias education. For example, one teacher affirms that she plans to build her understanding of how to include same-sex parents in her planned unit about families; another commits to focus on improving her "teachable/learnable moment" skills in responding to children's questions and comments about the hijab worn by a teacher; a third decides to take a class in Spanish, given the increasing number of Spanish-speaking families in her school.

At this phase in the journey, engaging in anti-bias education becomes a partnership among teachers and the program leader. One key indicator is that staff hold their leader accountable to the program's anti-bias education mission. John describes such a moment at his center:

> We had a conversation about whether to wear flip-flops or not at work, which led to a serious conversation around the cost of footwear. Some staff said, "I know you have expensive comfy leather sandals, but I can't afford them." I just had to laugh and say, "Well, I suppose I asked for that!"

Another marker of this phase is comfort working with families on anti-bias issues. For example, when teachers invite family members to come in and share something from their family culture, they sometimes encounter confusion about what "culture" means. Teachers now have the language they need to explain that *everyone* has a culture. The fact that the teachers can understand family culture in relation to themselves allows them to do this work in a more complex way with parents.

Becoming an Activist Beyond the Classroom

Program leaders are fortunate to have staff members who are ready to take a more active stance in pursuing the anti-bias mission, often in ways that no longer rely on the leader's direct facilitation. Sometimes there is the opportunity to hire a teacher who brings with them much-needed experience, awareness, and skills that will provoke colleagues' thinking and classroom practice. At other times, staff members embrace the professional development opportunities offered to grow in their understanding of ABE over time. These staff members are likely to be actively involved in social justice movements in their own lives.

In this phase, teachers initiate conversations with colleagues, parents, and children, as well as document and share their teaching ideas broadly. Most importantly, these staff members can challenge program leaders to do more in terms of equity, including identifying issues that have been overlooked or seemed too risky at the time. As allies and advocates, they are able to take on leadership opportunities such as leading a book discussion or a curriculum meeting focused on children's questions about diversity and bias. Director Karina Rojas Rodriguez sees the power in teachers being peer mentors:

> One of the things that we say is that we're never "a prophet in your own land." The teachers may not all be on the same page about ABE. But if we have one teacher who is really invested in this work, that teacher can then be the mentor of the other teachers—because it's coming from her mouth and not my mouth.

As you use these phases to help identify next steps in staff's anti-bias work, keep in mind that individual journeys always have their own specific variations. Individuals may also be in different phases of development on various anti-bias issues. While program leaders are responsible for guiding and supervising the professional development of staff members, we have also adapted and applied these phases to understanding the anti-bias journey of families (see Chapter 5).

RECOGNIZING CONTESTED GROUNDS FOR ANTI-BIAS EDUCATION

We use the concept of "contested grounds" to signify figurative spaces where diverging, contending views of what does and should count as core values, knowledge, policies, and actions open up possibilities for changes in thinking and practice. The generally accepted principles and practices of ECCE generate several pivotal contested grounds for anti-bias education thinking and practice. These include the role of ECCE, the sources and implications of developmental theory, the nature of children's identity development, and the impact of societal inequities on children. These issues reflect core contradictions in our society's ideology, policies, and actions regarding diversity and equity. We will discuss specific examples of contested ground in the following sections. Anti-bias education leaders must understand these contested-ground issues well because they do influence what they focus on and how they strategize. By seeking out and raising up stories from staff and families whose voices are often pushed to the margin, ABE leaders can include perspectives that run counter to mainstream views and that illuminate these contested grounds issues.

The Role of ECCE

Clarifying your own beliefs about the role of early childhood care and education in the larger society is a necessary aspect of building an anti-bias program. We view ECCE programs as a powerful bridge between the child's family and society. How this bridge gets constructed matters, profoundly affecting how young children experience their program. For example, is it a one-way bridge for primarily moving children into the dominant society, or a two-way bridge that enables children to become bicultural? Our diverse society is complex, with strong, contradictory themes and practices regarding how we treat human beings. The history of ECCE programs reflects these contradictions. Values of equality and supporting all children and families, regardless of their heritage and status in society, are strong themes in that history, as is the goal of preparing children to assimilate into the dominant society to be ready for society as it is, with its existing social and economic inequities.

These often-conflicting themes appear in the current debate about whether the role of ECCE programs is to enable children to thrive in their home culture and also successfully navigate in mainstream schools, or to push for children's assimilation into the dominant society by losing much of their heritage culture. An anti-bias approach goes further by asking how we transform mainstream schooling to create more inclusive approaches to teaching and curriculum. The ongoing debates and conflicting policies and practices about English-only early childhood education versus dual-language and bilingual education pose one example of the larger competing perspectives on the purpose of early childhood education as a bridge between family and society (Fu et al., 2019). These differing viewpoints also generate conflicting beliefs about the criteria for quality education and the need for and type of equity education. In the 2020 *Start with Equity* report, one of the core recommendations offered to dismantle racism in ECCE focused on the contested concept of "quality," arguing, "The field must explicitly include equity in the definition of quality and correspondingly, include it in every level of QRIS [Quality Rating and Improvement Systems]. A program simply cannot be deemed 'quality' if its programming, experiences, and outcomes are inequitable" (Meek et al., 2020, p.10).

The historical significance afforded family and community life in the ECCE field, as well as a strong thread of belief in the value of all children and families, creates a unique opportunity for building programs that foster a many-cultures and equitable understanding of child development and early childhood education practice (Isik-Ercan, 2021).

Development Theories and Practices

Child development theories and research, and the developmentally appropriate practices grounded in this knowledge base, have historically reflected the socialization norms and practices of the dominant group in the United States (Long et al., 2015). This thinking has traditionally pushed other cultural viewpoints to the margins, even in very diverse settings.

On the other hand, challenges to the dominant-culture-only approach to children's development and criteria for quality programs are a part of the current

ECCE discourse and principles (Virmani & Mangione, 2013). Advocating for culturally and linguistically appropriate care is affirmed in NAEYC's (2022) 4th edition of *Developmentally Appropriate Practice* and in their position statement on advancing equity in early childhood education (NAEYC, 2019b). Moreover, BIPoC educators are leading research examining diverse ways of learning and teaching that reflect marginalized cultural histories and worldviews (Paris & Alim, 2017; Ukpokodu, 2016). And Indigenous educators and researchers are contesting what knowledge should be valued by society (San Pedro, 2021; Tuhiwai Smith et al., 2019).

These additions to the knowledge base of ECCE are significant and positive, but much more requires doing in both research and practice. Building an ECCE program that integrates a many-cultures perspective obliges leaders and staff to accept that customary ways of thinking and working are not always the only ways (Gay, 2018).

Children's Identity Development

The questions of whether societal prejudices affect young children's development and how ECCE should address this influence also create contested ground. Traditionally in ECCE, the subject of young children and prejudice was largely invisible, although pioneering research about this subject began as early as 1926 and major work appeared in the 1950s. In fact, the Clarks' (1947) pioneering research played a key role in the U.S. Supreme Court's historic 1954 school desegregation decision. Active discussion and debate about children and the role of racism and sexism in their development reemerged in the 1970s and 1980s, influenced by the civil rights movement. By the 1990s, addressing the impact of the larger society on young children's construction of identity and attitudes became a part of ECCE discourse.

Many ECCE professionals now subscribe to this thinking, and it is supported in recent position statements by NAEYC (2019b, 2020). Advocates argue that it is both necessary and developmentally appropriate to integrate issues of diversity, equity, and inclusion that relate to young children's lives into the curriculum. Research about the negative impact of the various forms of prejudice and discrimination on children informs anti-bias education (Iruka et al., 2020; NAEYC, 2019b). Rukia Rogers, a Black educator leading The Highlander School in Atlanta, Georgia, shares how her White preschoolers were able to identify the unfairness of police violence against Black people and in response, after much intensive conversation, created memorials for Breonna Taylor and George Floyd.

> [One thing that's] been beautiful in our school was for our White children
> to be able to name [racism], but not only name it, but also name their
> power around it . . . The essence [was] the children having language when
> they were younger about who they are, their own Whiteness and culture

and their agency and power to make a difference, which was because,
I think, typically about them being able to name unfairness, being able to
take action.

Still, many early childhood professionals and families throughout the
country continue to believe that it is inappropriate to create curriculum
that explores issues of fairness and bias with young children (Reid & Kagan,
2022). Usually unaware of the considerable research to the contrary, some
insist that young children do not notice or have ideas about human differences and prevailing societal and family prejudices—what we call "differences
denial." Others believe that intentionally opening up issues of diversity with
young children results in their becoming prejudiced. This viewpoint has been
reinforced by politicians and school boards promoting laws and policies that
seek to ban ABE experiences that might lead to children feeling "discomfort"
because of their gender, race, or ability (Kim, 2021). And yet, many children
and families encounter the pain of bias as part of their lives in schools simply
because of their identities. Rideaux and Salazar Pérez (2020) argue that we can
turn to the lived experiences of BIPoC teachers to better understand the damaging impact on children of a differences-denial approach and how it can be
countered in the classroom. Being very familiar with the research and analysis
about children's identity and attitude development is an essential part of your
anti-bias leadership toolbox.

ANTI-BIAS EDUCATION—WITHIN REACH

Throughout the United States and internationally, ECCE programs are implementing the anti-bias approach (e.g., B. Brown, 2008; Mac Naughton & Davis, 2009;
Murray & Urban, 2012; Peters, 2020; Van Keulen, 2004; Vandenbroeck, 2007).
Reflecting ABE's dynamic quality, educators in various countries adapt anti-bias
goals, values, and pedagogical principles to the differing demographic, cultural,
historical, and political characteristics of their respective national and local contexts. These include unique identity issues and differences in early childhood systems and pedagogical approaches.

Anti-bias education leaders, wherever they are, must have a vision and be
strategic about working toward it. They must keep their eye on the journey
as well as the destination. In Chapter 2, we explore the qualities and capacities ECCE leaders will need for this undertaking. While the urgency to embrace
anti-bias education is great, the process of change happens over time. A slow,
continuous process can support real human growth, build skills, and elevate a
school culture committed to social justice. Still, we seek to avoid an approach
that leaves change to only what is acceptable and comfortable to those in our
society already with power. Fundamental and deeper shifts in our institutions
are needed.

In the end, anti-bias work humanizes us. Rukia Rogers sees our capacity to connect as a starting place:

Really invite your families, your teachers, your whole community to reimagine this world starting with young children. Invite your families, your teachers, your whole community to reimagine this world starting with young children. I really believe that when you invite people to share the bigger vision of what you're hoping for, and that the anti-bias goals are a means to get there, they will take the vision up with you.

CHAPTER 2

Best Practices of Early Childhood Program Leaders

The Foundation for Anti-Bias Leadership

Our heritage as a field has been the continual development of early childhood leaders who have been passionate, active dreamers with our eyes on the best interest of children.

—Valora Washington (1997, p. 66)

Anti-bias leadership builds on the core principles and best leadership practices of the early childhood care and education field. These include relationships of mutual caring and respect; sharing knowledge; reflective, intentional teaching; and collaboration among staff and between staff and the program leader. Overall, the leadership principles and practices for ECCE are also a strong foundational launching point for anti-bias education.

The leader role (as defined in Figure I.1) is central to initiating, growing, and sustaining quality ECCE programs. It is difficult for even highly educated and experienced staff to sustain their best work without supportive leaders. Leadership tasks involve thoughtfully negotiating the complexity of interactions with families, staff, children, and community members, all of whom carry deep personal meaning generated by caring for other people's children (Bowman, 1997; Carter et al., 2021).

The leader also plays a vital role in fostering anti-bias education values, relationships, and strategies as an integral part of an ECCE program's mission and daily practice. While dedicated teachers do make anti-bias education happen in their classrooms and can and should take on varied leadership roles, program leaders have the power to create the opportunities that integrate and sustain ABE throughout the program (Long et al., 2015; Nimmo et al., 2021). They can initiate organizational policy and structure changes that support ongoing anti-bias education in the classrooms and with families. Program leaders also can put into motion a strong professional development plan. Drawing on critical theory and research, Hard et al. (2013) conclude that "critically informed, intentional and strategic organizational [early childhood] leadership can play a pivotal role in creating changed circumstances and opportunities for children" (p. 324).

In this chapter we review the themes in current thinking and research about ECCE leadership and consider their application to anti-bias education transformation. First, we review key aspects of program leadership, and then we look at personal traits of successful program leaders and their implications for anti-bias work. We conclude with suggestions for professional development for ECCE program leaders.

KEY ASPECTS OF ECCE PROGRAM LEADERSHIP

In this section we consider the fundamental importance of facilitative leadership, program mission, organizational culture and climate, a community of learners, and collaborative relationships with families and communities to effective ECCE program leadership. As principles and practices, each of these elements interacts with and works with the other elements to build a strong, quality ECCE program. Similarly, they form the foundational core for anti-bias leadership.

Promoting Facilitative Leadership

Facilitative leadership relies on cooperation, consensus-building, and shared responsibility. It assumes that teachers and other staff are thoughtful professionals whose perspective, experiences, and insights are vital to building a quality program. At its best, it is transformational and empowering. Facilitative leadership also reflects a belief in all members of a staff working as a team, rather than as an unyielding hierarchy (Forester, 2013; LeeKeenan & Ponte, 2018; Schwartz, 2016). Facilitative leaders collaborate by exercising power *with*, rather than power *on*, staff and families. This does not mean that program leaders give up their leadership roles, but rather that they do not overdirect or simply impose their ideas without ongoing engagement of staff and families in discussion about program decisions (Stewart, 2019).

Program leaders set the direction and provide clear expectations grounded in values. Debbie and her colleague Iris Chin Ponte (LeeKeenan & Ponte, 2018) advise that while leaders should be "approachable and supportive," they also need to give themselves "the permission to lead" (p. 8). Leaders encourage and facilitate the development of self-awareness and reflection, confidence, and effective communication skills, provide a working knowledge of diverse child development and learning, and offer regular support for staff's efforts to make changes. They also engage staff in regular review of the program's mission and goal priorities, and ongoing individual assessment of each staff member's work (Carter et al., 2021).

The values-based approach of ABE means that staff members' authentic engagement with the journey is key. When teachers and other staff feel part of creating the mission, values, goals, and policies of their program, they are more likely to have a strong personal commitment to helping the organization achieve results. The NAEYC (2019b) *Advancing Equity* statement recommends that leaders "create meaningful, ongoing opportunities for multiple voices with multiple perspectives to engage in leadership and decision making" (p. 9). Research indicates that when a program leader thoughtfully considers the multiple perspectives of staff in reaching decisions and encourages collective responsibility for carrying out those responsibilities, then staff members have increased self-direction, motivation, trust, and belief in their own potential to contribute (O'Neill & Brinkerhoff, 2018).

Facilitating a Shared Program Vision and Mission

Because the program leader has the key role of "the keeper of the faith, the person who believes most deeply and cares most passionately for the central mission of the organization" (Neugebauer, 2000, p. 101), you have the responsibility for being the initial inspiration for your program's purpose. You take the lead in establishing and nurturing the program's vision, core values, and tone. Debra Sullivan (2023), a longtime leader in ECCE, tells us: "Good leaders not only realize that a better situation is possible; they have an image of what it looks like and how to get there" (p. 79).

While a vision statement is aspirational, expressing what you hope to accomplish in the long run, a mission statement describes the program's particular purpose and provides a framework for working toward the vision. Together, they act as inspiration and guide for a program's work, laying the foundation for developing annual goals and educational objectives. Creating vision and mission statements that spell out your program's commitment to anti-bias education is a crucial step in beginning and then cultivating change.

For a vision to become more than a statement on a piece of paper, you must engage the curiosity and involvement of the program's key stakeholders in generating a shared image of what this looks like and what it will take (Bloom et al., 2016; Carter et al, 2021). To do this, a facilitative and collaborative leadership approach is essential.

In Chapter 4, we look at ways to engage your staff in developing an anti-bias vision and mission statement for your program and to review and possibly modify them in subsequent years. Even though you may feel ready to forge ahead alone, the time spent on creating a *shared* vision and mission for anti-bias work will be worth it for the longer undertaking of implementing change and inviting accountability. Luz Maria Casio, a veteran director, implores us to take this process to heart:

> With a vision or mission statement, you make promises. This is a commitment to the families, the employees and the community. You can't just have impressive words. You have to be authentic and live your values. This means you put your heart in bringing these things to life, making them a priority. (Carter et al., 2021, p. 29)

Establishing the Organizational Culture and Climate

A program's vision and mission statements become living documents when they are actively infused into all aspects of the program's organization, relationships, and practices. They are a compass that helps guide the paths program leaders and staffs take as they make choices about what they are doing. The leader also initiates management systems and an organizational culture that reflect the program's vision and mission statements (Carter et al., 2021). Doing ABE calls on the leader's capacity to skillfully and intentionally manage systems such as budgeting, hiring, and policymaking in order for dreams to become reality. Both the visionary and management sides of leadership are essential.

A social–ecological perspective about organizational culture is well-suited to the many-faceted relationships in an ECCE program. In this approach, it is understood that each member of the community influences the collective values, mission, and style of the group's work. At the same time, the culture of the community shapes each member's attitudes and behavior. Therefore, a change in any component of the organization may affect all the others (Bloom et al., 2016). This perspective is also especially helpful for anti-bias education work, which requires systemic change in order to be lasting. Debbie and her colleague Iris Ponte clarify the concepts as follows:

> Culture reflects the expectations of a program, made visible in the way things are done while climate is often described as the "feel" of the program—its atmosphere. . . . Climate reflects the collective attitude of staff towards the program's beliefs, values, and norms. (LeeKeenan & Ponte, 2018, p. 21)

Shifting the culture of a program to be anti-bias is a long-term undertaking. Creating a climate that supports this cultural change is more immediate. Both are made possible through everyday leadership strategies, big and small. According to Bloom and colleagues (2016), quality ECCE programs share certain central organizational characteristics in their climate, including:

- *Collegiality.* The staff feels a unified team spirit, collective sense of usefulness and effectiveness, and freedom to express their thoughts and to share information and resources. Conversations about values, beliefs, and educational priorities are normal parts of ongoing discussions.
- *Innovativeness.* Quality programs adapt to change and find creative ways to solve problems. This spirit of innovation doesn't just happen on its own; the program leader cultivates it by encouraging risk-taking and an openness to try new ideas.
- *Professional growth.* Effective program leaders emphasize and provide ongoing opportunities for staff growth. This includes ways for staff to put new ideas into practice. Leaders also create a program climate that nurtures and stimulates the most skilled and dedicated staff, and mentor and coach those not yet performing as reliably. Multiple opportunities for growth take into account everyone's developmental journeys and life experiences.

Effective anti-bias programs establish and then build on these organizational dimensions of quality ECCE programs.

Supporting a Community of Learners

An active community of learners is the heart of building a quality ECCE program and culture of inquiry and adult learning (LeeKeenan & Ponte, 2018). Tashon McKeithan, Executive Director of the Child Educational Center in Southern California, sees community beginning with the model she provides as a leader:

> When I go into a conversation, I want to position myself as a learner as well. It's not that everyone's learning from me, right? That just silliness. But that we're all part of a conversation, to grow our crafts, and to make our environment better for children. That's my sole purpose.

Creating an amiable place to work requires teachers balancing their time between working alone or with a partner in their classrooms and spending time all together reflecting about and improving their practice. Through being members of a community of learners, staff have the opportunity to gain a deeper understanding of themselves, their relationships with one another, their work with children and families, and their knowledge of how children learn. Program leaders are both facilitators and members of this learning community. Multiple opportunities for growth take into account everyone's developmental journeys, life experiences, and identities (Bloom et al., 2016; Carter et al., 2021).

Ongoing, facilitated conversation among staff is pivotal to flourishing learning communities (NAEYC, 2019a, 2019b). An anti-bias approach requires that leaders courageously engage stakeholders in critical examination of who they are, what they know, and what they do. This includes reconsidering comfortable teaching practices and familiar "truths" about children and families that may not be inclusive or asset-based (Polson & Byrne-Jiménez, 2016). Some early childhood program leaders avoid the conversations that anti-bias growth requires. Ellen Wolpert, a veteran ABE leader and retired director of the Washington-Beech Community Preschool in Boston, Massachusetts, talks about ECCE directors asking her about how she keeps staff anti-bias conversations safe and comfortable.

> For me, the critical issue is how we encourage engagement in conversations that may sometimes be risky or uncomfortable. Comfort and safety mean very different things to people. Is this a concern about fear of disagreement, or conflict, or saying the wrong thing, or nonconfidentiality, or realizing that someone is not like you? Some people want guarantees that their own definitions of safety and comfort will prevail, but we cannot guarantee that. . . . But beyond the ground rules, the task is being open to a new *kind* of conversation.

Finding time in early childhood programs for staff to be a community of learners is another challenge, given the realities of insufficient staff and funding under which too many programs operate. Setting clear priorities is essential.

This may mean letting go of expenditures and activities that are less central to program values. Determined leaders find creative ways to carve out opportunities and time for staff members to meet often and regularly. Rejecting a "scarcity mentality" and instead being driven by vision rather than resources, Luz Maria Casio shares her approach as a director of a bilingual ECCE program serving low-income families:

> Because I want teachers to be passionate and reach for their dreams, I never say, "We don't have the money." Instead, I say, Let's figure this out." I especially never turn down a request for professional learning. I don't believe that our budget should sacrifice the need for teacher learning and only provide for the children's learning. They are tied together. (Carter et al., 2021, p. 258)

Building Partnerships With Families

Respecting the centrality of the family's role in a child's life is an early, enduring ECCE principle. NAEYC's (2019b) *Advancing Equity in Early Childhood Education Position Statement* asks educators to "embrace the primary role of families in children's development and learning" (p. 8). Leadership tasks include being in regular communication with parents in ways that respect their values, and actively welcoming their participation in the life of the program. Moreover, a social justice vision requires that leaders "position families as vital to the operation of the school/preschool [and] ensure that their voices are sought and validated through joint action" (Vasquez et al., 2016, p. 181).

Collaboration with families is essential for meaningful anti-bias education (Derman-Sparks et al., 2020; Derman-Sparks & Ramsey, 2011; LeeKeenan & Ponte, 2018). As Lisa Lee, a leader in creating ECCE programs that maintain collaborative partnerships with families, powerfully explains:

> Families honor us with the care of their children. Our daily interactions promote or discourage cultural pride, empowerment and a sense of self-worth and belonging in the children and their parents. Instead of seeing "deficits" and cultural differences as the problem, teachers who are allies appreciate the strengths and "gifts" that families bring to the learning experience. When we bring depth to implementing an anti-bias approach, we uphold their trust. (quoted in Derman-Sparks at al., 2020, p. 64)

Ongoing collaboration with families is how the leader and staff ensure that children's home and heritage cultures accurately become a central part of the daily life of the program. It also creates the environment in which it is possible to negotiate differences of ideas related to anti-bias concepts and activities. The leader provides professional development and encouragement for the staff to "be curious, making time to learn about the families with whom you work" (NAEYC, 2019b, p. 8).

It is essential that program leaders identify anxieties that staff may feel about building partnerships with families and find ways for them to move forward.

For instance, a staff members' unfamiliarity with how family views their child's autism could create unease for the teacher about how they can be of support. Providing opportunities for staff to increase their skills in working collaboratively with diverse families is part of the anti-bias program leader's responsibility for professional development (see Chapter 6 for ways to do this).

Being Present in the Local Community

Leading an equity-focused program that values families and seeks to be culturally sustaining requires leaders who are intentional in building meaningful relationships with the local neighborhood (Sullivan, 2023). Not only can your presence provide valuable insight into families and a model for staff to emulate, it can also muster support for your ABE goals. This is a challenging prospect given the long hours of child care and the reality that many ECCE professionals don't live where they work.

Khalifa (2018) offers suggestions for how school leaders can build their credibility locally, particularly in minoritized communities. These steps include being proactive in finding opportunities to invite community members into your program, as well as supporting your staff to be present in the surrounding community. For instance, a staff retreat might include a field trip to visit local advocacy organizations and cultural centers. Leaders also need to "find out what is important to the community" (p. 174) and be willing to offer their support around social justice issues even if they aren't directly impacting your ECCE program. This means being visibly and openly engaged in taking an anti-oppressive stance on issues of community concern, such as advocating for low-income housing in the neighborhood or participating in a racial justice rally. These kinds of community engagement can make it more likely that community members will offer support for your program's anti-bias efforts when needed. Taking a public stance as a leader requires a good deal of time and courage, so maybe take small steps at first. The rewards will be felt in the long-term sustainability of your ABE mission.

CORE ATTRIBUTES OF EFFECTIVE ECCE PROGRAM LEADERS

Leaders of early childhood care and education programs must have a highly developed ability to interact with parents, staff, children, and community members and be able to tolerate the uncertainty and frustration that often come with these relationships.

—Barbara Bowman (1997, p. 111)

The research and experiences of several leaders in the ECCE field point to a set of personal attributes that support program leaders in meeting their multiple roles, tasks, and demands, including anti-bias change. Several of the key qualities are:

- *Having the courage to lead.* This means understanding the risks and being aware of one's own fears and vulnerabilities, yet not letting fears prevent one from taking action (Sykes, 2014). "They are very aware that open hearts must be anchored in firm commitments to call out inequities and to move deliberately to disrupt and dismantle them." (Vasquez et al., 2016, p. 175)
- *Believing in human potential.* This strength-based approach to staff, colleagues, and families is fundamental to collaboration, trust-building, and innovation. "You see each child and adult as a capable, competent, and resourceful individual in need of coaching, mentoring, and emotional support." (Sykes, 2014, p. 12)
- *Servant leadership.* Ann McClain Terrell (2018) shares, "the servant-leader shares power and focuses on the development of those she works with as well as who she serves. The desired outcome is the wholeness of the people and the community and that those served will, in turn, also serve and build a stronger community." (p. 35)
- *Cultivating imagination.* Leaders inspire and welcome outside-the-box thinking by all stakeholders (Stewart, 2019). They understand that they can't possibly have all the answers. "Creativity is unleashed as people tap into their fullest abilities and capacities." (O'Neill & Brinkerhoff, 2018, p. 8)
- *Willingness to engage in ongoing self-reflection and renewal.* Leaders seek out critical awareness of their own histories and identities (Khalifa, 2018). "A leader must be willing to examine her abilities and attitudes in order to positively influence the transformation of others. Every journey begins at home" (Espinosa, 1997, p. 101). Through ongoing reflective practice, personal renewal, and continuing professional development, leaders construct the knowledge and hopefulness needed to act and inspire others. (Carter et al., 2021; Sykes, 2014)
- *Walking the talk.* Leaders "push the what-is to the what-might-be—thinking possibility, invention, and vision" (Kagan & Neuman, 1997, p. 60), and they live their beliefs (Khalifa, 2018). When program leaders set and enforce policy for staff but disregard it themselves, "it fosters a sense of resentment and disrespect toward the director, and a sense of detachment from and disregard for the program and its goals." (Zeece, 2008, p. 26)
- *Accepting and learning from mistakes.* Many scholars of best leadership practices talk about this trait. As Clifford (1997) puts it, "leaders must not turn from failure but see the opportunity to learn from mistakes; this drive for the truth also means leaders welcome dissent and see it as means toward a more complete understanding." (p. 104)
- Seeing *"turbulence as an opportunity for positive change"* (VanderVen, 2000, p. 122). Tension is often a sign that people really care about what's happening. When viewed this way, it becomes possible to move past discomfort and fear to a place of discovery and integrity (Carter et al.,

2021). Yet handling staff disagreement and discomfort is problematic for many ECCE program leaders and teachers who focus on care. An anti-bias program calls on leaders to overcome discomfort with conflict and embrace it as a precursor to change (see Chapter 7).

PROFESSIONAL DEVELOPMENT OF ECCE PROGRAM LEADERS

Effective ECCE program leaders need a broad knowledge base. They "hunger for knowledge" (Sykes, 2014, p. 13). Brown and Manning (2000) suggest four essential areas, which serve as a useful framework for assessing what you already have in your repertoire and what you need to learn:

1. Reflective knowledge of self
2. Knowledge about others, including understanding how adults learn
3. Knowledge about how organizations work, including leadership
4. Knowledge about the external world that surrounds the program

In Chapter 3 we look at how these four types of knowledge come into play when program leaders "read" the context and dynamics of their programs before initiating anti-bias changes.

Knowing about current research findings in child and human development theory and their applicability to children's programs, different supervisory styles and methods appropriate to a range of program staff, and different cultural styles of interacting are all necessary competencies for ECCE leaders (G. Morgan, 2000). We add familiarity with the research about young children's construction of identities and attitudes, as well as the core learning goals and pedagogical principles of anti-bias work.

Growth in program leaders' core knowledge comes through reflective practice and continuing professional development (Sykes, 2014). In addition to attending ECCE conferences, leaders should also participate in workshops on administration and social justice leadership by organizations with a mission outside the ECCE field. In order to develop the knowledge base needed for anti-bias work, leaders may need to access information from outside the early childhood field, including in places like neighborhood programs, cultural centers, and civil rights organizations. For instance, you might visit or connect virtually with a local center that advocates for people who are houseless in order to better understand the challenges being faced by your families.

Effective ECCE program leaders need ongoing connection with one another for mutual support, learning, and advocacy. "Your job can be much less stressful and much more rewarding, if you find ways to share, to communicate, to listen, to let off steam, to hear the steam of [your] colleagues, to join together to make much needed changes in public policy" (H. Morgan, 2008, p. 43). Participating in local support groups for ECCE program leaders and connecting with an experienced mentor leader are helpful ways to give and get support.

TAKING ON THE CHALLENGE

[The courage to lead] is born of the personal belief in the greater good benefiting all of us.

—Linda Espinosa (1997, p.100)

Being the program leader of an early childhood program is never an easy task. Early childhood program leaders have multiple, sometimes contradictory, roles. They are employer, guide, facilitator, boss, colleague, evaluator, and team member, as well as whatever role may be needed to keep the program functioning economically and programmatically. An anti-bias education approach requires the courage to open oneself up to the complexities of diversity, equity, and inclusion issues—and to the conflict and growth the work brings. While empathizing with program leaders because of the challenges they face keeping a program on its feet, especially during the social upheavals of recent years, Carter et al. (2021) also urge leaders not to be overcome by those challenges:

> It's easy to talk about your problems and the things that bother you in your work, but too often directors [leaders] neglect to describe how they would like their work to be. Letting your mind spin out new possibilities when you are so used to adapting and accommodating yourself to how things are can be a challenge. Breaking out of these confines can stir up old longings and remind you of how little you've settled for, how much more is possible, and they greater gifts you have to offer. (p. 27)

Even with strong program leader practices, change can be difficult and frightening. It can also be exciting and enriching and, often, deeply satisfying.

In this chapter we laid out the best leadership approaches the early childhood care and education field has identified through experience and research. By incorporating these practices into your own leadership work, you can make your center a wonderful place for learning for *everyone*—even with all the difficult realities of the conditions in our ECCE programs and field. These practices also provide a foundation for your journey to "shift the culture" of the program to an anti-bias education approach.

In the next chapters we relate ways to implement the central elements of effective ECCE program leadership and organizational culture, such as facilitative leadership, program vision and mission, organizational culture and climate, a community of learners, and collaborative relationships with families. We begin in Chapter 3 by exploring the important process of "reading" your program as a place to start on this journey.

Reading the Program and Preparing for Anti-Bias Change

Leading this work is not something you should take lightly . . . It's not a jacket you take on and off depending on how hot or cold it is. It's a cultural shift. A way of being.

—Caprice D. Hollins (2023, p. 9)

The commitment to build early childhood programs that embrace all children and families is the fuel of change. Leaders can make the most of this fuel through thoughtful, strategic planning that can guide the program's organization, people, and culture. Being a strategic leader involves making decisions about where to put your energy, the speed at which to proceed, and what will be the most effective route to your goals and objectives. Doing this successfully requires you to gather information about the people and contexts of your program, and to consider how this portrait can guide you in developing strategies to meet anti-bias goals. Otherwise, you risk moving too fast and causing unnecessary problems or, conversely, underestimating the support for forging ahead and moving too slowly, or not at all.

Preparation for the long road toward greater equity and inclusion in your early childhood program begins with careful research. We use the metaphor of "reading" the program, adapted from Paulo Freire (1985), to describe this process. Freire argued that literacy is more than simply reading words; it must be connected to the deeper meaning of understanding one's experience and place in the world. Likewise, reading your program is much more than taking an inventory of items. The steps include:

1. Gathering a baseline understanding of your program's context
2. Analyzing this information for insights relevant to anti-bias change
3. Making strategic preparations in response

Early childhood programs are complex and dynamic systems consisting of different players, relationships, culture, and history. Reading your program will help you identify your community's assets, its challenges, and the key people who will be part of or affected by your anti-bias work (Hollins, 2023; Jemal & Bussey, 2022). This process includes identifying all the people and groups who affect your program both directly (e.g., staff and families) and indirectly (e.g., neighborhood, funding, licensing, accreditation). You need to understand who will benefit from an anti-bias approach, who will be an ally in this work, and who is most likely to push back against change.

We have also drawn on the antiracism work of the People's Institute for Survival and Beyond by adapting their "power analysis" process (Shapiro, 2002). In this structural analysis, you identify the people, groups, and resources that could affect your program (as described later in this chapter) and examine how they might support or oppose your work. This analysis enables you to look below the surface features of a program and determine who holds power over your program, and who are the gatekeepers in your organization and community who can open or close doors to resources and support.

This chapter lays out a framework for establishing a preliminary or baseline understanding of the components of your program, and then discusses how to make sense of this information. Having a baseline will enable you to devise initial strategies to begin meeting your anti-bias goals. Finally, we suggest preparatory steps you can take based on your reading of the program. While this program reading typically takes place in the first few months of the year (or whenever you initiate an anti-bias approach), you will return to this process periodically to assess progress and determine next steps (see Chapter 8).

Given the demands of being a leader, you will need to make choices about the time and energy that you can invest in this "reading the program" process. Leaders are most likely to bring these steps informally into their everyday interactions and observations with staff and families. It is not necessary to complete all the detailed steps provided here in order to create change. Depending on your situation, you may decide to focus on certain aspects and spend less time on others. For instance, you may find that your program urgently needs to acquire more books about diverse languages, religions, and abilities—and you immediately take steps to improve the book collection. The process of change doesn't need to wait until you have everything in place. Balance the time spent on reading your program with taking action and learning from its outcomes. (See Appendix B at www.tcpress.com for a detailed worksheet on the "reading" process that you can use with the leadership team, the entire staff, or a family committee to develop goals and plans).

COLLECTING PRELIMINARY IMPRESSIONS: ESTABLISHING A BASELINE FOR PLANNING

To make strategic choices about how to move forward on the anti-bias education journey, you "read": (1) the physical and cultural landscape surrounding the program, (2) the program environment, (3) the program stakeholders, (4) the overall culture of the program, and (5) the program gatekeepers. Each of these components contributes to the initial portrait of your program's need and readiness for anti-bias work.

The Landscape

ECCE leaders understandably tend to focus on what is happening within their own centers, but anti-bias work also requires using a wider lens to be aware of the broader landscape of people, places, and local events surrounding a program. We have drawn on community-assets mapping as a tool for taking an inventory of the human and material resources, structures, and networks that exist for pursuing anti-bias goals (McKnight & Block, 2012).

Consider the following features of the surrounding community (along with examples) and how they might influence how you pursue your ABE vision:

- *What is the surrounding ecology of the program setting, such as location and environmental features?* Being located in a rural area could mean there is difficulty in recruiting teachers with diverse backgrounds.
- *What are the social identities of families and staff in the program and people in the neighboring community?* A surge in families who are refugees from conflict makes attending to trauma and resettlement issues a priority.
- *What are the social, cultural, and economic resources in the surrounding community and in the families' communities?* A mosque in the neighborhood offers outreach on religious diversity.
- *What are the important local issues, happenings, and politics?* A major employer in the neighborhood is moving out, and some families are at risk of losing employment.

To illustrate how differences might affect strategic choices, let us look at the contrasts in the landscape surrounding the program John led in New Hampshire and the ECCE center our colleague Karina Rojas Rodriguez leads in Seattle.

New Hampshire demographics are predominantly White and monocultural, with a relatively small, emerging group of recent immigrants who speak languages other than English. There is a large rural population, and significant pockets of poverty that tend to be hidden from view in mobile home parks. However, the closest neighborhood of John's program is the surrounding university. It is a unique environment, with more ethnic, racial, and linguistic diversity than the state in general, although much of that diversity is from international students and staff. John arrived at a time when the university administration was articulating a clearer and stronger mission regarding equity and inclusion. This move, including the appointment of a high-level position responsible for diversity matters, signaled institutional-level support for an anti-bias approach.

Karina's program, the Southwest Early Learning Bilingual Preschool in urban Seattle, Washington, presents a very different cultural landscape. Her program is situated in a politically liberal city with considerable public support and resources intended to reach equity goals in education. The demographics across all social identity categories are much more diverse than in New Hampshire. The children and families largely reflect the surrounding low- and middle-income neighborhood. While most families qualify for publicly funded ECCE, there are other, often White families who choose the program because it is bilingual and high-quality. Collectively, the families and staff reflect diversity in race, ethnicity, ability, family structure, religion, socioeconomic class, and, of course, language. Karina's program includes staff, families, and community members with more experience living and working in diverse communities than in the relatively monocultural village of the public university in New Hampshire.

These contrasting social landscapes indicate the importance of reading beyond the walls of the program to create your program's anti-bias strategies. In John's program, socioeconomic class became a central aspect of identity exploration in his early anti-bias efforts. In Karina's program, being bicultural and bilingual is a primary focus. While the languages of the families are primarily Spanish/English, she and her staff welcome families with different languages, including from the East African immigrant community. This composition of families has also meant, for instance, actively seeking to engage families with diverse religious identities in the inclusive values of anti-bias education.

The Program Learning Environment

The physical environment of a program and the availability of needed time, space, and personnel provide a stage for anti-bias education at the classroom level. Document what resources already exist in the program and what you need to add. Broad questions include:

- *Does the program have learning materials that accurately and respectfully reflect the backgrounds, languages, and heritage of all the children, their families, and the people in their community?*
- *Does the program have resources for the staff to learn about anti-bias education, social justice, and cultural awareness (e.g., books and journals, online sites, professional development)?*
- *Does the program have access to technology (e.g., telephone apps, loaner laptops) that could help staff in sharing, articulating, and learning about the anti-bias mission?*
- *Do teachers have time and space to discuss anti-bias issues with colleagues, children, and families?*
- *In what ways does the infrastructure of the facility support or inhibit anti-bias efforts?* The building or playground may or may not be accessible for children or adults with physical ability differences such as using a wheelchair or being a blind person.
- *Do you assess and document children's leaning using tools that are authentic and culturally responsive?*
- *Are there administrative policies and processes (e.g., admissions, tuition structure, communication methods) that could affect inclusion of families of all backgrounds?* Some families may not have access to electronic communications.

Several anti-bias education resources offer specific suggestions for creating an inventory of the program environment (e.g., Allen et al., 2021; Derman-Sparks et al., 2020, pp. 180–181; Ramsey, 2015, pp. 29–37). In Chapter 4, we discuss strategies to involve staff in review of the program environment as part of their anti-bias professional development.

The Stakeholders

The stakeholders include the individuals who actively participate in and have a direct investment in the success of your program. Each stakeholder may define program success differently, but the changes that come as you pursue an anti-bias mission will touch each of their lives in some way. They can potentially be a source of support or of opposition.

The key adult stakeholder groups within ECCE programs are the program leader/s, the teachers, and the families. Depending on the structure of your program, you may have additional stakeholder groups with varying degrees of participation in the program and effect on anti-bias efforts. These groups include other program administrators and educators with leadership responsibilities, office personnel, interns and student teachers, volunteers, and auxiliary staff (e.g., cooks, custodians, and bus drivers). You should determine what you need to know about these groups and individuals as part of the preliminary read of the program. For instance, you may not be the supervisor for auxiliary staff members who enter the center after hours to clean, but you could be very reliant on their efforts.

To be an effective anti-bias leader, you need to get to know and build positive relationships with the members of all the stakeholder groups at your program. However, the dynamics and depth of the relationships with various stakeholders will vary. For example, teachers are employees and colleagues with whom you interact every day. In contrast, you see families less frequently and in a different professional role. As a result, you focus on collecting different kinds of information about each stakeholder group, beginning with yourself as program leader.

Leader Profiles. You can generate a portrait of your anti-bias leadership capacity through critical self-reflection. The following questions are helpful in gauging one's readiness for leading anti-bias change:

- *What is my leadership style? How do I make decisions and engage others in these decisions?*
- *What is my comfort level with risk-taking and working through conflict with others?*
- *How do I view my social identities? How do they influence my anti-bias commitment and my relationship-building with staff and families?*
- *What experience and knowledge do I have regarding anti-bias education?*
- *What are my values and long-terms goals for anti-bias education? How do these align with or differ from staff and family values?*

Teacher Profiles. Children are at the heart of a program's anti-bias mission, and as such, teachers are the key players in implementing an anti-bias approach at the classroom level. They have primary responsibility for knowing where children are in relation to the ABE goals. Program leaders, in their roles as mentors and supervisors, are in a unique position to learn about each teacher's readiness to implement ABE. You are looking for entry points to begin the process of change depending on where each teacher is in their own anti-bias journey. For instance, if your teachers have personal experience with diverse identities and bias, or are more familiar with the theory of oppression and privilege, you are likely to engage in a more challenging anti-bias dialogue than if teachers have little experience or understanding of bias. Julie Bisson, the experienced child care director at Epiphany Early Learning Preschool in Seattle, shares how complex and important it is to not make assumptions about where a teacher is in their ABE journey:

> I got a little bit too relaxed, assuming that people who sought out [our program] were really familiar with and passionate about ABE, then come to find out when this teacher was giving their notice, they were telling me "I've always been uncomfortable with [your ABE approach]." And I had no clue! It turns out that the teacher really has a sort of color denial mentality. They feel like [the center] has made [bias] a bigger issue for kids than it needs to be.

Try to get a preliminary read on the following:

- *What is each teacher's awareness of their intersecting social identities (e.g., race, ability, and economic class)?*
- *What fears or concerns do the teachers have around addressing diversity and bias?*
- *In what ways are the teachers' curious about and/or committed to anti-bias values and goals?*
- *What are the teachers' relevant skills and experience? Are there teachers who speak the languages of the program's families? Are there teachers who have had PD in addressing bias with children and families?*
- *Which teachers are public advocates for an anti-bias approach?* A teacher shares stories about the children's questions about bias in a display outside their classroom.
- *Which teachers could act as leaders or mentors to colleagues? Do those teachers have the respect and trust of their peers?*

Your preliminary read of the teachers' readiness for anti-bias education will primarily come from everyday informal conversations and during formal supervision and staff meetings. Being intentional about raising anti-bias questions and conversation topics and looking for opportunities to do this as they arise daily are key. In reality, your initial impressions are likely to be broad and tentative. Given the complexity of ABE work, it is important to be aware of and challenge your assumptions about teachers and instead be open to new information.

Interview teachers about their hopes and dreams for the program and their early school experiences. As you listen, look for key words such as *privilege, culture, identity,* and *bias,* stories about their experiences that suggest awareness of social identities and biases, and interest in anti-bias concepts. Since teacher awareness may not be so explicit, it is also important that you listen carefully for language that shows an openness to or respect for diversity. The activities described in Chapter 4 provide further ways to read where teachers are at the beginning of school and throughout the year.

Families. Having a sense of where the children's families are in relation to ABE is also helpful. However, this will take time. While you may have a goal to know and connect with every family member, their willingness to share information about themselves will vary. The depth of the relationships you form is likely to vary greatly and will continue to develop over time.

Beyond the general family demographic information (e.g., ethnicity, languages, family structure, religion, and economic class) you collect to describe the landscape of the program, your reading of individual families is likely to be limited at the beginning of the school year. If you have been a member of the local community or have lived in the neighborhood for some time, you may have knowledge of families from your experiences. In addition, you are likely to get to know family members on the governing board or advisory committee because you are involved in early and continuing discussions about philosophy, curriculum, personnel, and funding.

Later in this chapter, we share the process of identifying family members who may be potential allies for your anti-bias mission. You may also get indirect or explicit indicators of families who have concerns about or objections to anti-bias values. As with the teachers, you should be wary of early impressions that may tend to focus on extremes of either support or opposition. Be open to a more complex and nuanced understanding of families and their perspectives. For instance, a White family that voices concerns to you or their teacher about their child hearing stories about racism may still be supportive of these conversations happening in the classroom. In Chapter 5, we explore the long-term process of getting to know families during their time at the program in order to develop a partnership in this work.

The Culture of the Program

Effective early childhood leaders understand that every program has its own dynamic culture that both shapes and is shaped by its members over time. When we talk about anti-bias education involving a *shift* in the culture of a program (to one that is more inclusive of all differences), we are using the term *culture* broadly to describe the program's values, rules, and practices. Like an anthropologist, a leader who is new to a program can often observe and identify the culture more easily than someone who has been immersed in its daily life over time. If you have been at a center for many years, you will have to make a conscious effort to step outside of the culture and take a fresh look at it, given that you have been a participant and contributor.

All the program components we have identified for information-gathering (landscape, learning environment, and stakeholders) are part of the culture of your program (Hollins, 2023). In addition, the following are some important elements to look for:

- *What are the power dynamics among the staff members?* Some staff members tend to speak up and participate in committees and other decision-making bodies? One of the teachers is respected as an elder?
- *What are the formal policies in staff and family handbooks?*
- *What implicit rules and language have the community passed down orally over time?*
- *What are the key rituals and traditions in the program community?*
- *In what ways do staff members and families reflect or differ from the program culture?*

This information is important to anti-bias change for a couple of reasons. First, you will discover which individuals and groups appear excluded or less visible in the program, as well as which ones seem to hold more power and influence. In addition, implicit (informal) rules often reflect important but unexamined values that long-term staff and families have accepted as set in stone. For instance, community members may assume that male teachers would never work in the infant classroom or that all families know how to access ability accommodations. With awareness of the program's culture, you can avoid harmful mistakes by building trust, awareness, and buy-in *before* rushing in to nix a much-loved but not inclusive tradition, such as an annual holiday carnival.

Gatekeepers

Gatekeepers are people or groups that have power over a program's operations by virtue of their institutional position and role. They may control access to people, resources, and knowledge, and create regulations that are relevant to anti-bias efforts. Potential gatekeepers include oversight organizations and funders (e.g., governing board, foundations), various regulatory groups, the school district, and town council. Leaders themselves also act as gatekeepers.

An anti-bias leader looks carefully at these gatekeeper roles and works creatively to minimize the obstacles. Later in this chapter, we consider the possibility of gatekeepers acting as allies and resources. Here are some of the questions you can use depending on your particular circumstances:

- *Does the administrative entity that oversees your program (e.g., board, school district, agency) have any written criteria, standards, or policies that can support your anti-bias education efforts?*
- *Does the program depend on funders for support of operations and capital projects?* Your program hopes to implement a sliding scale for tuition to give greater access to low-income families.
- *Does the building owner have particular values with regard to diversity that might align or contrast with anti-bias values?* A religious organization that owns a facility may insist on adherence to values that support or conflict with aspects of anti-bias education.
- *What items in the applicable regulations (e.g., licensing and accreditation criteria, building code) might support or interfere with your anti-bias work?*

Leaders as Gatekeepers. As a program leader, you play a gatekeeper role in terms of admissions, hiring, policy development, and budgeting. By looking critically at these administrative structures, you can identify ways to remove obstacles to an ABE mission and create opportunities for action. For example, you can open the "gate" into the program by prioritizing anti-bias skills and experiences in your staff hiring process and by being proactive in seeking more diversity in admissions by outreach to local cultural organizations.

Oversight Bodies. There may be individuals and organizations that have varying degrees of oversight responsibility for your program's operations. These include community and institutional groups such as religious and social service agencies that act as umbrella organizations for an ECCE program. A nonprofit program has a board that makes decisions regarding policy, budget, and personnel. Head Start and other government-funded programs are accountable to advisory groups or to school, district, state, and federal personnel. Even when an oversight body has a stated DEI mission, leaders can still encounter obstacles to their ABE efforts. Miriam Zmiewski-Angelova shares her own experience as director of an ECCE program:

> It was really hard to be in, ironically, a cultural space, to be talking about cultural work, to be constantly trying to figure out ways to harness it—and to have pushback [from the Board] on anything that really was creating more equity, because some of those things may not be as profitable. Like things that you can provide for families to ensure that they feel whole are often those things that cost a lot of money. I was willing to sacrifice financial profits for the sake of making it better for my families. . . . And so, you really got to make sure that all the way up to the top, everybody is keeping the larger vision of. . . . we're creating a place that children feel is a second home to them.

In addition, you need to consider the various funders (e.g., individuals, foundations, government) that, while not directly involved in program oversight, may be important contributors to your annual budget or specific capital projects. In particular, you need to know if an anti-bias initiative could jeopardize funding, or conversely, if there are organizations that might be particularly interested in financially supporting such efforts.

Regulators. Licensing, accreditation, and other regulatory bodies (e.g., local council, state, federal) are the most visible gatekeepers for early childhood programs. These requirements create boundaries (some real, some imagined) that can get in the way of innovative anti-bias efforts. Some programs may also be subject to local building code regulations or even insurance requirements that could affect operations.

Because of their role in interpreting and enforcing rules, those who monitor your compliance with licensing can make your life difficult around anti-bias efforts. Licensors can also prove to be important sources of support. We have found it useful to find out your licensor's understanding of and commitment to anti-bias education up front and to figure this information into how you approach anti-bias issues that arise.

Regulations are a source of support and obstacles to anti-bias work. NAEYC's *Code of Ethical Conduct and Statement of Commitment* (2011) and *Early Learning Program Accreditation Standards and Assessment Items* (2019a) stipulate that diversity work is an important element of early childhood programs. On the other hand, licensing criteria can get in the way. An anti-bias program leader seeks to negotiate a constructive and reasonable solution to these issues. For example, a licensing requirement that infants sleep in individual cribs clashed with a family's cultural use of a hammock at home. The approved solution was to hang the hammock diagonally inside the crib at the center (Derman-Sparks et al., 2020). Later in this chapter we discuss the possibility that regulations and those responsible for them can be allies.

MAKING SENSE OF THE BASELINE FOR STRATEGIC PLANNING

In this phase of reading a program, you carefully consider the meaning of the baseline information that has been collected, maybe over months, about the landscape, learning environment, stakeholders, gatekeepers, and program culture. By taking stock of the anti-bias readiness of key stakeholders, and identifying potential allies, opportunities, and obstacles, you can generate informed initial strategies for embarking on anti-bias action. As you start carrying out your initial strategies, you will evaluate the outcomes, continue to gather new information about the program, and then make new plans accordingly.

Take Stock: Readiness, Opportunities, and Obstacles

At this point, you have inventoried the features and resources of the program environment and surrounding landscape, developed a preliminary understanding of key stakeholders, and formed a broad understanding of the program culture. Next you focus on the task of figuring out the level of readiness of yourself, the teachers, and the overall program and community to engage in anti-bias action (Hollins, 2023). Then you can consider the potential opportunities and obstacles to the anti-bias mission.

An *opportunity* is any factor that has the potential of opening up forward movement in achieving your program's anti-bias mission. One example would be discovering that a parent is the executive director of a local refugee and immigrant organization. You can identify and activate this opportunity by inviting the parent to lead a helpful professional development workshop for the staff. In contrast, an *obstacle* is a factor that can slow, complicate, or even stall your shifting of the program's culture. These obstacles can also be internal issues, such as fears and uncertainties about the consequences of change. You can mitigate, reframe, or eliminate obstacles through creative problem-solving, staff professional development, or adjusting plans and goals. For instance, lack of funding can limit the materials for anti-bias efforts (e.g., purchasing dolls for anti-bias story telling). Thinking creatively, you could reframe the situation as an opportunity to bring staff, families, and community members together to raise funds or to make learning materials. This deliberative process of recognizing opportunities and creatively problem-solving obstacles helps you feel empowered rather than overwhelmed or ambushed by the challenges of anti-bias work.

Leader Readiness. Regardless of commitment to an anti-bias approach, each leader brings very different skills, knowledge, experience, and awareness to the task. For instance, a leader may feel at ease in moving forward with discussions and professional development related to social and economic class in part because of growing up in a working-class or poor family (opportunity). In contrast, the same leader may feel very uncertain about supporting families around international adoption without taking time to do some reading first (obstacle).

Knowing your capacity for anti-bias work will help you understand the strengths you bring to implementing anti-bias values (opportunities), as well as where you need to grow (obstacles). For instance, a leader's fears and uncertainties can be an obstacle to taking the risks needed for this work. With self-awareness and support from colleagues, you can turn fears into opportunities for growth. Debbie's and John's backgrounds provide relevant examples. Debbie points out her strengths and challenges:

> As a woman of color, I had a life history that helped me have a realistic view of how racism operates and understand the urgency of seeking broad inclusion. On the flip side, I am very conscious of not having teachers see me as the go-to person on Chinese culture. As a leader, I was organized and hands-on—strengths I harnessed in my work with staff. With such a passionate anti-bias vision, my challenge at times was to know when to let go and allow teachers to make mistakes.

John contrasts his own style to Debbie's:

I am very aware of my cautious personal style, which both supported my strategic thinking and challenged my willingness to take risks. I also crossed gender-role norms by being a man in the field of early education; this offered me a unique insight into the challenges for boys in developing a healthy gender identity.

Leaders are also intentional about how they articulate, and when they share, their anti-bias commitment with others. For instance, John recalls:

At my first annual goal-setting meeting at the center, I decided to share my goal broadly as "Explore and implement strategies for expanding the social and cultural diversity of the curriculum, pedagogy, and community." I chose this approach because I did not see explicit anti-bias goals coming directly from individual meetings with teachers. By articulating a broad goal, I hoped that most staff would feel included in the dialogue and action of the first year.

These kinds of choices require that leaders have clarity about their anti-bias strategy.

The leader's history in a program is an important consideration in how to proceed with anti-bias efforts. For instance, when you are new to a program, there is often an expectation that you will make substantive changes in policy and practice (opportunity). At the same time, it is important to take time to observe the culture of the program and its context before you initiate significant changes, like working on anti-bias goals. If you are an experienced leader, especially one who has been at the program for years, you probably have established a good deal of trust and social capital within the community (opportunity). Teachers and families are less likely to question your motives and competence in initiating change. The respectful relationships built over time will have a positive effect on any conflicts that occur.

Finally, a leader's energy and workload are important elements of readiness. It is crucial to acknowledge that there are many demands on you—from problem-solving to meeting the needs of staff and families, paying attention to regulations and standards, and creating and managing the budget, to evaluating staff, dealing with the facility, and building relationships in the larger community. This reality has been especially true during the challenges encountered throughout the pandemic, from the emotional toll on staff and families to the complexities of changing health regulations. Although anti-bias education is not a separate part of the leader's curriculum, but rather integrated into everything you do, it still requires your time and conscious effort. Conversely, this work can energize you and the teachers because of the creativity, emotional investment, and connection to deep values that it entails. In the end, there is always a way to move forward in your anti-bias efforts that respects both the need for a healthy and sustainable workplace *and* the urgency of change.

Teacher Readiness. The leader seeks to uncover where each teacher is in understanding and experience with anti-bias education. Everyone is going to experience some discomfort and trepidation as anti-bias changes occur and the culture of the program begins to shift to a many-cultures perspective. However, you can more effectively move the work forward by carefully reading where people are on their anti-bias journey and responding with thoughtful scaffolding and strategizing.

Drawing on the ABE journey framework presented in Chapter 1 (and noted in parentheses below), you can construct a general awareness of where teachers initially fit in this framework as individuals and as a staff. The following broad categories are useful as starting points, but your first impressions of teachers are likely to be incomplete.

- *Averse* (Before the Journey Begins): The teacher may seem uncomfortable talking about diversity, talk or act in discriminatory ways, and/or have expressed objections to an anti-bias approach (e.g., a teacher complains about a Bhutanese family using their heritage language at the center). You may also see a differences-denial approach of "we are all the same" (e.g., when observing in a classroom, you notice that a teacher ignores a child who asks, "How come Eliza smells funny?").
- *Beginner* (Beginning to Face the Issues): The teacher seems unaware of or has little experience with different social identities but, at times, appears to recognize what they don't know. When faced with an anti-bias challenge, the teacher looks to a colleague they view as the "diversity" person. They listen intently in anti-bias PD, but may seem confused or unsure about asking questions.
- *Learner* (Committing to the Work of the Anti-Bias Journey): The teacher is open to talking and thinking about diversity and is willing to take on new challenges. This teacher may already be using aspects of an anti-bias approach in the classroom but does not take an activist stance (e.g., you observe children playing with dolls of different skin colors).
- *Mentee* (ABE as a Way of Being in the Classroom): The teacher has begun to actively integrate ABE values into all that they do at the center, especially in the classroom, but also increasingly into other interactions. They ask ABE questions, are curious, take some risks sharing about themselves, and generally keep making progress in this work even when they encounter problems.
- *Mentor* (Becoming an Activist Beyond the Classroom): The teacher has expertise and experience in anti-bias education, professionally and personally (outside the program), and can take the lead with colleagues. These teachers will be important allies in moving forward with change (e.g., the teacher offers suggestions about how to ensure that the upcoming harvest festival is accessible to families of all socioeconomic backgrounds).

One factor that can affect where teachers are in their developmental journey is their history in the program. Veteran teachers may be comfortable with the status quo and resist change (obstacle), while newer teachers may be more open to trying an anti-bias approach (opportunity). Over the long term, high teacher turn-over can become an obstacle because it makes it difficult for a leader to gear train-ing and expectations to varying levels of familiarity with an anti-bias approach. In these situations, the leader may choose to focus on teachers viewed as potential mentors of their peers (opportunity).

Program and Community Readiness. Just as we can consider the readiness of the various stakeholders to engage in ABE, Caprice Hollins (2023) argues that the cul-ture of the organization also cycles through developmental stages that can be ob-served, considered, and inform action.

One place to start is to look for the aspects of identity that are meaningful to the key stakeholders in the program in the context of their backgrounds and the philosophy and traditions of the program. Consider how these factors might help people make a connection to anti-bias values and issues. For example, John describes a surprising discovery at the center he directed:

> While nearly all the families spoke English, I found that 25% of the families spoke more than one language at home. As a result, a workshop on dual-language learning proved very popular and led to a parent-facilitated, follow-up dialogue. This, in turn, led to recommendations for changes in the children's curriculum and the program.

The community landscape also presents potential opportunities and obstacles in relation to bias and equity issues. Knowing these helps avoid unwelcome sur-prises and increases the possibilities for networking with allies in the community. For instance, the town mayor and police chief are hosting a neighborhood bar-beque to create greater connection between residents and newly arrived families with refugee status (opportunity). On the flip side, some in the community may be campaigning through the local media to retain traditional Christmas celebrations in public programs for children (obstacle).

The program leader must also consider the possibility of opposition to anti-bias efforts from people in the larger community. For example, later in the book we look at a community where there was an attempt to stop an ECCE program from including children's books and posters showing two mothers or fathers. This speaks to the need for program leaders to move strategically and to be aware that, sadly, social justice values continue to be controversial in many places. Indeed, the current political climate includes a flurry of state and local legislation, referred to as anti-woke/anti-CRT, designed to silence educa-tors who engage colleagues and families in ABE. Most leaders and programs will not have to face these kinds of extreme obstacles. However, it is wise to not be naive and unprepared and to be aware that some kind of external op-position is possible. In Chapter 7, we offer some specific strategies for respond-ing to both internal and external attacks on a program's anti-bias values and actions.

Identify Potential Allies

Leaders identify allies and their potential to contribute individually and institutionally to their anti-bias efforts to shift the culture of the program. An *ally* is a person or group who shares and strives to implement your anti-bias values, supports and publicly endorses your anti-bias efforts, understands the challenges involved in the work, and provides access to resources and networks. As they develop their anti-bias understanding and skill, some allies become true collaborators and take on leadership tasks. In social justice movements, the term *ally* also is used specifically to refer to people with dominant identities acting in support of and in solidarity with people who are different from them. This definition is particularly relevant to program leaders who have marginalized identities. For instance, a program leader who uses American Sign Language to communicate might reach out to attentive allies who identify as non-disabled for support against accusations by staff of not being capable of meeting the expectations of their position.

An ally has one or more of the following characteristics:

- Open to new ideas
- Asks thoughtful questions about bias, equity, and diversity
- Listens carefully
- Indicates willingness to take risks in supporting anti-bias values
- Demonstrates experience and knowledge relevant to anti-bias education

A program leader's immediate allies come from staff and families. However, not all stakeholders are allies, and not all allies are stakeholders. They also come from the program's gatekeepers and from the leader's network of community and professional colleagues. While gatekeepers and community groups may be more distant from the daily work of a program, they can still play significant ally roles, such as being conduits to a range of resources. Building relationships with individuals in the various stakeholder and wider circles is central to finding allies. This work does not happen overnight. It means being observant and being ready to take advantage of opportunities that arise.

Staff Allies. Pay attention to signs of staff members' interest in, explicit support for, and willingness to implement anti-bias education. Another indicator of their anti-bias commitment is holding themselves and their colleagues accountable to anti-bias values. Some staff members may have personal experiences with diversity and bias, or may have knowledge about issues such as cultural relevancy, social justice, or children's identity development. These qualities all provide useful entry points for anti-bias initiatives.

Signs of potential allies appear during everyday discussions, in supervision sessions, in staff meetings and workshops, and in annual survey comments. You can encourage these signs by responding positively when a staff member makes a suggestion related to the anti-bias mission. For example, John recalls:

A teacher at the center proposed that the entire staff read a book she had found insightful about examining the discomfort that often comes with social justice work [Jacobson, 2003]. While not necessarily the book I would have chosen at that time, I decided it was important to act on this opening from the teacher and for the staff to read something recommended by a colleague.

Another approach to uncovering allies is to initiate a voluntary staff anti-bias taskforce or discussion group that meets after hours. While this strategy does not guarantee that all the participating teachers will be effective allies, and it may exclude interested staff who cannot attend for family reasons, it is one way for you to gauge interest and commitment.

Family Allies. Family members make powerful allies because they have a voice as program clients and are in a position to have expectations of the program. Unlike the teachers and program leader, they are not responsible for providing a service to other families and are not constrained by professional boundaries. For example, a parent or guardian can speak up compellingly in a family workshop about personal experiences with racism without being as concerned about offending others or revealing their own confidential information. A parent's request or complaint related to anti-bias values can relieve the program leader from always having to be the one setting expectations for staff. Parents can also be advocates, such as when a parent in John's program emailed him their concern about the lack of teachers reflecting the different cultural groups in the center.

Indicators of potential allies among the children's families come during both one-on-one and group meetings. The intake interview at the beginning of a family's entrance into the program is one opportunity to gauge interest. Pay attention to specific experiences and expertise that family members have with diversity and social justice issues. For instance, you could discover that a family member is an advocate for the rights of people who are houseless at a legal office or are active volunteers at a local queer resource center.

Test the waters by inviting parents and guardians to join hiring and other committees and see how they respond to discussions related to anti-bias goals. For example, a parent member of a hiring committee might express concern about a job applicant's lack of experience with family diversity or encourage the committee to hire a blind candidate despite the reservations of others.

ECCE Colleagues as Allies. Building relationships with other ECCE directors and programs that share a commitment to anti-bias education is also vital. Julie Bisson talks about what that meant for her as a White director reaching out to BIPoC colleagues as both mentors and allies:

It's really helped that there's been a critical mass of People of Color who just regularly helped me remember that I had no other choice, that it wasn't an option not to make ABE an important part of what we did. I worked really hard to develop authentic relationships. The mentorship and the allyship with people of color especially didn't just come easily. You have to earn that.

Attending local director support groups and participation in local and state committees of professional organizations are ways to locate allies. These colleagues may be at different phases in their own understanding and practice of anti-bias education, but may still offer significant support. Attending conference workshops about diversity and equity work is another opportunity to identify professional allies.

ECCE colleague allies offer support in multiple ways. First, you can share experiences and ideas, as well as access new strategies and activities. Second, you can think and problem-solve difficult issues with colleagues in person and through email, Zoom, and social media. A third benefit of networking is getting emotional support and friendly reality checks.

The stress and complexity of anti-bias leadership can wear you down. Leaders periodically need to unload and check in with colleagues who have similar values and responsibilities. Finally, you can collaborate with other program leaders on professional development opportunities in order to share trainer costs and connect your teachers to staff from different cultural contexts.

Community Groups and Networks. Community, state, and national advocacy groups outside of the ECCE field that focus on identity, diversity, and social justice issues are another potential source of ally support. They have relevant information, resources, and experiences, and can help with problem-solving and strategies. For instance, a local bookstore owner could provide you with access to used books to borrow for staff professional development on gender identity issues. At another program, a relationship with a Latinx community center might provide access to Spanish translation services and information on local cultural celebrations. Miriam Zmiewski-Angelova shares how, as the director of Daybreak Star Preschool in Seattle, her mutual engagement in the community became a source of allies, resources, and sustenance:

If I'm wanting to sustain myself and my anti-bias work, I need to make sure I'm showing up. I can't only be going to events in the Native community, or the Black community. I'm making sure that . . . if someone has extended an invitation to something, to try to make the best effort I can, to attend in some way. And just see how I can be helpful and supportive because I find that if you're if you're looking for folks to be allies, you want to make sure it doesn't feel transactional. So better to show up and be helpful. [You're] going because you're going to learn a lot by just being present. I learned a lot by just like, showing up at stuff.

Some social service organizations also have conferences where ECCE people can meet professionals from other professional fields who may become allies.

For example, Louise reaped valuable knowledge and encouragement over the years through her relationship with the national anti-racism educational and organizing group Crossroads Ministry, which is an interfaith group working on social justice.

Gatekeepers as Allies. One of the most strategic and difficult places to identify allies is among people who have power and authority over the program or in the community. While ECCE program leaders have considerable power to make decisions independently, many are typically accountable to a higher authority. This could include the director of the agency that oversees the program, a district superintendent, or a college dean. In some cases, the people acting as gatekeepers are not early childhood professionals, but come from other social service backgrounds or other professional roles (e.g., business manager).

Even though they are not always in direct or regular contact with the program, the people in these positions can be valuable as allies because of the power they have in relation to funding, public relations, and policy. It is important for you to be intentional about developing relationships and finding opportunities to share the program's anti-bias education goals and efforts. For instance, a board member for a community child care program shows interest in the program leader's collaboration with a community garden, which is growing vegetables for a local food pantry. Realizing that the board member might share the program's social justice values, the leader invites them to be part of a meeting to discuss plans to engage the children in the project. Later, the board member's support proves helpful in locating funding for new garden beds and in securing city council approval.

Regulators (and regulations) are gatekeepers that can also be allies in your work. Accreditation typically includes explicit criteria that support both cultural relevancy and anti-bias education in the program and classroom. For instance, when John's program was undertaking accreditation some years ago, a search at that time of the NAEYC (n.d.) online accreditation TORCH site using the term *bias* came up with the following statement:

> The criteria are designed to be inclusive of all children, regardless of ability, culture, language, ethnicity, religion, or socioeconomic status. Teachers are expected to counter potential bias and discrimination (1.D.01 and 3.B.04) and to help children build their understanding of diversity. (2.L.03)

As the leader, you have a responsibility to be aware of these criteria and use the language to promote anti-bias efforts with staff and families. With some creativity and relationship-building with gatekeepers, you can often find constructive solutions to apparent obstacles. To illustrate this point, John recounts the following story:

> I had been encouraging teachers to take children on field trips into the local community as a way to increase their access to more diversity and

potential anti-bias curriculum. Families, staff, and students often used the university's shuttle bus service to visit various places on and near campus. Unfortunately, the state licensing regulations dictated that a child under kindergarten age could not be on a bus without a safety belt and car seat. I talked with the head of licensing, someone I regarded as an ally through our membership on a child care task force, and pointed out that children in the city ride public transportation every day. She advised us to appeal through the formal process and subsequently granted us a variation on our license for younger children to ride the bus with parent permission.

SETTING THE STAGE FOR ACTION

In this chapter we have provided examples of how reading the program can help with generating thoughtful strategies for anti-bias action. This baseline portrait can also help you take beginning steps that help get the ball rolling or set the stage for the long term. This final section offers some doable suggestions for starting to act.

Adjust the Program Structures

Policies and Procedures. Creating program policies that affect staff and families is one of the program leader's core responsibilities. After reviewing formal policies, you can make immediate changes to policies that present obstacles to anti-bias goals and add ones that proactively support them. This step would also include a review of administrative paperwork to ensure that it is inclusive of all families. One example is the application and intake forms that include spaces for only a mother and father, rather than being inclusive of the range of family structures. Another possibility is to have dual-language forms for families who are more comfortable using their heritage languages.

It is important for you to recognize that policies—whether formalized in print or informal and based on tradition—are not written in stone, and you can rethink, modify, or eliminate them. You must also decide whether to simply change the policy or go through a more deliberative process of discussion with staff and families to arrive at a more helpful policy. The choice depends on an analysis of priorities: Is this a straightforward or urgent change that needs to happen quickly (e.g., the application form), or is this a complex issue that presents an opportunity for engaging stakeholders in a learning process that leads to a sense of democracy and visibility? For instance, the policy (and practice) regarding holiday celebrations is often one that requires rethinking (see Chapter 5).

Admissions Priorities. After reviewing the program's racial, language, and other demographics, you may decide to be more proactive in seeking families and children with particular backgrounds and identities. To change admissions for the following year, prior planning is necessary. You may have the authority to adjust policies and forms to reflect priorities, or you could focus on community outreach to increase the diversity of child and family backgrounds in your applications.

At John's program, he worked with the parent advisory committee to include specific language that identified increasing the diversity of family backgrounds as an admissions priority. He also found that he was able to create small shifts in the demographics of the families by eliminating or limiting policies such as alumni and sibling priorities for new spaces that tended to reinforce the status quo. Debbie redesigned the school brochure at her program to make it more accessible in language and format (e.g., adding more images and less text). Both John and Debbie also undertook targeted outreach to local religious and community organizations with populations that might increase diversity of family backgrounds.

Budget Allocations. While we believe it is possible to implement anti-bias education within any budget, the allocation of funds does reflect the program's priorities. Program leaders have varying degrees of decision-making power over the annual budget and the funding of specific components, with some having full jurisdiction over it. However, even when they share budget decision-making with oversight administrators or agencies, leaders typically have the ability to make small and incremental, but important, changes in the distribution to specific budget items.

For instance, you can decide to make sure that there are funds for immediately expanding anti-bias learning materials. As needs get identified, it may be useful to decide to dedicate most of your classroom materials budget one year to a particular aspect of anti-bias work, such as ensuring that all classrooms have books reflecting all the heritage languages spoken by families or sending a classroom team to an anti-bias professional development workshop.

While some budget changes can happen immediately, others require long-term planning—maybe over several years. The leader is involved in making the case for the expenditures and seeking even incremental changes each year. For instance, in programs with fees, the leader may be able to adjust how tuition is structured (and create a sliding scale, as is the case in John's program), or build a scholarship fund (as Debbie was able to do, in part by instituting a new application fee).

Hiring Procedures. A staff that comes from diverse backgrounds and has the capacity and commitment to support anti-bias education is vital. These qualities become part of the criteria for selecting new teachers and also provides candidates clarity about the program's values. Because openings can arise at any time, you need to develop a plan early on that includes hiring practices that can attract a diverse pool of candidates (e.g., proactive outreach into specific communities or community-based advertising media) and meet program goals. Proactively seeking teachers with important capacities, such as speaking or signing in languages other than English or having experience teaching in diverse settings, is legitimate if clearly defined in the position announcement.

Challenging our assumptions and implicit biases is critical to using inclusive hiring practices. For instance, make sure you don't rely on easily known candidates or candidates who "fit in" to the status quo, rather than assessing clearly defined qualities and skills. Selecting diverse hiring committees and including interview questions about inclusion and equity also improve anti-bias hiring. Possible interview questions include the following:

- Give an example from your experience of figuring out a difference between a parent's views and your own beliefs or program policies. What did you do, and what guided your choices about how to respond?
- We work hard to make sure that our programs are respectful and inviting places for children and families of all cultural backgrounds. What are some examples from your own experience of things you have done to ensure a welcoming environment?
- If you overheard a preschooler make a comment to another child that rejects or demeans an aspect of the child's social identity, what would you do?

Prepare Yourself

As a leader, you also change yourself. Having assessed your own readiness for the journey ahead, you should develop a plan for professional growth. You may need to do further reading and learning about the adult anti-bias developmental stages or about implementing anti-bias work with children. You may decide you need to learn more about facilitating anti-bias discussions (see Chapters 4 and 6).

While leadership is vital, you will not be doing this work by yourself; progress does not just depend on you alone. As you generate a plan for preparing yourself, it is also important to have collaborators on the journey ahead. As discussed in the section on identifying allies, you will find support from both within and outside your program. Identify them as early as possible, and do not be shy about asking for help.

Leadership is a strategic balance between what you want to accomplish and what you can actually do. You seek to do what is within your reach and within your power. Shifting the culture of your program to an anti-bias community requires a mix of thoughtful pragmatism (What is happening here? What is our capacity?) and visionary optimism (We will get there! It is possible!).

A DYNAMIC AND CYCLICAL PROCESS

The aim of an anti-bias leader is to realize deep and lasting change in all the components of the program. This does not happen quickly. While a long-term view of change is often in tension with the urgency of social justice (When do we want it? Now!), we believe such a view is essential to shifting the culture of a program.

Reading the program is a preliminary step, as well as a dynamic, cyclical process. Using the initial read as a preliminary baseline, you can begin to act. Throughout the year, you should periodically revisit what you know and assess what is happening. Based on the analysis at each point, you can develop a new set of strategies to meet anti-bias goals.

We now turn to the specific strategies and activities for working with teachers (Chapters 4 and 6) and families (Chapter 5) over the long haul of the anti-bias journey.

CHAPTER 4

Fostering Reflective Anti-Bias Educators

First and foremost, the leader needs to be deeply invested in this work. They then need to present it to the staff as an invitation to explore issues of diversity and be sure there is time and opportunity for staff to be engaged.

—Teacher

Becoming skilled at anti-bias education in the classroom is an ongoing journey that calls on educators to engage in a cycle of practice and reflection about themselves and their actions. They do much more than acquire new materials and develop new activities. Anti-bias education cannot be mastered in a one-time workshop or by reading a book. Most teachers largely learn how to implement ABE on the job, in specific settings with specific children and families.

Anti-bias leaders provide the necessary time, space, resources, support, and facilitation for teachers and other staff to be part of the process of change. They build a community of learners that enables everyone to explore and grapple with anti-bias issues. A collaborative style of leadership, facilitative leadership, (LeeKeenan & Ponte, 2018; Schwartz, 2016) empowers staff members to first begin and then take ownership of their anti-bias work (see Chapter 2).

All early childhood programs have a staff with a range of awareness and experiences with diversity, inclusion, equity, and anti-bias education. Some staff members are just discovering diversity work; others have experience doing some type of diversity and anti-bias work in their previous professional development (PD) or classrooms or have been exploring their own issues of identity. Some may have more experience of ABE than the program leader; others may reject an anti-bias approach. As the program leader, your charge is to find ways to provide a variety of learning opportunities for all of the staff, given their diverse range of awareness, experiences, and curiosity. You should scaffold the anti-bias education growth of the individual staff members, as well as the forward movement of the group as a whole.

This chapter offers a range of strategies and activity examples, organized in two main sections. First, we describe ways to build the community of anti-bias learners. Second, we offer strategies for engaging staff in learning about and starting to implement an anti-bias education framework. Throughout this chapter, as well as subsequent ones, composite quotes from teachers, leaders, and parents are used to introduce the various sections.

Drawing from a social constructivist framework, we assume that, as with children, teachers at different places in their learning and development will engage with and take away different understandings from the same learning experience Therefore, while the activities we describe can work for teachers at any stage in their anti-bias journey, keep in mind where they are on their path. We also suggest revisiting activities you have previously implemented. Similarly, as with children, strive to match experiences you offer with the challenges and strengths of those you are teaching, rather than assuming that any specific activity is the best—or only—way to learn about a particular topic. All the strategies and activities are applicable to teachers; most may also be used with the entire staff (see the definitions in Figure I.1 in the Introduction).

BUILDING A COMMUNITY OF ANTI-BIAS LEARNERS

> When we put effort and care into anti-bias education, we see and feel it throughout the entire school.
>
> —Teacher

Anti-bias work grows best in an environment where collegial, mutually respectful relationships among staff and between staff and the program leader are the usual practice and where a culture exists that fosters open conversation and dialogue, reflection, and risk-taking. Creating a caring and welcoming environment in which staff feel respected and trusted from the very first day is essential. As pointed out in Chapter 2, this is a central tenet of effective program leadership in ECCE, and many resources already exist that offer strategies for creating collegial relationships. Here are strategies for establishing and deepening anti-bias culture and interactions.

Create a Climate for Taking Risks

> I've learned anti-bias education is messy work; you [the director] have given us permission to make mistakes. I know you've got my back, especially when I am trying things that I don't always feel comfortable with!
>
> —Teacher

Once you lay a foundation of mutually respectful relations with staff, it is time to begin engaging teachers in reflection and conversations about their intersecting identities, their biases, and anti-bias issues. These conversations inevitably lead to personal disclosure that can feel risky and uncomfortable at different times. Some teachers embrace the opportunity to stretch their thinking and consider new perspectives. Others feel unsettled by the disequilibrium they experience as they gain better self-understanding, uncover biased attitudes, and encounter challenges to their worldviews. Some people, particularly of dominant social identities, experience embarrassment or guilt about their lack of awareness and role in perpetuating bias. In these situations, adults confuse feeling discomfort with being unsafe. These are not the same dynamics (DiAngelo, 2018; Oluo, 2018). In contrast, people of marginalized identities may feel frustration and anger as they revisit and reveal hurtful and often traumatic experiences in their lives.

Many anti-bias education leaders mention that their goal is to move from a culture of kindness to a culture of courage. Anti-bias education conversations need spaces that are both brave and safe. A *brave space* encourages dialogue, where people of all social identities and lived experiences are accountable for sharing and coming to new understandings. This process is often hard and typically *uncomfortable*. A *safe space* provides a break from judgment, unsolicited opinions, and having to explain yourself. It also allows people to feel supported and respected (Arao & Clemens, 2013).

Constructivist theory tells us that if people feel supported in their learning, disequilibrium and its accompanying discomfort can lead to growth. As the program leader, you have the responsibility to create a climate for discussions in which participants will not feel under attack. At the same time, you must help everyone to understand that feeling discomfort is a part of the anti-bias journey. Avoiding uncomfortable conversations does not lead to growth. It simply results in keeping things as they are, rather than creating new perspectives and practices. In Chapter 7 we focus on the central role of conflict in anti-bias change.

Setting Community Commitments. Developing and practicing community commitments helps create a safe and brave environment for risk-taking in anti-bias discussions. Doing so establishes the agreed-upon way of interacting, or agreements, from the very beginning of the program year. Parker Palmer (1997) refers to two kinds of norms as a useful framework. *Structural norms* define when, where, and how long staff meetings will take place and rules for the conversation, such as maintaining confidentiality, active listening, and respecting silence. *Interpersonal norms* are those that allow a group to feel safe, such as speaking from one's own experiences, suspending judgment of others' narratives, and being honest. At the first staff meeting of the year, you should engage everyone in setting the community agreements, brainstorming the question, "Share one commitment you can agree to make to be able to participate fully in and contribute to the building of our learning community together." Revisit these community agreements periodically at subsequent meetings, and change or add additional ones as needed.

In creating the "rules of engagement" at the Child Educational Center in California, director Tashon McKeithan emphasizes it is everyone's responsibility to ensure our environment is safe, and everyone is respected and supported. She uses these prompts to initiate discussion:

How do you want to feel when you are at work?
How do we make it happen?
And when we don't, what is our responsibility?

Modeling Leader Risk-Taking. When program leaders model risk-taking around anti-bias topics, they encourage staff to go beyond their comfort zone and risk opening themselves to new ideas and ways of working with each other, families, and children. As one teacher at Debbie's program explained to her:

> The director needs to model anti-bias education. You share a lot of your experiences with us, your messiness is public, you make very clear what the stance and the expectations are for teachers, for parents, for kids. Then you have our backs when conflicts come up: that is really important.

As the program leader, you can model risk-taking by acknowledging and doing something that is uncomfortable for you, sharing mistakes you have made as leader, and acknowledging that you don't know all the answers. John relates an example about modeling taking risks:

> At one of our staff retreats, I talked about my experience as a man in early childhood, a young teacher in a profession in which there are very few men. I found that one of the very early questions from interview committees (made up of parents) was about my policy regarding giving children affection. I didn't recognize it at first—but, in retrospect, I realize there was an underlying homophobic agenda. My female colleagues weren't getting the same questions. I also discovered that a dad on one committee, a professional in the legal system, ran a criminal background check on me— this was many years before these checks were legally required. Sharing this information with my staff as their director was very personal and somewhat emotional. People listened intently. I have always felt it is important for the leader to be a participant with the staff as well as share your expertise.

Tashon McKeithan, at her program in California, asks her staff to share their "blooper reel," not their highlight reel, because we learn from the bloopers.

> In early childhood mistakes are magic, we learn from them—and that does not only apply to children. We have to model for our children that it is OK to make mistakes.

A program leader can also use their own anti-bias journey as a learner to provide staff with a window into the process and to encourage their risk-taking. Director Karina Rojas Rodriguez at the Southwest Early Learning Bilingual Preschool in Seattle shares the following wisdom with her teachers:

> I've been in your space. I've been a teacher who didn't know a lot about anti-bias. I've been learning as I'm going. One of things I've learned is it's OK to not know what you don't know. It's OK to ask questions and to say, yes, I do have a bias. And it's OK for you to share it with me. Because then we can work together and we can experience this disequilibrium.

Educators Supporting Each Other. Nadia Jaboneta (2019), in her book *You Can't Celebrate That! Navigating the Deep Waters of Social Justice*, describes the important strategy of having thought partners and a community of anti-bias colleagues in your program. You can rely on these thought partners again and again to share observations from the classroom, get feedback for next steps, and find support for meeting the challenges of doing anti-bias work. Some of these thought partners can be your teaching team, other teachers in your program, or the program leader. Often Nadia came away from these conversations feeling unsettled and full of questions. Yet in the long run she knew that disequilibrium is the springboard for new learning.

In the next two sections are activities and strategies to use with staff in the beginning of the school year or when groups transition. Most can be adapted for use in virtual PD sessions by using breakout rooms. The first category of activities is about getting to know one another and our multiple intersecting identities. The second category of activities is about understanding anti-bias education. You can use activities from both categories at the same time throughout the year.

Get to Know One Another

> I have learned the importance of self-reflection and deeply looking into my own values and beliefs and unpacking my own history. Without doing so I do not believe it is possible to move forward with the work nor be able to think about how we might engage children in thinking and talking about diversity.
>
> —Teacher

One of the central themes of anti-bias education is educators knowing who they are and sharing their identities and life experiences with one another. This ongoing interchange deepens collegial relationships and sets the precedence for learning about families and children. You can use the following getting-to-know-each-other activities at in-person staff retreats or staff meetings at the beginning of and throughout the school year.

Potato Activity. This is an icebreaker, intended for staff for whom talking about human diversity is new or uncomfortable. It is a playful way to help people start to take risks and think about differences, including those staff in the *difference denial* stage. The purpose is twofold. One is to get participants talking about differences—in this case, the many ways a potato is a potato. The second is to introduce the idea that learning opportunities for exploring diversity exist in daily early childhood activities and materials. To implement the potato activity:

1. Arrange enough potatoes on a table for at least one per person.
2. Ask participants to describe what they see as the characteristics of potatoes; record their responses on a large sheet of paper or projected screen.

3. Invite each person to choose one potato and to study it closely (5 minutes).

4. Collect the potatoes, and put them back in a large box.

5. Ask participants to find their potato. Then ask, "How did you identify your potato?" Record answers next to the first list.

6. Ask the group to consider differences and similarities in the two lists. Words in the first list tend to be broadly descriptive (e.g., *brown, lumpy, different sizes, roundish*), while phrases in the second list are individualized, suggesting a unique potato (e.g., *has a frown, two dots, fits in the palm of my hand*).

7. Engage participants in reflecting on the activity: "What did you do to get to know your potato?" "What did you learn from this activity?" "How can you apply these ideas to how we view people?"

As the program leader, you should facilitate the brainstorming, adding your own reflections, which are the central ideas you want participants to consider:

- There are many different ways to think about people (as there are with potatoes), once you get to know them.
- As with potatoes, people are complex, made up of many characteristics and identities.
- A potato, like a person, is both a member of a larger group and a unique individual.

How Did You Get Here? This activity warms up a group to engage in dialogue and raises issues of identity and the complexities of our stories. It can be as short as 10 minutes and can be followed by a quick debrief or commentary. Introduce the activity as follows:

1. Everyone has a story (or stories) about how they came to be at this workshop today. Your story might be how you literally got to the workshop this morning, it might be about your journey as an early childhood educator, or, even more broadly, how you came to this city or country as an immigrant. You get to decide.

2. Pose the following questions to the group. Give everyone a minute or two to recall the stories they want to share. Invite participants to write or draw out their story to help jog their visual memories.

    How did you get "here"?

    How did this "journey" shape who you are today?

The following activities invite staff to go deeper into their consciousness-raising process. In the film *Reflecting on Anti-bias Education in Action: The Early Years* (LeeKeenan, Nimmo, & McKinney, 2021), teacher Veronica Reynoso shares the importance of getting to know her cultural identities:

Being a teacher of color, I think it is a lot easier answering the children's questions, because I am very comfortable with my identity and my culture (and have had many years to develop that). It is such a vulnerable place, because you are sharing a lot about yourself, and they are sharing a lot about themselves.

Cultural Identity Narratives. Storytelling with staff about who they are rests on the premise that they all grew up and now live within a cultural framework that affects relationships with one another as well as their work with children and families. This activity makes these influences visible by naming and exploring participants' backgrounds. In the beginning of the year, Miriam Zmiewski-Angelova, former director of the Daybreak Star Preschool, serving predominantly urban Native families in the Seattle area, asks staff to share where their names come from and the meaning.

A person's name has important meaning because these are the qualities that the parents wanted to instill or are their hopes for their child . . . We all have a story, we all have a story of how we got to where we are . . . learning each other's stories, beginning with our origin stories, is a way for making connections with each other, working through the hard things, knowing that things take time.

Some people find it difficult to publicly share their stories, so it is important to acknowledge the risk-taking. You should break the ice by telling your cultural story first. Providing structure to the activity with clear goals and outcomes also provides safety. There are no "right" questions to open up cultural storytelling about oneself. Questions should come from reading your group, beginning with ones that make sense to the group. As staff get to know one another, then you can scaffold questions that deepen the conversations.

Topics that stimulate stories about family culture and heritage include talking about:

- A meaningful family cultural artifact and why it is significant
- The reasons for one's first and family names
- A favorite ritual or holiday and what was important about it
- How an individual's family came to live in the United States

You should facilitate the storytelling, inviting individuals to clarify and expand their stories, and engaging the group in reflecting on the similarities, differences, and themes that emerge from the stories.

Culture in Your Bag. This activity can be done on the spot as an icebreaker with no preparation. It reflects the concept that we carry our culture with us all the time. In this activity everyone has a partner. In pairs, the participants share what is in their bag (pocket or wallet) and what these objects reveal (either literally or metaphorically) about their identity and culture. For example, one teacher pulled out a set of keys and said it reminded her of her parents being immigrants and entering this country. After the participants have a chance to share in pairs, they can then share in the large group. To encourage relationship-building and active listening, the partners in each pair introduce each other to the large group by relating the partner's story in brief.

A variation of this activity is to have each person create a cultural bag as an assignment completed at home. The participants put five things in a brown paper bag that represent who they are and their culture. Then they share their bags at a staff meeting in one of several ways; for example,

- Each participant can share his or her bag and explain the significance of each item.
- The anonymous bags can be arranged on a table. Each person picks a bag, looks at the objects, and then tries to guess who it belongs to and why.

In all of these variations, the main purpose of the activity is to have participants gain a better understanding of what is meant by culture and from this perspective to get to know one another. Sharing a brief text like "Culture: A Process That Empowers" (Phillips, 1995), which succinctly clarifies the core ideas, can help teachers understand the concepts better.

Uncovering Attitudes We Were Taught. Asking staff to identify and examine their attitudes about diverse identities is also key to their growth in anti-bias work. At the beginning of this activity, it helps participants' sense of safety if you say a few words about how we all learn negative attitudes as we grow up. As with other activities, you can model being open about this topic. Responding to the following questions from *Anti-Bias Education for Young Children and Ourselves* (Derman-Sparks & Edwards, 2020, p. 30) provides places to start:

- What is your earliest memory of realizing that some people were different from you and/or your family (for example in racial identity, ability, family structure, religion, economics)? How did you feel about yourself in relationship to the people who were different from you? How did you feel about them?
- What did your family say about people whose social identities were different from your family's? Did their behavior match their words?
- What did you see or not see about people who were like you in books, movies, on the Internet and social media, TV, and advertisements? What messages did this give you about your social identities?
- Did you know or know about anyone who didn't behave in the ways expected according to stereotypes about their social identities? What did you think about those people?

Diversity Rounds. The objectives of this activity are to become more aware of one's multiple identities, to work with others to define social identities, and to think more deeply about what diversity means. Leading this large-group activity, you ask participants to group and regroup themselves in four or five different ways. Based on the prompt the leader calls out, participants talk with one another to define and form their own categories. Sample prompts may be:

- Where were you born?
- If known, what is your birth order?
- What kind of school did you attend growing up?
- When you think of your social identities, what comes to mind first?

As each group forms, participants discuss:

- What does it mean to you to be (a member of this group)?
- How important is this group to how you define yourself?
- How is our group unique?

This protocol was created by educators and affiliates with the School Reform Initiative (2014a). Complete directions for this activity are available at the SRI website (www.schoolreforminitiative.org).

Identities Web. This identities web activity rests on the premise that everyone has many personal and social identities. This activity is an effective way to explore what these are and the distinctions between them. The idea of "social identities" as distinct from "personal identities" may be new for many staff, so it may be necessary to review the concept before introducing the activity (refer to Chapter 1 for an explanation of these concepts.).

1. On a large piece of paper (or on a computer), draw a circle with your name in it in the middle.
2. Using one color, draw spokes out from the circle for 5 personal/individual identities that you recognize as important to who YOU are as an individual. These could be individual qualities, personality traits, interests, and strengths; for instance, funny, educator, foodie, detail-oriented. This is how you define or "see" yourself as an individual.
3. Using a second color, draw new spokes for each of your social identities—starting with those that seem most significant to who you are in the world and your work as an educator. Refer to the "My Social Identities Portrait" worksheet on p. 31 of the Anti-Bias Education text (Derman-Sparks, et al., 2020), for example, woman, Asian American, Jewish. This is how society defines and groups individuals in the United States based on access to institutional power. You may want to include other relevant terms and categories not on these lists (e.g., immigrant, Spanish

speaker) or that have relevance to where you are in the world. These identities can be thought of as "imposed," as they serve the purpose of distribution of social power. The categories that define the "norm" may vary according to the social and political contexts of your home country. When exploring social identities, participants may need room to discuss and come to terms with the realization that group memberships they may hold dearly ("I speak Spanish," "I grew up working-class") are also defined and stereotyped by the dominant society in negative terms about which groups get access to power and resources.

4. What overlaps or connections do you see between your personal, and social identities? Draw in these connections with lines to create a web in any way you like. These lines can also show intersections between different areas of your social identities (e.g., gender identity and economic class).

Take a partner on a "tour" of your identities map. You decide what you are ready to share. Finally, take time to discuss the following questions:

- What messages did you get about your social identities from your family, schooling, and media?
- Which social identities are most significant to you? Which areas do you feel uncertain about sharing? Which seem less important to you as an individual?
- How might these social identities play a role in your work with families, children, and colleagues (i.e. as assets and/or challenges in your equity efforts)?

COMMITTING TO AN ANTI-BIAS EDUCATION FRAMEWORK

I used to think that showing my anti-bias attitude meant not highlighting or bringing up differences, but I have learned that discussing and celebrating these differences in a more active way is a very powerful tool against bias.

—Teacher

In the first months of a program year, the leader should provide regular opportunities for the staff to advance their grasp of the core concepts of anti-bias education.

Introduce Anti-Bias Education

Workshops and staff meetings that introduce and review the purpose, values, and goals of anti-bias education reflect the program leader's commitment. Learning activities about anti-bias education begin at staff orientation and the first staff meeting of the year and continue regularly as an incremental series of experiences.

Director Tashon McKeithan found the concept of emotional intelligence (Goleman, 2005) useful for preparing staff to hold challenging conversations about anti-bias topics, particularly with White educators and families. Emotional intelligence refers to the ability to identify and regulate one's emotions and understand the emotions of others. Tashon views the concept as an entry point to anti-bias education.

> Having language to discuss emotions is critical to anti-bias education. Working on emotional intelligence development helps with building a level of trust. We can't say we are fine, when someone asks how are you, when we are not . . . We need to know how we are really feeling, distinguish being jealous and envious, scared and angry. Having honest conversations is messy work and we are going to make mistakes, and we're going to say the wrong things at times, and that is OK.

Director Miriam Zmiewski-Angelova used metaphors from Indigenous cultures to describe anti-bias education to her staff.

> It is like a woven mat, these strands in the mat are the principles and components . . . that are woven together and create a really strong foundation for how this whole thing looks. You can't pick and choose, can't start pulling things out of it, because you don't like it, because it's uncomfortable, or because a barrier might be in the way. . . . With anti-bias education, it's really important that you make sure you have representation of those cultures that are relevant to the classroom that you have. What does your classroom look like right now? Bring in the backgrounds of the educators, the languages, the families, the key stakeholders in the community, cultural important figures. How do you weave them in, in a way that, feels respectful and feels whole. Make sure that there are opportunities to keep looking back at that whole woven piece. And, what can we continue to improve upon? What can we strengthen?

Below are several introductory sessions to use with staff. They include an exploration of the rationale for anti-bias education, a discussion on how ABE differs from other approaches to diversity, and self-reflection activity that focuses on the meaning of anti-bias education for each person. This section concludes with an outline for organizing staff meetings focused on ABE.

Noticing Differences. Ask staff to think back to their work with children or their own childhood experience for examples in which a child/children noticed another child or adult who was different from them in one or more of the following ways: disability, race (skin color), language, gender, sexual orientation/family composition, religion, or ethnicity. What are the comments or questions that are voiced when they notice the difference? The goal is to have participants think about the wide range of differences and the different ages when children notice differences. After staff have had time to think and write silently, they share their comments in pairs, and then the whole group. As the facilitator, you write the comments and child's age on chart paper (e.g., 4-year-old: Why does he talk funny? 3-year-old: Why is her skin dirty? 5-year-old: Look at that person using a wheelchair). You then ask the participants to discuss how adults respond when they hear these comments and questions from children. Examples of responses have included:

- Ignore the comment
- Reflect the question back to the child
- Get more information from the child
- Answer the child very matter-of-factly
- Correct the child with adult's desired response

In processing this activity, the main point is for staff to understand that while children are aware of differences at very young ages, how adults respond to the children's responses makes a huge impact in how children think about these differences. The adult response can reinforce that it is not good to ask questions about differences or that it is okay to notice differences and okay to be different. As a follow-up, you could provide a handout on children's developmental stages of awareness of differences (York, 2016).

Diversity Education Continuum. The purpose of this activity is for participants to learn the differences between anti-bias education and other responses to diversity found in ECCE programs. The program leader first gives a mini-lecture that provides a framework for the staff to think about the differences.

1. On a piece of chart paper or computer slide, you can draw a big line with two arrows at each end to show that this is a continuum. There are four terms on the line, from left to right:
   Differences denial————Tourist curriculum————Bias-free——Anti-bias
2. Explain that this continuum represents different ways to think and teach about diversity and equity. Give the participants a definition for each term, and the core ideas you want the staff to understand about each approach to diversity education.
3. Ask participants to relate their own school experiences to the four terms on the continuum, write their ideas on the chart paper or slide in columns under each term, and use their examples to supplement the core ideas. It is important to note that the first two responses are intended to maintain dominant perspectives as the "norm."

- In a *differences-denial* response, the learning environment, curriculum, and teaching ignore and avoid human diversity and social bias.
- In a *tourist* approach, cultural differences are emphasized and often exaggerated as exotic. Children learn superficially, and often stereotypically, about different cultures around the world, as a tourist would when visiting different places.
- A *bias-free zone* approach focuses on creating an authentic, nonstereotypical classroom environment that acknowledges similarities and differences. The approach is limited because it does not explicitly acknowledge the need for children to have tools to actively counter bias outside the classroom.
- *Anti-bias* perspective places diversity, inclusion, and equity goals at the heart of everything we do in early childhood. It recognizes that very young children are observing, experiencing, and actively making sense of social identities and biases in the world around them. It is an active and activist approach that respects each child's and family's background and reality, while directly addressing the impact of social stereotypes, bias, and discrimination in children's development and interactions.

Becoming an Anti-Bias Educator. Considering the meaning of anti-bias education for themselves and their work is another important beginning-of-year discussion for staff, as it also becomes a way to check changes in thinking as the school year progresses. Your staff needs a basic foundation of anti-bias education, which can be found in resources such as *Anti-Bias Education for Young Children and Ourselves* (Derman-Sparks et al., 2020), *Don't Look Away: Embracing Anti-Bias Classrooms* (Iruka et al., 2020) and *Anti-bias Education in the Early Childhood Classroom* (Kissinger, 2017) (See Appendix A for more suggestions www.tcpress.com). Introduce (or review) the four goals of anti-bias education listed in Chapter 1. Then ask staff to think about relevant questions, such as the following from Derman-Sparks et al., 2020, p. 19, and to share their responses with their colleagues:

- What do you hope ABE could do for the children you teach? For their families? For yourself? If your hopes are realized, how will it benefit them?
- What anxieties or concerns might you have about implementing ABE in your particular setting or community?
- Where could you find support for doing ABE within or outside your program?
- What seems most interesting and inviting about becoming an anti-bias teacher? Which anti-bias goal interests you most right now?

As the leader, you should contribute to the staff's discussion of these questions. Seeing you as a learner who is willing to be open and vulnerable about where you are on the anti-bias journey invites the staff to take more risks.

Using Film to Provoke Discussion. The film *Reflecting on Anti-Bias Education in Action: The Early Year*s (LeeKeenan, Nimmo, & McKinney, 2021) is an introduction to and provocation for discussion about ABE. Closed-captioned in English, Spanish, and Chinese, the film is available for free streaming from the website https://www.antibiasleadersece.com/the-film-reflecting-on-anti-bias-education -in-action/. Organized around the four anti-bias goals, the film is a series of classroom vignettes of teachers working with children and reflecting on their identities, contexts, and practice.

A discussion guide (LeeKeenan & Nimmo, 2021) is available from the website to help teachers reflect on what is possible in their own classrooms and programs. After viewing the film in its entirety or by chapter goals, facilitate a staff discussion of the following questions:

- What strategies do you see teachers using in the film to support anti-bias education?
- What enabled the teaches to take on this type of curriculum? What might the teachers need to have done before they started?
- How would you involve families in anti-bias work? How would you approach their questions, concerns, and support?
- What might you do differently in your classroom and program? What challenges might you face? How do you apply ABE in your context?
- How do your intersecting social identities influence this work?

Staff Meetings. Staff meetings are an ongoing opportunity to infuse learning about anti-bias education. While you ensure that anti-bias issues are included on the agenda, it is important to involve staff in planning the specific agenda items as a way to encourage individuals to take more ownership of the proceedings. Anti-bias growth requires that participants actively engage in the process of change.

At staff meetings, teachers can routinely share documentation of their classroom anti-bias work. This may include stories about children, issues, challenges, questions, and effective—as well as missed—learning opportunities. Their colleagues' feedback and discussion provide support and teaching ideas, which help teachers improve their classroom practice. These staff meetings also play a key role in creating a learning community that allows for risk-taking, critical reflection, and growth.

Program leaders can organize a system of professional learning communities where different teaching teams sign up for a particular staff meeting and share a specific question or anti-bias dilemma they have in their classroom. These communities can work in both virtual and face-to-face spaces. The teachers bring photos, a work sample, a short video clip, or a transcript of a conversation to the staff meeting. After viewing the documentation and hearing the teacher's questions, the rest of the group discusses the issues. As leader, you could share issues that come up for you as well, modeling the kind of communication anti-bias education work requires.

Figure 4.1. ABE Staff Meeting Discussion (60 min) (Nimmo et al., 2021, p. 26)

1. **Connections/Icebreaker**: Share one thing important to you about your identity. (*5 min*)
2. **Review meeting agreements**. Anti-bias education requires community commitments that help create a safe place to have honest and brave conversations. These commitments can be collaboratively developed by the group or provided by the facilitator. (*5 min*)
3. **Choose ONE of these activities** for each staff meeting: (*45 min*)
   - Have classroom teams each take turns sharing documentation about an anti-bias strategy, curriculum idea, or dilemma that occurred in their classrooms. This may require giving teams advance notice to prepare materials for the activity.
   - Analyze children's books for anti-bias issues.
   - Read an anti-bias/equity article together and discuss using the following framework:
     » *Connect: How do the ideas presented connect to what you know about ABE?*
     » *Extend: What new ideas did you gain that extended or broadened your thinking?*
     » *Challenge: What challenges or questions have come to mind? (Project Zero, 2015)*
   - View all or part of the film *Reflecting on Anti-Bias Education in Practice: The Early Years* (LeeKeenan, Nimmo, & McKinney, 2021; 48 min.). Use the guidebook for prompts and questions (LeeKeenan & Nimmo, 2021).
   - Provide anti-bias questions for small-group discussions. Use small groups of four staff members to encourage more personal conversations. Choose ONE of the following questions per meeting:
     » *Anti-bias goals: What are four anti-bias goals, and how do I implement them?*
     » *Raising self-awareness: What moments have come up in my work with children and families that triggered my own social identity, history, or bias?*
     » *Physical environments: What is in my physical environment that reflects anti-bias goals and values?*
     » *Pedagogy: How do I actively encourage children's critical thinking about differences and stereotypes?*
     » *Families: How do I involve families in anti-bias work? How do I respond to families' requests respectfully and fairly when there is conflict about beliefs and goals?*
4. **Closure**: Share in dyads something important you learned today and can apply tomorrow. (*5 min*)

An alternative approach is to engage the teachers themselves in a specific anti-bias education activity that is intended for children, and then talk together about what children can learn from the activity. For example, the teachers could make an "all about brown group collage," working together with a range of beautiful brown materials (e.g., cinnamon, pine cones, pine needles, sand, silk fabrics, feathers, spices). After discussing what the children might learn, you can review child development issues. For example, some children have negative associations with dark colors, and many begin to connect negative associations with dark skin during the preschool years (Ramsey, 2015). Anti-bias educators need to counteract those stereotypes (see Chapter 6 for more ideas on staff meetings and professional development about ABE). See Figure 4.1 on how to organize a 60-minute staff meeting on ABE.

Articulate an Anti-Bias Mission Statement

Even though anti-bias education has always been part of the mission of this school, our level of engagement shifted when we began to have more focused conversations about it.

—Teacher

Every program practicing anti-bias education needs a clear written statement about its mission, goals, and values. This can be a stand-alone mission statement that focuses on be anti-bias education, or embedded in the overall program philosophy, core values, and mission of the program. These statements become a part of the program's policies and are visible in the program's staff and family handbooks.

An anti-bias mission statement is the operational framework that lays down what a program will do about anti-bias education. It is a foundational building block, giving direction and accountability markers to what the leader and staff hope to accomplish. As program leader, you should have a clear sense of what an anti-bias vision and mission encompass from the start, but it can't be just one person's idea. Establishing a mission that really becomes part of a program's ongoing organizational structure, culture, policies, procedures, and daily practices demands collaborative participation of the educators. Take some time to do this, but do not let the process get bogged down so that it becomes a way to avoid making anti-bias changes. Once your program has agreed on a DEI/anti-bias mission statement, it then becomes a framework for taking stock of where you are, what you have done, and where you want to go next.

When a program has an established anti-bias mission statement, it is not necessary to reconstruct a new one every year. However, you do need to reestablish staff understanding and sense of ownership of the mission each year and ensure that terminology remains inclusive.

The Program's First Anti-Bias Mission Statement. Asking staff to state their ideas about "What would your center look like if it were an effective anti-bias program?" is a valuable beginning step for developing your program's mission statement. Next, involve staff in considering what impact the NAEYC (2019b) *Advancing Equity in Early Childhood Education Position Statement,* the NAEYC (2011) *Code of Ethical Conduct and Statement of Commitment,* and the general philosophy of your program have on your anti-bias mission.

If your staff is small, it is possible to draft your mission statement together. You can write a first draft, based on the staff's thoughts in the discussion previously described, and invite their feedback. In the case of a large staff, drafting a mission statement all together becomes cumbersome. Establishing a staff leadership task force is one effective way to begin the mission statement process. Start with staff whom you have identified as sharing an anti-bias perspective, who have done some type of DEI work in their classrooms, or who have explored their own issues of identity. In John's first year as director at his center in New Hampshire, he formed the Diversity, Equity, and Bias Taskforce (DEBT) with five interested teachers, as he describes below:

> Together we drafted a diversity mission statement, which incorporated the staff's vision of an anti-bias program [see Figure 4.2]. I provided examples from other schools and the anti-bias education goals to help us get started. While I was concerned that this could be a distraction from action, it was vital to name the center's vision of anti-bias education work and have a public document that set a basis for accountability.

> Broader language from the university's diversity statement was intentionally included in our mission to ally the center with the larger institution. This language is helpful in being explicit about the range of human diversity. We were also careful in using words like *strive* to indicate that the program was not there yet, but making a concerted effort.

> The task force distributed the draft mission statement to all staff for feedback, discussion, and reaching consensus about the final version. We made it available to families, in handouts, on the bulletin board, and on our website, thus making public the center's desire to honor diversity. Two

Figure 4.2. Example of a Program's Diversity/Anti-Bias Mission Statement

Diversity/Anti-Bias Mission Statement

We believe that human diversity is integral to the care and education of young children and to all those who touch their lives. Diversity in our community means a fully inclusive campus community that is enriched by persons of different races, genders, ethnicities, nationalities, economic backgrounds, ages, abilities, sexual orientation and gender identity or expression, and religious beliefs. Our goal is to promote awareness and acceptance, affirm equity, and take an active stance against bias in our community.

We strive to respect and value the differences in each child and family in our community through all that we do. We value the development of strong relationships with families and colleagues in order to better understand how we can respond to cultural and historical differences in experiences, values, and practices. We offer an environment that welcomes and celebrates the sharing of family history and culture in the classroom in meaningful ways. In our curriculum we are intentional in providing children with opportunities to explore similarities and variation, and we are responsive to the questions that emerge.

We support children in being active participants in their world by connecting them to their community in ways that foster an understanding of diversity and an ability to effect change. We are committed to an open and ongoing dialogue among colleagues, families, and the students we mentor, seeking insight into how we contribute to social bias and the process of change. As adults we strive to be models of active participation in our field by speaking out against bias and seeking equity.

Note: Adapted from "Diversity Commitment" by Child Study and Development Center, 2005.

important outcomes occurred: We began connecting with families who fully supported the diversity work, and families began to explicitly hold us accountable to the mission statement. Each year we read the mission statement in training to keep it alive.

When an Anti-Bias Mission Statement Exists. Attaining staff engagement with the anti-bias mission when it has already become part of the program's culture calls for other strategies, as Debbie explains:

> At the center I directed in Massachusetts, anti-bias education has been part of the policy handbooks for many years. It is fully integrated into the core philosophy and framework goals for the school. However, the community reviews the core values underlying the statement each year at an early staff meeting and also at an early meeting of families. The objective is for the community to understand and feel involved with the mission statement. When I was the program leader, we read and examined the mission statement and core frameworks together in small groups using the Four "A"s Text Protocol [for the full protocol, see School Reform Initiative, 2014b.] Then the whole group discussed the following prompts:
> * What assumptions does the text (diversity statement) hold?
> * What do you agree with in the text?
> * What do you want to argue with in the text?
> * What parts of the text do you want to aspire to (or act upon)?

While changes to the underlying values of the program's existing anti-bias values and mission statement usually weren't made, Debbie and her staff did use this process to modify sections that they felt did not fully capture core values or needed clarification.

Set Anti-Bias Implementation Goals

Once the program has an anti-bias mission statement, the next step is to set specific implementation goals for making the anti-bias approach come alive. Considering the four anti-bias education goals as the core framework, you will also develop three types of specific goals that are typical of high-quality programs: program-wide goals, classroom team goals, and individual staff goals.

Program-Wide Goals. These are goals that affect the entire program and draw on the contributions of all the staff and, potentially, families. Examples of goals that explicitly seek to implement your anti-bias approach include updating the program's collection of diversity and anti-bias books, expanding family education opportunities, and offering teachers PD on specific anti-bias topics. While program anti-bias goal-setting needs to be a collaborative process, the program leader sets the expectation for implementing these goals, making clear that all educators need to engage in the anti-bias commitment. John offers an illustration of this:

When I began my work at my center in New Hampshire, the teachers' proposals for goals that we could work on together did not include any reference to diversity. I decided to add an explicit, but broad, anti-bias goal to the list and connect this to the teachers' espoused humanist values of care, community, and respect. I felt it was important to create an initial starting place for our anti-bias efforts.

Another time for the program leader to take the lead in revisiting and setting program-wide goals is when anti-bias efforts lag or stagnate.

Classroom Team Goals. Teaching teams set the goals for their specific classroom's work, within the framework of the school goals. Examples of classroom goals include enhancing the types of props the teaching team puts in the dramatic play center to make it more culturally relevant to the population they serve, introducing the use of storytelling to facilitate discussions with children about differences and bias, observing the children's thinking about gender, and developing activities to scaffold learning experiences about gender. After the teachers identify their classroom goals, they share them in writing with the program leader, who coaches teaching teams through supervision on how they plan to work on their goals and help them revisit the goals periodically throughout the year.

Individual Teacher Goals. This level of goal-setting includes each teacher's personal growth, practice with children, and relationships with the families of the children in the class. The framework of the anti-bias mission statement, as well as the program-wide and classroom team goals, set an initial direction. Individual goal-setting enables teachers to begin each year at their own level of anti-bias education ability. These initial individual goals also give the program leader information about where each teacher is on the anti-bias journey.

Figure 4.3 is a sample of individual teacher beginning goals and more advanced goals. Teachers specify what they will work on, how they will do it, and what kinds of support they need from the program leader.

Develop a Critical Eye About the Learning Environment

Providing a physical learning environment that is free of misinformation and stereotypes and rich in diversity is another major component of shifting the culture of a program. It is essential to incorporate changes in the physical learning environment to reflect the program's anti-bias mission statement, goals, and professional development. As program leader, you should facilitate educators developing a critical eye about the materials they provide to the children.

Book Survey. This is an example of one specific activity for cultivating a critical anti-bias education eye. Teachers and other staff educators work together to review all the children's books in the program. To get on the same page about the issues to consider, they first read a checklist tool, such as the one on

Figure 4.3. Individual Teacher Goals

Anti-Bias Goal	What I Will Do	Support I Need from My Supervisor
BEGINNING TEACHER GOALS		
Become more comfortable responding to children's comments and questions about differences.	Respond to their questions; keep track of the comments and questions.	Give me suggestions on how to respond.
Read more books on same-sex families to the class.	Research what books are available and appropriate for my age group.	Find funds for me to purchase the books. Give me suggestions on how to introduce a book. What should I tell families?
MORE ADVANCED TEACHER GOALS		
Write a story about a child who is homeless to use with persona dolls (see Chapter 6).	Read and research more about the issues for a child who is homeless.	Help me find appropriate resources; meet with me to review the script.
Document my skin color curriculum.	Keep notes; find time to write them up. Prepare a conference presentation.	Give me some structure to keep me accountable; find funds for me to attend a conference.

the Teaching for Change website (https://www.teachingforchange.org/selecting
-anti-bias-books; see Derman-Sparks, 2013a). After reviewing the books, the
teachers and other staff educators discuss which books they want to continue
to use and what to do with books containing misinformation and stereotypical
images and/or messages of particular groups. For example, some books may
not be appropriate for young preschoolers, but useful to open up conversation
with older children about why a book may be "unfair." They also identify what
people and ways of life are missing in their collection and prioritize purchasing
new books.

Scavenger Hunt. This activity introduces the topic of the learning environment.
The program leader creates a list of classroom materials that could be used for
anti-bias education in the program. The educators divide into several teams, and
each group looks for the items on their list. Examples of items that could be included are the following:

- A book with characters experiencing poverty, such as food scarcity or homelessness/houselessness
- Art materials to make self-portraits reflecting all the children and staff
- Posters showing diversity of family structures and identities
- A resource to learn about local Indigenous peoples of this land
- Charts (numbers, colors, songs) labeled in different written and signed languages
- Dolls with different skin tones and abilities

When the scavenger hunt is over, participants gather the materials they have found in the school and then discuss how they could use these materials with children for anti-bias education. During the discussion and analysis, the program leader may find that some materials found by the teachers are problematic or incomplete in some way. For example, a teacher may bring a poster of two Asian children but with very stereotypical clothing or gender roles. The leader and teacher discuss how they could use this poster with the children: "When would these children wear the kimono? Is it for a special occasion?" The teachers could also discuss how to adapt readily available early childhood materials to explore anti-bias concepts, such as adding photos of children of different racial or ethnic backgrounds to the unit blocks.

*   *   *

Once educators have assessed their anti-bias teaching materials and identified what they still need (or need to dispose of), you should look at ways to allocate available funds or figure out other ways to acquire the materials. For instance, by building relationships with businesses in the community, you may be able to obtain donations of materials or funds to support workshops with families and staff to make materials. Engaging staff members in researching and making decisions about new purchases *and* thinking creatively about how to best use limited resources is in itself a useful anti-bias PD experience.

BEING A LIFELONG LEARNER

There are many effective ways to introduce and engage teachers in anti-bias education and to start them viewing themselves as advocates for inclusion and equity. It takes work and creativity—but it is doable. As the program leader, your charge is to spark and lead the process of program change, collaboratively develop and keep the mission and expectations clear, and facilitate the staff's professional development. This does not mean that you need to know all the answers. By modeling being a learner, taking risks, and working collaboratively with staff to figure it all out step by step, you live the anti-bias approach. And many of the directors we interviewed commented on the importance of creating authentic, honest relationships among the staff. "Empathy is the root of social justice work, says Rukia Rogers, director of the Highlander Center in Atlanta. "We need to honor our past to build toward our futures."

In Chapter 5, we turn to strategies for program leaders to engage with families. Program leaders have a vital role in ensuring that families are aware of, come to appreciate, and support anti-bias education. In Chapter 6, we return to a focus on teachers and the professional development and strategies needed to support their continued anti-bias journey.

Engaging Families and Growing Anti-Bias Partnerships

Families do and don't feel like they fit in for a whole range of reasons. We want to be heard, valued, and included in ways that seem meaningful and valuable to us.

—Parent

We are all learning as a community side by side . . . when our engagement with families is rooted in love and relationships, we can tackle those really big subjects together.

—Rukia Rogers, center director

Family engagement is fundamental to building a meaningful anti-bias education program. The program leader is responsible for fostering family belonging, trust, and engagement, as well as promoting strong teacher–family relationships. As leader, you make sure that the program's anti-bias values, mission, and goals are transparent to the community, put into practice a range of strategies for family participation, and facilitate problem-solving when there is a disagreement over anti-bias issues.

In this chapter we begin with outlining a framework for working with families and discuss differing levels of family engagement within anti-bias education. We then describe a variety of strategies directors can use to engage with families. In Chapter 6 we discuss how leaders can support teachers in their daily work with families.

THE FRAMEWORK FOR WORKING WITH FAMILIES

Families must first feel accepted, respected, and part of the program's community in order to engage actively with anti-bias issues. The foundation for working with families begins with the program's willingness to embrace reciprocal partnerships (Gonzalez-Mena, 2012). Families know about their children in ways educators do not, and, conversely, educators know about child development, group settings, and learning in ways families do not. It requires both learning from and teaching each other through regular exchanges of information, observations, and questions. In anti-bias family partnerships, early childhood programs see families as reservoirs of knowledge and expertise, central to understanding the children they serve

(Gonzalez et al., 2005; Yosso, 2005). While both home and program need to be open to learning from each other, the program leaders and teachers set the tone for dialogue and learning. Program leaders and teachers must also integrate what they learn from families into their pedagogy, and in their environments and curriculum.

An Inclusive View of Families

Having an inclusive definition of families is essential. Families come in many different constellations beyond the heterosexual nuclear family, including single-parent families, same-sex families, extended families, blended families, foster families, and adoptive families. All families also belong to various social identity groups (e.g., racial, Indigenous status, economic class), which affects their everyday lives. These differences can mean that families vary in their relationship to and experiences with specific anti-bias issues. In a program with an ABE approach, families should be able to answer "yes" to the question, "Do I see who I am, who my child is, who my family is in the program's staff, environment, and curriculum?"

Learning about families is a process, not a one-time event. It begins at the start of the year and then continues as families develop more familiarity, comfort, and trust with the teachers and program leader. Families differ in when and how much they choose to disclose about their lives. Program leaders, as well as teachers, should take this into account in how they learn about the families they serve. As teachers' skill in building relationships with families grows, they feel more confident about how to raise sensitive topics (Park et al., 2014).

Building an effective anti-bias family partnership incorporates best ECCE practices. At the same time, leaders need to be mindful that traditional notions of "parent involvement" can reflect assumptions about the time, energy, and emotional availability of different families. These notions may also include implicit bias that families who cannot get involved in traditional ways are not interested in the education of their children. Programs need to provide multiple ways for families to engage with the program, both individually and collectively, since families differ in their life experiences, expectations of school, the communities they are part of, and how they raise children. For families who have experienced marginalization, particularly in schools, the program leader should also support opportunities for them to meet with other families who share similar issues and contexts (Foubert, 2022).

Program leaders should value the contributions all families make, from getting their child to school prepared for the day to being on a family advisory board. Participation should be made as accessible as possible by having events at different times, providing child care and food, and offering translation. Leaders should not expect families to take part in everything, but to take advantage of offered opportunities that mesh with their skills, energy, and availability. Regardless, ensuring that your program offers an equitable and culturally sustaining education for all children should never be dependent on a family's level of participation (Foubert, 2022).

Levels of Family Engagement With Anti-Bias Work

Everyone in the community is at their own comfort level with anti-bias education and different topics.

—Parent

Coming to understand what the goals of ABE are, how young children develop their identity and attitudes, and how ABE infuses all aspects of a program takes time and effort. Families come to a program with varying levels of commitment to its mission and members. Some families may have explicitly chosen a program based on the anti-bias mission, while others may be there due to reputation, convenience, or other more pragmatic considerations. Furthermore, families come to anti-bias education from diverse starting points. For many, anti-bias education is a new concept and approach. Some may have some general but vague ideas about what it means. Even families who chose the program because they agree with its commitment to ABE may find that actually participating in the community is asking more of them than they had expected. In addition, various issues going on in families' lives may affect their responses to an anti-bias approach. Some families may be interested in and even committed to anti-bias education, but may not be in a place to participate due to the complexity of their lives or prior trauma. For instance, a parent who experienced bias due to their heritage language may feel too vulnerable. As the program leader, it is your responsibility, in conjunction with the teachers, to identify where a family is in relation to anti-bias work, and to decide where and how to start meeting varying levels of interest and engagement.

One frequent question about involving families in ABE is how to do this without making them uncomfortable. Opening up issues of identity and bias is inevitably uncomfortable at times. This is because prejudice and discrimination hurt individuals—directly when they are the targets and indirectly when they face how they may have participated in hurtful behavior. Most people learned to be silent about prejudice and discrimination at a young age. Some may think that talking openly about bias is impolite or too controversial. Therefore, the more useful question is, "How do we create a supportive place for people to begin or continue engaging with anti-bias education from wherever they are?" This requires building a community where all members feel that they are seen and heard, and that they belong. It also means considering and respecting at all times each person's place on the anti-bias engagement progression.

Family engagement with anti-bias education not only occurs at different levels, it also moves through the progression with varying speed and duration. This progression can be a useful guide for you in choosing relevant family-engagement strategies.

1. Families first learn about the anti-bias commitment and mission of the program. This happens during preadmission tours and orientation meetings with the program leader, and by reading the family handbook

and mission statements. Families are visible in the physical environment with photographs and other documentation. Depending on the prominence of your anti-bias efforts outside the program, families may enter at Levels 2 or 3 below.

2. Families begin to understand what being part of an anti-bias community means through family education opportunities about specific anti-bias topics, as well as informal storytelling and interactions with teachers, the director, and other families.

3. Families begin to participate in classroom activities and initiate conversations with teachers or the program leader about anti-bias education. They may share family cultural practices and traditions in their child's classroom (e.g., send family artifacts, record a story in their home language, or demonstrate a holiday ritual), help create anti-bias learning materials, and work with staff to resolve disagreements regarding anti-bias issues and teaching practices counter to their cultural beliefs.

4. Families become allies of anti-bias efforts. They advocate anti-bias values and actively engage with other families and the staff in related issues and activities. They participate in family and family–teacher discussion groups, and provide input to the anti-bias program.

5. Families provide leadership. They take the lead in initiating new anti-bias strategies and related activities, participate in making decisions about the program, and actively bring their anti-bias perspective to various program groups (e.g., co-leader of a diversity group, program advisory group, or teacher search committee).

The year will typically begin with families reflecting a range of anti-bias levels. Many will be at Level 1 or 2, and some are at Level 3. However, in programs that form with an explicit anti-bias mission, many families may be ready to engage with anti-bias work at Levels 3, 4, and 5. As the year progresses, most families advance in their understanding and involvement. While the proportion of families at the leadership level is usually small, they play an indispensable role in shifting the program to an anti-bias culture. Later in this chapter we discuss strategies designed to engage families at various points in their participation.

INTRODUCING ANTI-BIAS VALUES AND EXPECTATIONS

I learned that anti-bias is very broad and not limited to race, culture, and ethnicity, and it's a lot more than just celebrating different holidays.

—Parent

Families begin learning about a program's anti-bias mission even before the program year begins. This education begins prior to admission, orientation and intake, and continues during the year as families build familiarity and trust with the teachers and the program leader.

Preadmission

Programs have opportunities to reach out, educate, and inform potential families about anti-bias education before enrolling their children. This outreach may be part of efforts to diversify the demographics of your program. In addition to having explicit language about your anti-bias approach in application and promotional materials, we have found it is important to be intentional about including anti-bias education language as a priority in any tour of the program that families attend. On her admission tours, director Julie Bisson of the Epiphany Early Learning Preschool in Seattle talks about anti-bias practices that have become foundational in each classroom in her center, including their ABE children's book library, the use of persona dolls, and the family holiday boards.

Intake and Orientation Process: Who Are You as a Family?

The intake process is an opportunity for families to *begin* to share information about themselves and their home and heritage cultures. Make sure that the wording and questions of application and admissions paperwork reflect respect for diversity and acknowledges that the child's primary caretakers may be other than a mother or father (e.g., using "guardian one" and "guardian two"). The intake questionnaire should include specific questions about languages spoken at home, important traditions, cultural beliefs about childrearing and education, and how families identify their race, ethnicity, Tribal affiliation, religion, and family structure. Make it possible for families to answer the questions orally, signed, or in writing, and provide translation as necessary to help ensure that all families feel welcome in the community.

Family Goal Form. Completing this form early in the school year enables families to describe their child's unique characteristics, interests, likes and dislikes, strengths and challenges, as well as list their hopes and expectations for their child. This information is gathered annually, as the goals for their children may change from year to year. Reviewing families' responses provides important learning for you and the teachers.

Program Open House. By inviting families to visit the program before a child attends, you offer an informal opportunity for families to see the classrooms and chat with you and the teachers. An alternative would be to structure a few days of transition for new families in which parents engage in observation and conversation at the program while the child attends.

A gathering at a local playground or park at the start of the year offers families a chance to begin to connect with one another and for staff to begin to learn about families through informal conversations. Debbie offers the following example:

> At a summer (pre-school) picnic, we first learned that a dad was using a wheelchair and were able to be proactive about preparing the program for his visit. In another situation we discovered at an open house that a grandmother was the primary caregiver for one of the children enrolling.

Family Handbook and Program Website. Anti-bias goals, values, and relevant policies should be visible in your program's family handbook and website. Being clear about the program's goals for staff–family relationships lays a foundation for turning disagreements about anti-bias education into meaningful solutions and growth. John explains how staff–family relations were developed at the center he directed:

> The staff generated the following goals as part of defining an anti-bias partnership with families:
> - Ensure families feel welcomed and included as valued members of the center community
> - Commit to the inclusion of different perspectives and searching for common ground
> - Pay attention to the needs of the entire community, rather than just individuals

Parents on the advisory committee reviewed the goals and considered, "Can we hold the program accountable to work on meeting these goals?" Once staff and families agreed, the goals became part of the policy handbook. When new families came for an admissions tour, they received a handout that included these goals for developing a partnership with families.

John also developed a policy for adult conduct as a proactive strategy to help create a safe place for discussion and conflict (see Figure 5.1 for an excerpt).

Figure 5.1. Example of an Adult Conduct Policy

Conduct of Adult Community Members Policy

As members of a community, adults at the center should strive to provide the children with a model of civil and respectful behavior. Interactions between adults should support a caring and safe environment for everyone.

Given that differences in opinions can arise, it is important that adults are aware of the behavior children observe when there is the potential for conflict. Children can learn a great deal by seeing how adults approach and solve differences in a positive way.

Regardless of the problem, we expect community members to approach differences in opinion with an open mind and with respect for the other person and program policies. Language or behavior that is disrespectful, discriminatory, or abusive to others, including children, is never acceptable at the center.

Note: Adapted from *Family Handbook* by Child Study and Development Center, 2011, p. 31.

Teachers found the language helpful because it provided clarity about the difference between conflict and disrespectful behavior.

Frequently Asked Questions. Knowing that anti-bias education is a core value in the program is one step. Welcoming and thoughtfully responding to their questions comes next. Once a family starts attending, the reality is often different from what a family expected. Families who are part of privileged social-identity groups (e.g., White, heterosexual, cisgender) may have a hard time understanding the benefits of anti-bias education for their children. They might equate the inclusion of other cultural and social perspectives in the curriculum as a loss for them and question where they fit in. Others may really believe that their culture is the superior and only "right" way to live. Some may also worry that by embracing anti-bias values they will come into conflict with other members of the dominant group, including members of their own extended family.

Families from socially marginalized groups (e.g., immigrants, BIPoC) may also express pushback to aspects of anti-bias education (Derman-Sparks, 2011). They may not trust how others will teach their children about identity or want to protect their children for as long as possible from the hurt of knowing about prejudice. They may hold prejudices toward an aspect of social identity or have internalized negative ideas about their own groups. Some families whose first language is not English may object to early childhood programs cultivating both their home language and English because they worry their children will not learn English sufficiently to progress successfully in school. They may not be aware of research demonstrating the limitations of an English-only approach in mastering a second language, as well as the harm of losing the heritage language at an early age (Fu et al., 2019).

Over the years, we have found that certain questions about anti-bias education always come up. Debbie explains how responding to these questions was handled at her center in Massachusetts:

We created a Frequently Asked Questions (FAQ) document for families, involving teachers and families in its development. We felt that putting the FAQ document in the family handbook and on our website would provide answers to some common questions, jumpstart families asking others, and provoke discussion. We began writing the FAQ with questions from our fall family meetings and our annual parent survey, which asks, "What do you want to know about anti-bias education?" Some of their questions included:
- What do children learn in an ABE environment?
- What is the role of families in anti-bias education?
- How does anti-bias education relate to bullying?
- How do teachers decide what to teach? What types of similarities and differences are discussed with the children?
- How is anti-bias education integrated into the school day? What is the relationship between play, academics, and ABE?

- Is anti-bias education appropriate for young children? Will my child learn or acquire biases about others?
- How does the school discuss similarities and differences between families, in terms of their parenting styles, beliefs, and values?
- What do I do if I disagree with the school's anti-bias philosophy? Is there room for discussion when a family's approach is different from that of the school?
- How is anti-bias education related to special education inclusion?
- How are the teachers trained to use anti-bias education? How can teachers teach ABE in a responsive and sensitive way to children whose identities are different from their own?

The yearlong process of developing answers to these questions served as one way to engage families in anti-bias work and build a teacher–family partnership. Families engaged in dialogue about anti-bias issues and heard a range of views and beliefs. The process of sorting, examining, and responding to the questions at a staff meeting (What were parents really asking by this question?) was a professional development opportunity. Debbie worked with a teacher and a parent to put the final draft together. As a result, everyone reached a deeper understanding of different perspectives, and new families had another entry point for their participation in ABE. See Figure 5.2 for an example of the questions included

Figure 5.2. Example of a Frequently Asked Questions Handout

What do children learn in an ABE environment?

Children learn about similarities and differences in people and communities. They are encouraged to act in ways that reflect anti-bias values and to stand up for things they feel are unfair. ABE is integrated into the classroom activities. It is both planned curriculum within the structure of the day, as well as natural "teachable moments" based on children's social interactions, conversations, and play. Anti-bias curriculum topics come from the children, families, and teachers, as well as historical or current events. When children ask questions about differences, adults listen in order to facilitate conversations and responses.

How does ABE relate to bullying?

ABE is an example of an anti-bullying, pro-social curriculum because we are proactively teaching children how to fairly understand and respond when they encounter difference. Exploration of power and conflict are a natural part of this process.

Creating and maintaining a classroom community where everyone feels safe and respected is an essential part of the teacher's role at every age level. During the first weeks of school, teachers develop "ground rules" or "classroom agreements" with the children. These may include words such as "We take care of each other. We don't use words or actions that hurt others." Teachers lead discussions and activities that foster understanding others' points of view and differences. Problem-solving strategies are directly taught.

Note: Adapted from "FAQs about Anti-Bias Education at the Eliot Pearson Children's School" (Eliot–Pearson Children's School, n.d.).

in the EPCS Frequently Asked Questions Handout. Another example of an FAQ section is available in the *Reflecting on Anti-Bias Education in Action: The Early Years Guidebook* (LeeKeenan & Nimmo, 2021).

Anti-Bias Education Newsletters. Periodic newsletters, emails, postings on a family bulletin board, blogs, and website stories are visual and oral forms of communication that offer opportunities for you and the teachers to build on and reinforce discussion about various anti-bias issues. You can share stories and video about what the children are doing related to anti-bias education and offer ideas for responding to their questions about their own and others' identities. You may also use these outlets to include short pieces about your thoughts, observations, and recommendations on current anti-bias issues such as offering perspectives on a holiday, like Indigenous People's Day or Thanksgiving; connecting anti-bias education to current topics such as bullying and obesity; or expressing concerns about stereotyping in a new children's movie. In addition, these communications are an opportunity to model talking about social identities by sharing something significant about your own background and experiences in relation to anti-bias work. Director Julie Bisson has an "Anti-Bias Learning" section in her weekly electronic newsletter, where she shares new ABE children's books, public webinars on anti-bias topics, and anecdotes from the classroom, or asks for family input about an anti-bias dilemma. Similarly, Director Rukia Rogers shares examples of the school's anti-bias curriculum and in-depth projects on The Highlander School's Facebook page with detailed documentation, including photos and text. Families and other staff can make comments and ask questions on the social media page.

Create Family Visibility and Connection

Not only is every child different, every family is different. From their culture, race, ethnicity, background, dynamic, home life, and beliefs, you can't assume two families from the same place will be the same.

—Parent

No matter how families come to a program, every family has the right to feel visible, welcomed, and supported to be full participants in creating the community. Program leaders and staff need to ask themselves the following questions:

- Do families feel included and welcomed?
- Do families feel they can share their opinions?
- Do families feel reflected in the program and encouraged to share who they are?

The practices and activities described below are intended to help you build inclusion of all families. Some activities are specifically for the beginning of the year, while you can implement others throughout the year.

Reaching Out. The leader's responsibility is to reach out actively to all families, being observant and conscious of who may not be feeling comfortable in the community. It is very important to be aware of your own comfort levels as you initiate interactions. Do you tend to gravitate to some families because you are more comfortable with them, while avoiding others? These preferences can reflect your social identities and experiences. Reaching out can happen informally throughout the day or during program-wide events, such as a school potluck dinner or class breakfast. Debbie describes ways she reached out to families at her program:

> I tried to be in the front lobby during arrival and departure to greet families as they walked through the door. As a parent said to me, "I loved seeing the director every morning greeting my child and me when I walked in the door." We also hosted an informal midweek morning coffee in the entrance area to allow families to grab a cup of coffee or tea on their way to work if people had time. We also provided virtual coffee/tea chats with the director on a regular basis. This was another opportunity for me to check in with families briefly who might not physically be coming into the school building.

Director Karina Rojas Rodriguez at Southwest Early Learning Bilingual Preschool invites families to a tea party before the school begins each year. Families spend time in the classroom, chat with her and the teachers and get to know each other.

> It is a way for families to see the school and classroom and because we're quite diverse, we serve about 13 different languages in our school . . . they're going to be in community and they're going to build community. We're going to be there to help with translation, use body language and gestures to communicate when we don't know the language. Our goal is to really build the bridge between a family whose children are playing and introduce them to each other, so they can have the relationship from the beginning.

Virtual Connections. During the pandemic, directors, teachers, and families found creative ways to connect via virtual video platforms. With many families working from home, these applications provided more opportunities for families to participate in school life, such as popping in to read a story, sharing what they are cooking for dinner, or offering a cultural tradition or artifact. "Home visits" can be a successful virtual experience when clear goals about the purpose of the visit are set. These goals could include: (a) to exchange information, including family values and program goals, and (b) to get to know each other better with an activity such as a teacher reading a book to a child with a family member. However, it is important to remember that some families may feel uncomfortable with a "camera" peering into their private lives and spaces. Offering a screen background is sometimes an option. Be aware that some families may need help in accessing technology for virtual meetings, such as a loaner mobile device or support using the apps.

Family Walls. One place to set the anti-bias tone is in the entrance area of the program. Invite each person in the school (both children and staff) to provide a photo of their family to decorate a bulletin board in the entrance area. Family is defined explicitly in a broad way and left to the family to choose whom they show. It could be the people who live in your household, your extended family around the world, or you and your grandma. Put a world map in the center of the bulletin board and invite people to put dots on the map, to show "which cultures are part of your family." The word "cultures" in the plural is used to acknowledge that more than one culture can make up a family. The bulletin board sparks conversation about both difference and similarity and acts as a focal point for everyone to connect.

You can also suggest that community members make drawings of their family or a collage of photos to represent their family. Individual classrooms can ask families to bring in photos to put in the children's cubby or on a classroom bulletin board or to make a class family book.

Welcome in Different Languages. Signs, resource materials, and books in languages spoken or signed by the families in your program play an essential role in enabling them to feel at home. Welcome signs in different languages on the program door or in the entrance area make a difference. Set up an adult space that includes literature, magazines, parenting books, and copies of the program newsletters in the home languages of your families. Translation services may be difficult or expensive for some programs. Asking families to help you with this task often makes them feel validated and empowered. If they cannot do the translation, they may be able to find a resource to help you with the task.

Family Artifact Bag. This activity is designed to encourage family sharing in the classroom. Each teacher obtains a drawstring cloth bag that is designated as a family artifact bag. Each child in a class takes home the family bag one time during the year. The family puts different family artifacts into the bag, and then the child and a family member come to school to share the items in their bag with the classroom. Photographs of each family and their artifacts from the bag can be used to make a scrapbook or bulletin board display.

Family Boxes. In this activity, each family decorates the inside of a shoe box to represent their family in any way they choose. Families use photos, words, drawings, paper collage, clay, and small toys to decorate their box. Materials should be made available for use at home, and families should be encouraged to use a variety of materials and interpretations. Families bring completed boxes to the program, and staff members join the boxes together with tape to make a family wall. Families are asked to explain their boxes to the children in the class, or the teachers can get the explanation by phone or email, or when families pick up their children. The wall of family boxes sparks conversations among families.

Family Book Bag. To carry out this activity, the staff first decides on a topic that will provoke anti-bias conversations, and then each classroom creates a book bag that includes a relevant children's book (appropriate to the developmental level of the class) and a journal. The book bag goes home each night with a different child. The family reads the book together and then draws a picture or writes about the book in the journal. Each semester the program chooses a different focus for the book topic, such as families, ethnicity, ability, gender, or activism.

Getting to Know Me *Book*. The Southwest Early Learning Bilingual Preschool (SWEL) has modified the idea of the child portfolio to a *Getting to Know Me* book. The book embraces many aspects of the child from both home and school. Documentation from three perspectives is included—from the child, the family/parents, and the educators. Director Karina Rojas Rodriguez explains:

> Through documentation over the course of the year, the book shares
> who the child is within their culture, their language, anything about the
> child the family wants to share, how they identify, their values regarding
> education . . . In Mexico where I am from, we believe that if you're
> the educator, you are the person that I'm going to trust 100%. But we
> [educators] want to let the families know that there is a balance, there's a
> dance between home and school. . . . you can share what you do at home,
> and we share what is happening at school regarding your child . . . and it's
> a reciprocal relationship.

Holiday Boards. At Epiphany Early Learning Preschool in Seattle, holiday boards are used for families to share how celebrations, traditions, and holidays are acknowledged in their families. In November, each child is given a piece of poster board and directions to make a poster using words, photos, drawings, recipes, decorations, and other artifacts showing their family's celebrations during the year. The posters are returned to school sometime in February. Director Julie Bisson comments,

> But the real excitement is when the kids talk about their poster with other
> kids in the classroom. Each poster is shared at a meeting time, and the
> parents are invited to and often come in to help their child talk about their
> poster. The kids note the similarities and differences . . . "I do that too," "I
> saw Santa too," "We eat beans also."

FAMILY ANTI-BIAS EDUCATION AND DIALOGUE

The climate of the school allows for dialogue and a brave and safe place to exchange ideas.

—Parent

In creating opportunities for families to develop their understanding of anti-bias education, the program leader considers the various ways adults learn (e.g., small groups, hands-on activities, large-group, and media), preferred communication styles, and where families are in their anti-bias journeys.

In this section we share an example of a particularly effective family anti-bias education approach developed by Ellen Wolpert when she directed an all-day preschool located in a housing project in Boston. The community preschool served families with low incomes, including many recent immigrants from Haiti and Central America. Monthly staff–family gatherings of 2 hours or less were at the core of the program's work with families. Sessions were scheduled at the end of the preschool day, so families picking up their children could stay and participate. Dinner and child care were provided.

The staff–family gatherings enabled families to learn about the anti-bias approach by experiencing the activities their children were doing as well as staff professional development activities. The sessions also explored the ways people learn and are affected by bias; shared values and strategies for dealing with bias with their children; and ways to challenge bias in themselves and in their environment. Ellen also used staff planning for the gatherings as a time to develop the staff's anti-bias awareness.

Topics for the staff–family gatherings came from the following sources:

1. Areas of bias that staff and/or families identified as important to learn more about
2. Curriculum themes that were emerging from observations of the children in the classroom
3. Issues in the community or the media that were likely to affect the children

Ellen always introduced discussions about issues of bias by first having participants look at their past and current experiences in pairs or small groups. The sessions repeated key issues over the year to meet the needs of new families and to provide opportunities for people in the program to share their experiences and changes of perspective with newcomers.

Following are four examples of Ellen's topic-focused discussion sessions. While these sessions reflect her specific context, the underlying strategies could be adapted to any setting and community.

Identity and Memories of School

As a foundation for later discussions about ABE, this first staff–family gathering of the year aimed to facilitate people making connections between their own experiences and their hopes for their children.

1. Introductions:
    a. In groups of three, each person talks about themself for 2 minutes: name, relationship to school, anything you want to say about your family, where you are from, things you are curious about or like to do, your ethnic background, and anything else you would like to share about yourself.
    b. Each person introduces themself to the group: name and one or two things you would like the group to know about yourself.
2. Exploring school experiences:
    a. In small groups, talk about "What experiences in school made you feel good about what your family is like, ethnic and racial background, economic situation, physical differences, and gender identity?" "What experiences in school made you feel not good about these parts of who you are?"
    b. In the whole-group discussion, shares thoughts from the small groups. Then everyone discusses, "What do you think teachers, school administrators, and other staff could have done differently to better support positive feelings about who you are?"

       The resulting discussion tends to reveal the varying school experiences of adults based on their social identities. In the process, adults see both points of connection (familiarity) and differences (unfamiliarity), which challenge our assumptions. The discussion also provides an opportunity to identify what families want for their children and what the educators want for children in their care.

Ethnicity and Language

This discussion topic is a response to children's comments about languages in their classrooms that reflected both curiosity and disrespect. For instance, children laughed and teasingly said, "You talk funny," when a child whose first language is Spanish pronounced "juice" as "yuice."

1. Discussion begins in small groups about what experiences participants had (as a child/as an adult) in these situations:
    a. Learning a new language
    b. Not being understood
    c. Not understanding others

     d. Being uncomfortable with languages, dialects, and accents different from one's own

     e. Not respecting or being respected because of language or accent

Responses by family members can be very personal, for instance, sharing the fear of losing the ability to speak with grandparents and other relatives as they learn English.

2. The whole group hears from small groups and then addresses these additional questions:
   - How does this issue affect your children?
   - What language experiences have they had?
   - What have you, other children, or other adults done in response?
   - What would you like to have done in your child's class related to this issue?
3. The program leader describes what the center is doing about language issues, followed by families discussing these questions:
   - What do you think about the suggestions for dealing with language issues?
   - What ideas do you have?

The earlier discussions about prior experiences can create a helpful bridge to the program leader's presentation of what the program is doing and wants to do.

Unlearning Stereotypes About Indigenous Peoples

Children often see and absorb stereotypical images and information about Indigenous peoples from the media and society throughout the month of November. This staff–family gathering focuses on what happens and how to challenge the misinformation.

1. The whole group brainstorms what they have learned about Indigenous peoples from their country of origin. As part of this process, the program leader displays a collection of common stereotypes in cards, children's books, and clothing as a way to stimulate memories.
2. Small groups play a series of games with photo cards depicting contemporary Indigenous people doing familiar activities (e.g., reading to children, playing football, cooking, and engaged in various occupations). Participants talk about what they think children learn from playing with these cards and then consider how the photos differ from what they had thought Indigenous people looked like, what they do, and the sources of any misinformation and stereotypes.
3. Small groups share their findings regarding stereotypes and reality, along with ways to help children learn about all of our lives in school. Typically,

some participants will express indignation that they had never learned the truth in school and that the media and peers continue to expose their older children to stereotypes and misinformation.

Community Activism

This staff–family gathering addresses Goal 4 of anti-bias education activism with children (see Chapter 1) in a creative and fun way. The activity is based on an experience at Ellen's center. Teachers read their children the picture book *The Streets Are Free* (Kurusa, 2008), which is based on the true story of the children of the barrio of San Jose de la Urbina in Caracas, Venezuela. It tells what the children did when the mayor did not keep his promise to build a playground in their neighborhood. After hearing the story, the children in Ellen's center turned her office into the office of the mayor and acted out the story! The staff decided to share what the children were doing with the families, as a positive way to discuss taking action in the face of unfairness.

While this activity was very specific to Ellen's context, it reveals some core ideas that can be applied in any program: (1) children's literature is a powerful way to share complex ideas, (2) young children can identify unfairness and be active in finding solutions, and (3) it is important to recognize that families come from diverse neighborhoods and communities.

This session unfolded as follows:

1. Small groups of family and staff received copies of the book illustrations changed to look like a reporter's photos of an incident happening in the neighborhood. Each group had the task of assigning captions to their photos.
2. The small groups then shared their captions with the whole group, and discussion explored the different perspectives about the photos.
3. The program leader, role-playing a member of the neighborhood, then told the group the story in the book from the neighbor's perspective.
4. The whole group then discussed the difference between their various perspectives of the story and those of the people who live in the neighborhood.
   - They considered how people have different perspectives even when they see the same incident, and the importance of getting the perspective of the people involved in that situation.
   - This then led to a discussion of what happens in their own neighborhoods when "outsiders" repeat only the negative events and don't know the daily life of people in their communities.
   - Finally, the leader led a discussion about activism in the story: How do you feel about the story? What do you think about the children going to the mayor? How do you feel about our reading stories that include protest and demonstration?

PROMOTING FAMILY PARTNERSHIP AND LEADERSHIP

Beyond families engaging in education discussion and participating in activities for the children, an anti-bias approach requires building support and partnership among families and leadership of families in the program's work.

Building partnerships with families can go hand-in-hand with helping them develop a deeper understanding of ABE. Relationships are at the core of ABE work, which includes establishing ways that the members of your program get to know each person's identities. At Rukia Rogers's program in Atlanta, home visits and playdates are scheduled when a new family joins. They make space and time for all staff and families to engage in conversations. For example, quarterly family meetings are led by their classroom teachers. Rukia's program also has a parent council, which includes two families from each classroom, and a social justice committee. Rukia explains,

> During these times, we are getting to know the families and they are getting to know us in deeper ways. During the beginning of the year, based on our observations and questions from the children and families, we collectively make a declaration of intent on a topic we want to pursue as a community. This past year we had a focus on food equity, who has food and who doesn't, and how do children perceive the rights of the natural world. During our meetings we share with families our observations and invite them into the conversation to get their perspective/input, and very often to take action with us around a particular issue. For instance, writing letters to the mayor, participating in a march with the children. We think of parents, in partnership to raise their children, as opposed to our program as a service. This is a village.

Family Support System

An ECCE community with an anti-bias focus provides ways for families to raise their experiences with prejudice and discrimination in the school or in the larger society and opportunities for families to support and be allies for one another. Depending on the specific situation, the program leader and staff may also offer support directly.

Being Available. As the program leader, be comfortably accessible to all families throughout the year. John and Debbie used the saying, "My door is always open"—both figuratively, physically, and virtually. They wanted families to feel safe to share concerns and discuss anti-bias issues as they arose. Debbie offers these comments:

> My office was off the front entrance, and I tried to keep my door open (unless I was having a meeting), so families could pop in any time they wanted without a special appointment. Families often are more willing to

share difficult issues with an open-door policy. Sometimes parents just need someone to listen, not talk. Ensuring that a parent feels heard, especially when sharing issues that are emotional, can go a long way in building trust. Other times, I needed to offer a resource, information, or a recommendation for further support, such as a social worker, adoption group, or other support group. Because anti-bias issues are complex, it is often helpful not to respond in depth at first and essentially say, "Let me think about that and get back to you." This provides you time to think through the issues, collect information, and consult others.

Resource Access. Some programs have a family resource area with books, pamphlets, and articles on a range of parenting issues. Access to websites and other electronic resources provides another useful source. Families might have access to the Internet at your program or be offered photocopied materials. In an anti-bias program, the resource library includes specific materials on anti-bias topics for families to read at the center or borrow. The program leader can use what they learned by "reading" the program (see Chapter 3) to gather a portfolio of support networks and resources. This can include researching literature on issues such as families raising children adopted internationally, interracial families, children with cross-gender identity, or whatever specific concerns arise from the families in the program to share with families.

Diversity Dialogues and Affinity Groups. Functioning as a support and learning group, a Diversity Dialogues group met monthly at Debbie's school in Massachusetts. The group was co-led by a family member and a staff person. Debbie notes:

The group defines diversity broadly, and anyone in the community may attend. At one point, some White families felt they were not welcome because they did not see themselves as "diverse." As the director, I used this situation as an opportunity to clarify that everyone has a culture and that together we create diversity. Diversity exists in the relationships between us, not in those who are different from us. The group also changed the name from "Diverse Families Group" to "Diversity Dialogues," which helped to alleviate the concerns of some White families that they would not be welcome.

Over the years topics for the meetings included adoption, multiracial families, religion, class, and handling bias when it occurs. Families often brought up dilemmas about identity or bias issues in their own and their children's lives, and asked for ideas about how to handle these situations. Sometimes the group read a specific article together or watched a video clip to jump-start the conversation.

Depending on the family community and history of working on anti-bias education, you may find that in addition to diversity dialogue groups, support groups for a particular sociocultural group are needed. These affinity groups (i.e., BIPoC, LGBTQ+, disability, etc.) often help their members feel safer to open up about the challenging issues of social identity, prejudice, and discrimination. Affinity groups do not preclude diversity dialogue groups; they can operate simultaneously, and people can choose which format they prefer. Individuals may choose one type of group and then move to another. Any format that enables people to talk about themselves and their children is useful. John describes his thinking on this topic:

> I decided to begin the initial diversity dialogue group at my center by personally inviting parents from marginalized social-cultural groups in the community where the center is located. I also invited overt allies of the anti-bias mission. I thought it was more important at first to ensure a critical mass of group members committed to a dialogue about bias and equity rather than opening the dialogue group to everyone and risking diverting attention to the concerns of families less comfortable with an anti-bias approach.

Debbie talks about bringing together families that shared similarity in identity and issues at her prior center. In this anecdote Debbie uses identity-first language to describe the group (see Figure I.1), but we also stress the importance of encouraging the affinity group members to discuss and agree on the terminology that is preferred by the participants:

> We formed a support group specifically for families who had disabled children. Being an inclusion school, we soon found that other families also had questions about children with learning differences. In response, we expanded the group to friends and families of disabled children. The school's Educational Rights Coordinator and a parent facilitated this group, which met monthly on topics including advocacy, the special education IEP process, managing transitions, and the issues for siblings of a disabled child.

Families as Allies of Anti-Bias Education

I used to think that showing my anti-bias attitude meant not highlighting or bringing up difference, but I've learned that discussing and celebrating these differences in a more active way can be a powerful tool against bias.

—Parent

Identifying family members who can become advocates and allies for anti-bias education at your program begins with the reading of the program (see Chapter 3). As the year progresses, there are several forms that family advocacy and leadership might take.

Families Advocating for Identity Differences. Some differences in a family's social identities are less identifiable than others. Skin color, language, and physical disabilities, such as cerebral palsy, are typically more discernable—but not always. Families may deliberately hide some of who they are out of concern about acceptance. Some differences, such as emotional and behavioral challenges, can be hard for community members to comprehend because families do not feel able to share them openly. In an anti-bias community, one of the goals is to support families to feel visible and audible in the community and be able to express all aspects of their identities.

One strategy to achieve this is inviting families, if they are willing, to share their child's disability differences, whether obvious or not. This process empowers the family to take ownership and frame the child's disability in the way they want. This kind of sharing requires a lot of trust, and some families may not be ready to make this step, especially if they are still coming to terms with the disability themselves. Other families often become more empathetic once they understand the child's situation and challenges and the ways they can provide support. We have found that this kind of sharing (and visibility) helps to disrupt the concept of "normal" and celebrate differences in the community. Some families may visit the classroom and talk about their child's differences, for example, reading a book about autism, bringing in a hearing aid to share with the children, or explaining how to communicate with their child whose nonverbal using sign language or a picture exchange system. In one center, a parent came to talk about his own learning disability and how he felt growing up having difficulty learning to read. Other families have written a letter to the classroom community.

Figure 5.3 provides a sample letter written to the classroom families by the parents of a child with Down syndrome.

Family Leadership and Initiative. There are several ways to intentionally promote anti-bias leadership. Invite and encourage family members to serve on program advisory boards, governance councils, and hiring, outreach, and fundraising committees. Include families with teachers in panel presentations at program meetings and external conferences. As noted previously, families should also be supported to create their own groups for dialogue about shared identities and issues. John funded a team that included an administrator, a teacher, and a parent of a disabled child to attend an inclusion leadership meeting at the state capital. He also selected parent/family members for staff hiring committees to ensure a diversity of perspectives. John explains:

> Over the years I was proactive about including parents who came from
> underrepresented groups in the community in various leadership roles.
> These opportunities to be involved in decision-making not only shared
> power with a broader range of perspectives but also sent a concrete message
> that all voices were valued. On a hiring committee, we (teachers, parents,

Figure 5.3. Sample Letter From the Parents of a Child With Down Syndrome

Dear Families,

We are the parents of Matthew, your child's classmate at the center. Thank you for your warm welcome. Like all parents we have been anxious about our son starting school, and your openness and kindness have helped us feel easier.

We are looking forward to coming in this Thursday to speak with the class about Down syndrome and what this means specifically for our son. Matthew was born with Down syndrome and it is something unique to him. It makes him who he is just as each of your children have things that make him or her unique. Matthew likes to play cars, dance, sing, and read books, just like his friends. However, he approaches these activities differently than most do and needs extra help and time learning to do all of them. As with everyone, there are things he is really good at and there are things that are frustrating and challenging. Like any parent we want our child to be confident and proud of who he is.

We also feel charged to share with others about Down syndrome and to provide current and accurate information. Since Matthew was born, we have learned a lot. We have also learned that many people have questions but are hesitant to ask. We are always open to answering any questions that you or your child has. The center has a variety of resources and books too. Please feel free to contact us anytime.

Sincerely,

Matthew's family

and administrators) came to know each other both professionally and personally as we discussed the values and teacher attributes that were most important in an anti-bias program. Parents were able to see the thought and commitment that teachers had for an inclusive program, and we built relationships with allies among our parents.

I realized it was important to be alert for family leadership opportunities that can emerge from program-wide activities. For instance, after seeing how engaged some parents were at a parent and teacher lecture on dual-language learners, I personally encouraged four parents (all of whom were on the advisory board and had first languages other than English) to organize and facilitate a follow-up conversation specifically for families with children learning two or more languages. The meeting proceeded without my involvement (other than organizing time, space, child care, and food) and resulted in a set of recommendations and questions that were shared with teachers.

We recommend that you encourage family initiative and leadership by including families in advisory and leadership roles whenever possible. Families (and teachers) can be on a hiring committee, help develop policies, and provide input on committees. However, you are ultimately accountable for the bottom line and alignment with the program mission and values. You must be clear about why, when, and in what ways you can truly share decision-making power with families, as Debbie's story illustrates:

> During one of my first years at my center in Massachusetts, a parent came to me about wanting to hold a Halloween parade throughout the school and into the surrounding university campus. I thought this could be a helpful dialogue and opportunity for the whole school, and I offered to take up the topic at the advisory board meeting with all the parents and teachers in attendance. The meeting was one of our best-attended sessions, and the topic generated many emotions. Some people felt holidays were important traditions; they just wanted to have some fun and take photos. Other people, including most teachers, felt it was not developmentally appropriate, that children would be afraid, and that it was feeding into the materialism of the holiday.
>
> It became evident that for many families the desire to have a Halloween parade was about their own needs rather than because the children wanted it. Others brought up the point that some people do not celebrate Halloween and that would make them uncomfortable. After the meeting a small group of teachers and parents drafted their ideas into a new holiday policy. I reviewed the final policy before it became part of the family handbook. Below are some key points about holidays that became part of the formal holiday policy.

- Find a balanced approach to holidays without exaggerating the experience or ignoring it.
- Any holiday experience in the school needs to be meaningful to the children and developmentally appropriate, and foster understanding and respect for one another.
- Recognize similarities and celebrate differences. Group holiday celebrations according to the seasons, and look for parallels across cultures; set holiday activities in the context of people's daily lives and beliefs; and connect them to specific children, families, and staff.
- Families are welcome to share their special traditions.
- Listen carefully and respond to children's comments, questions, and feelings about holidays.

MAKING *ALL* FAMILIES VISIBLE

Engaging families in your ECCE program and growing anti-bias partnerships requires a leader to use many versatile strategies. The goals include creating family visibility and connection, bringing staff and families together to pursue anti-bias values, and providing systems and opportunities for mentoring of family leadership. To be most effective, use and adapt strategies and activities that match the assets, needs, and dynamics of the specific group of families with whom you work.

Another crucial task for an anti-bias leader is fostering the teachers' knowledge and skills for creating positive relationships and partnerships with the families whose children they serve. In the next chapter, we look at the issues and strategies for doing this important work, as well as other ways that you can continue to deepen the teachers' capacity for anti-bias education.

CHAPTER 6

Deepening and Sustaining Anti-Bias Awareness, Knowledge, and Skills

> There is dedicated time to do the work. I have been able to talk about anti-bias issues
> to my classroom team, and to bring dilemmas to staff meetings and to my supervision
> meeting with the director. There are many professional development spaces for anti-bias
> discussion!
>
> —Teacher

The anti-bias journey calls for reflective practitioners who regularly assess where they are and where they want to go next. Accordingly, you continue to generate opportunities throughout the year for your staff's growth in knowledge of anti-bias education, critical reflection on practice, and skills in teaching and working with families. The strategies and activities in this chapter assume that there is now a solid core of teachers who are ready to move forward with the next steps in realizing your anti-bias mission.

In this chapter we pick up where Chapter 4 ended and begin by presenting several professional development strategies for integrating, deepening, and sustaining anti-bias work. Then we build on the theme of Chapter 5 and consider what program leaders can do to facilitate teachers' collaborative work with families.

ENHANCING THE PROFESSIONAL DEVELOPMENT OF ANTI-BIAS TEACHERS

One of the challenges of leading the professional development (PD) of an early childhood staff is offering activities that scaffold the varying levels of awareness, knowledge, and skills. Not only do adults learn and engage with change in different ways, they also join a team of staff at different points in time and bring with them varying kinds of experience. Your initial reading of the program (Chapter 3) and ongoing documentation (Chapter 8) will guide you in making appropriate choices of PD experiences and strategies that are best matched to your staff's readiness for anti-bias education. Inevitably, you will need to cycle back to the strategies shared in Chapter 4 when you have new staff enter the program or you feel a need to revisit and strengthen foundational ABE concepts.

Director Julie Bisson at Epiphany Early Learning Preschool in Seattle reflects on integrating experienced and new staff:

I begin each year like I need to continue moving our ABE practices forward. We have a mentor teacher system in place to support and bring along any new teacher. The mentors meet with the new hires to go over our ABE approach, talk about foundation practices, and find out the questions they have . . . We use a team approach, where everyone has time outside the classroom to read articles, watch the ABE video, and talk together. Every classroom team has an hour-and-a-half team meeting every week. And anti-bias is often on that on the agenda for that meeting. . . . What are we seeing? What are kids saying about differences and fairness? . . . I think if you don't keep going, then you'll never go anywhere.

In the following sections we look at ways you can support teachers who are ready to go deeper into anti-bias education at various points in their anti-bias journey, and eager for deeper levels of engagement and collaboration. First, we consider your role in supporting staff to identify potential anti-bias curriculum and plan for their classrooms. We then discuss how you can engage in supervision, coaching, and mentoring of your teachers around anti-bias goals, and finally outline various PD modalities you can use to support anti-bias work.

Integrate Anti-Bias Education Into the Daily Curriculum

Our curriculum was so much more responsive with an anti-bias perspective. It became an intentional and explicit way to help our students as we explore our social, emotional, and cultural selves.

—Teacher

Once teachers have a foundational understanding of what anti-bias education encompasses and have begun implementing specific strategies, you focus on expanding their ability to fully integrate ABE into the ongoing curriculum. The goal is to ensure that teachers advance beyond simply implementing activities from a curriculum guide, no matter how well constructed, by challenging them to think about the particular group of children and families with whom they work at any given time. This process includes considering the neighborhoods and communities these various families are nestled within (Nimmo, 2008).

Identifying Potential Curriculum. While the four anti-bias core goals form the curriculum framework, specific learning opportunities and activities arise from the observed needs, questions, and backgrounds of the children in any program (Jones & Nimmo, 1994). Your ongoing observation of classrooms provides an opportunity to engage teachers in thinking about children's questions, comments, and responses regarding diversity and fairness and to help them identify starting points for specific anti-bias curriculum themes and activities. Your objective is to help teachers brainstorm how they can build on a child's (or children's) specific comment or interaction and to plan ways to explore the issue with the whole group. Thinking about curriculum together in this way reinforces the daily, ongoing, and emergent nature of opportunities to build anti-bias curriculum. For instance, the teacher has put out play dough in several skin tones from light to dark brown. One of the children picks up a darker brown piece of play dough, says, "Amelio's one is yucky; I don't like it," and throws it down. Other children imitate this child. Happening to observe this incident, the program leader tells the teacher about it during a lull in the action. After thinking about possible underlying reasons for the first child's behavior, the teacher decides to create a variety of learning opportunities over the next week to enable all the children to explore skin colors, learn the purposes of the color in skin, and gain appreciation for the beauty of all skin colors. The teacher also plans to listen carefully to further comments from the children, to better understand their thinking and to help them develop further activities as needed.

Sometimes the provocation for curriculum may come from an event outside the classroom. Your role is to help teachers make the potential anti-bias connection to the event. John tells this story to illustrate how you can support a teacher in identifying an opportunity to explore values and beliefs regarding economic class with children. In this example, the objective was to help the children become more aware of *all* the members of their community:

> I asked a facilities employee to look at a piece of rotting wood on our tree house while he was at the center fixing a door. He went out of his way to replace the wood, so I asked the teachers to invite the children to share their thoughts about what he had done in making their house available again for play. They wrote thank-you letters with pictures and posted them off to him. My thinking was that the children could appreciate that there are many people who work hard (often after hours) to ensure the center is clean and maintained—that it's not magic—it requires skill and hard work. I shared my reasoning with the worker, and he appreciated being valued and welcomed. This issue had been part of a larger discussion with teachers about auxiliary staff being more visible in our community. The teachers talked about trying to be more cognizant of when facilities workers were at the center. Rather than seeing them as a disruption or having nothing to do with the curriculum, they realized that they could say to the children, "This is Louisa—she's here to help get rid of the wasps. Let's say thank you to Louisa for doing that!"

Planning Guide for Teachers. Using the following steps for developing learning experiences helps teachers think through, in a more systematic way, how to implement anti-bias education with their particular group of children. This guide is an adapted version of a teacher's framework used at the Eliot–Pearson Children's School (Kuh et al., 2016).

Step 1. Observation/Documentation: Data-Gathering (see Appendix C for a worksheet to record observations focused on specific anti-bias topics).

- What are the children saying in their conversations with each other and teachers? What are the children asking about or showing us through their play and actions?
- What are families talking about?
- What issues and questions are provoked by the children's environment?
- What are teachers thinking about?
- Given your observations/documentation, what are the possible entry points for doing anti-bias curriculum?

Step 2. Reflection: Teachers share and consider their data together, both in staff meetings and in individual meetings with the program leader.

- What are the issues that emerge from the children?
- What are the emotions behind these issues for children?
- How are the adults (teachers, families) responding to these issues?
- What are some questions and topics that might be of interest and developmentally/culturally appropriate to explore with children?
- What issues and feelings arise for teachers and for families in relation to the identified issues for the children?

Step 3. Curriculum response: Learning experiences that address, explore, and expand on the children's questions and issues.

- What are our criteria for choosing specific topics to explore?
- Given a specific topic, how could we respond in the moment, generate learning experiences in the long term, and revisit or expand a topic with children?
- How do we implement curriculum that supports diverse learning styles and knowledges?
- How do we make the topic accessible and concrete for children?

Step 4. Assessment

- What worked and didn't work? Why?
- What have we learned with and about the children?
- What have we learned about ourselves? What was challenging?
- How do we share with families and our colleagues what we have done in the classroom?
- How do we solicit feedback from the children, families, and other staff in the community?
- Where do we go from here?

Program-Wide Curriculum Anti-Bias Focus. Another strategy for integrating anti-bias perspective into the classroom is to implement a schoolwide curriculum on a particular topic. This approach draws on the resources of your entire staff and encourages both peer mentoring and greater sharing of what classrooms are doing in their anti-bias curriculum.

Topics that provoke anti-bias questions could be anything that can lend itself to looking at similarities and differences. For example, the topic of shelters/homes could be the curriculum topic. All people have a right to some form of shelter, but each is different, and not everyone has the shelter they need. Some shelters are permanent, some are temporary. Some people live in a house, an apartment, a condo, a tent, a multifamily house, a houseboat, a motel, or a car. What makes a shelter a home? Each classroom could study shelters, read books about shelters, and make shelters out of blocks, sticks, cardboard boxes, and other materials. Debbie describes another curriculum example at the center she directed:

> We conducted a schoolwide curriculum about anti-bias topics. Each classroom focused on a "social identity category"—the 3-year-old class focused on family diversity, the 4-year-old group focused on racial identity, the kindergarten focused on class and privilege, the 1st/2nd grade focused on ability differences, and the afternoon mixed-age group focused on home culture and language. While we understood that these identities intersect, we used this study to examine whether we were exploring all these areas of identity and to hone our skills. (See Chapter 8 for information on how this curriculum was documented and shared.)

In any kind of schoolwide curriculum there are four key points to remember:

- Choose a topic that has potential for all age groups and can be explored in multiple ways. Consider intersectionality of issues in the topic. For instance, if your program decides to explore religion, this curriculum topic might include reading children's books about the role of spirituality in Indigenous cultures.
- Provide opportunities (e.g., at staff meetings) for educators from across the program to meet regularly to share, plan, and problem-solve together. These conversations become effective PD experiences.
- Encourage family participation in the curriculum by sharing the topic with families and getting their ideas, questions, and concerns right at the beginning. Some anti-bias topics are controversial for programs, such as talking about religious beliefs, Indigenous knowledges, or social class issues. Allowing families to raise their concerns up front is being proactive (see Chapter 7 for how to deal with conflicts that may arise). Teachers can hold an end-of-the-investigation celebration where children share what they learned. At these events, teachers have some of the curriculum activities for families to try out. For example, families can have the opportunity to mix their own skin-color paints and make their

own self-portraits using the paints, just like the children did as part of a racial-identity study.

- A schoolwide newsletter or blog on the topic is one way to share what is happening in the classrooms with families across the school. Each classroom writes briefly about their particular classroom; the program leader writes about why this topic is important to young children and includes a section on resources and children's books on the topic.

Considerations When Designing and Planning ABE Curriculum. It is important to think about your context when considering specific curriculum activities and provocations (to initiate the activity) to use. Below are some useful questions you can ask teachers to consider when planning anti-bias education provocations and activities for their classrooms.

Identity and Relationships: Does this curriculum connect authentically to you, your children, families, or networks?

Knowledge and Accuracy: What do you know about this issue? What is the source and accuracy of your information? What don't you know?

Timing and Context: When is it meaningful to introduce this curriculum to this specific group of children and families?

Preparation: What people, resources, and information need to be in place for this curriculum to be effective?

Pedagogy: How will you share this curriculum with colleagues and families and respond to the questions and responses it provokes?

Continuity: How will you continue this curriculum into the future to ensure depth and complexity?

Supervise and Coach Teachers in Anti-Bias Work

Through supervision and coaching, you have a direct, continuing opportunity to guide a teacher's anti-bias growth. Use positive and critical feedback, ask provocation questions, and scaffold suggestions to help teachers move to a new step in their work. Individual supervision meetings are safe places to discuss and support a teacher's professional goals and needs. Intentionally scaffold how you work with teachers, considering the stage of each teacher on the anti-bias journey. Finding the point where each individual can move to a next step, but not be pushed into too much disequilibrium, is key.

While supervision and coaching teachers are an essential part of your responsibilities, how you organize these sessions depends on the characteristics, dynamics, and needs of the program. These include, but are not limited to, size of staff, number of staff per classroom, and time you have in the face of all responsibilities. Debbie explains how she handled supervision at her program (see LeeKeenan & Ponte, 2018, for more details):

I held regular (weekly or biweekly) individual supervision meetings with the five lead teachers. They came prepared with their agenda, questions they had about curriculum, children, or families. I responded to and supported the teacher, and also introduced appropriate scaffolding and resources, based on what I assessed that particular teacher needed. I integrated an anti-bias lens into my questions and support. I learned when to challenge a specific teacher to the "next level," and when I needed to hold back for a bit. I based these decisions on my knowledge of the teacher's readiness, resiliency, and abilities. Sometimes I provided a prompt or focus for the teacher to implement (e.g., Keep track of who plays in the dramatic play area and block area. Is it limited to a particular gender? Why do you think that happens? Is it something you want to shift? What can you do?).

Conducting regular observation of teachers was another way I supported and coached staff. I held a pre-conference with the teacher, asking questions such as, "How can this observation help you? What do you want feedback on?" For example, the teacher might ask if she is using different language based on gender in the block area. Sometimes I initiated an observation session; sometimes a teacher requested an observation of a learning experience about which they wanted feedback. During an observation, I took notes on what was working, including specific language the teacher used and actions about which I had questions, and noted suggestions for improvement. During the post-observation conversation, I asked the teacher how they felt the lesson went (What went well? What would you change?) before I gave my feedback.

Supporting Teachers in Having Challenging Conversations With Children

Teachers need support on how to hold conversations based on young children's questions about what they see and hear in their world related to diversity, bias, and fairness. Here are guidelines to help teachers feel more comfortable holding clarifying and brave conversations with children (adapted from Derman-Sparks et al., 2020, pp. 55 & 61).

- *Make it safe for all the children involved.* The teacher's first job when children are distressed is to stop the action and to be a safe and assuring presence for all the children. In particular, attend to any child who is the target of bias.
- *Find out what the children know.* Then, without judgment, find out what the children are feeling and thinking and how they make sense of the situation. Listen carefully and reflect the children's thinking back to them. Name the feelings.
- *Always respond.* Silence gives children the message that this topic is taboo and robs them of the vocabulary to discuss it. If you need more

time to respond, say, "That's an important question. Let me think more about it and get back to you."

- **Tell the truth.** Clarify misinformation as factually and simply as you can: "Here's what I know about this idea." Emphasize: "We are all the same. We are all different. People have different ideas. That's OK."
- **State the justice issues** as they relate to the child's question, comment, or behavior. "What is fair/unfair, kind/hurtful? How do we know?" Empower children to speak up for themselves.
- **Give the children something to do to make it better. State the safety issues.** What do the children need for processing their feelings as well as clarifying misinformation? Let the children know there are people who work to fix problems. Create ways for the children to do something age-appropriate about the situation. Speak your program's values: "In our program we . . ."; "This is what we believe . . ."; "Here's how we treat people in our school . . .".
- **Talk with families.** Once a sensitive issue comes up with a few children, most of the children will hear about it in a short period of time. It is important to alert all the families about the issue (without using individual names). Offer a brief explanation of what you have done to address the issue and ask families for their ideas.

Model Anti-Bias Teaching in the Classroom

As the leader, going into the classroom to model working with the children on a specific piece of anti-bias curriculum demonstrates to the teacher how to make complex ideas developmentally and culturally appropriate and how to engage children to think and talk about a specific anti-bias issue. You can also model teaching an anti-bias activity when a teacher is unsure about how to handle an anti-bias issue. Modeling gives you and the teachers a common experience to reflect on together during supervision meetings. Teachers can then do follow-up activities with the children in ensuing days. It also emphasizes the importance you give to this work and models risk-taking. Debbie notes:

At the beginning of the year, I visited each classroom to read one of my favorite books that focuses on diversity. With teachers less familiar with ABE, I might read a book such as *Bread, Bread, Bread* (Morris, 1993), which has photographs of people all over the world eating different types of bread. The anti-bias theme in this example is about similarities and differences in how people living in diverse cultural settings make and eat food—some are like what the children's families do, and some are different. We discuss questions such as: What do you notice about the different types of breads? How do you think they are made? What types of grain are the breads made from? What kinds of bread do you and your families like to eat? How are these similar or different from breads you are seeing in the book? I also encouraged the children to ask questions about the similarities and differences they notice in the people and settings in the photographs. Next, I brought samples of different types of bread (challah, manto, steamed bread, injera, and tortillas) to taste. Over the next several weeks the teacher might then do bread baking and invite different families to come to the classroom to share the type of bread they eat in their homes.

The program leader can also use modeling to help teachers consider a more effective way to teach about a specific topic or problem-solve an anti-bias issue. Debbie shares a story about helping a teaching team that was struggling with how to best support a Muslim child being ostracized by his classmates.

> I met with the team to find out the problem and what they were already doing. The teachers shared there was a pattern of children not playing with Fahad, a new child in the classroom, calling him names, saying his food is stinky. The teachers were directly addressing the comments and saying that's not OK because words can hurt. They also encouraged Fahad to speak up and share how the comments made him feel. The teachers were reading books with Muslim characters to the class. I suggested the use of a persona doll to make the issue more explicit and do some problem-solving with the children. The teachers were nervous about using the persona doll, so I offered to model. The next week, with the doll on my lap, I introduced Bilan to the group: "This is Bilan, she speaks 2 languages, English and Somali; she lives with her mom and auntie in an apartment down the street. She loves to play with dolls and read books. She just moved to a new school. But she is feeling sad because no one is playing with her, and other kids are making fun of her name and the hijab she wears on her head." I asked the class, "What do you think we can do to help Bilan?" The children made comments such as, "That's not nice." "I like her head scarf." "I like to play with dolls." And Fahad said, "I will be your friend, I speak Somali too." It was a moving moment—he felt connected to the doll. Afterwards I debriefed the session with the teachers and we discussed next steps, including how they would use Bilan, the persona doll, in the future.

Persona dolls are a powerful tool to help children embrace diversity and equity and develop social skills and empathy while reflecting on their own experiences (Brown, 2008). Persona dolls are toddler-size dolls that have their own unique personality and life history. Through storytelling, the dolls help children understand differences and culture, bias and prejudice, and develop critical thinking and the skills to stand up to unfairness. The dolls also help children who may feel marginalized to see someone like themselves (Al-Jubeh & Vitsou, 2021).

Mentor Leadership Capacity of Teachers

Leaders build teacher capacity and ability to take the initiative in anti-bias education through a process of mentoring over time. Encourage teachers to participate in leadership opportunities and use these as occasions to mentor their skills and dispositions. Mentorship involves a supportive relationship of careful guidance for teachers in which you ask questions, provide expertise, and engage in dialogue. This relationship continues in the many one-on-one and more personal interactions that you have with teachers throughout the day.

Leadership Groups. These groups may be a mentor or representative teacher group, a schoolwide diversity task force (including family representatives), or a family advisory board team. The program leader might send a leadership group to a conference, diversity workshop, or special PD event, with the expectation that the leadership group will share what they learned with the rest of the staff. This could be through a presentation to the whole staff, distributing handouts and summary notes, and meetings with the others in their stakeholder group.

One example is John's creation of a Diversity, Equity, and Bias Task Force (DEBT) at the program he previously directed:

> I asked five teachers who had begun to raise questions regarding diversity to commit to participating on the task force for 2 years. The group met monthly during school time, beginning with concrete tasks such as reviewing the intake questionnaire, before moving on to development of a diversity mission statement [refer to Figure 4.2]. This task force was an occasion for me to challenge perspectives in a way that was difficult in larger all-staff meetings. I expected committee members to take responsibility for raising diversity issues in their team meetings with peers. Over several years, the group read books together, developed guidelines on anti-bias issues for the staff, facilitated anti-bias workshops, and hosted a series of evening forums for families we called "Diversity Dialogues." Later we branched out with a second key task force focused on the inclusion of children with varying abilities. This group of teachers engaged in similar activities to DEBT and created an inclusion action plan for the center.

Cross-Program Study Groups. Setting up study groups with a combination of staff, teachers, and families is another way to grow anti-bias work. These groups encourage individual teachers and family members to take leadership as meeting planners and facilitators. Then program leaders move into the role of co-learner. At Epiphany Early Learning Preschool in Seattle, quarterly Family-Teacher Anti-bias Meetings meet to discuss different anti-bias topics and dilemmas. Other programs organize groups that become an affinity group for the participants (e.g., BIPoC families, friends and families of disabled children); others may work as action groups on behalf of the whole school community. The Highlander School in Atlanta has a social justice committee that organizes events and activities for the whole school community, for instance, sponsoring a schoolwide diversity speaker or creating a resource binder on anti-bias resources for families.

Provide Multiple Opportunities for Learning Together About ABE

There are several ways for the program leader to create experiences for staff to continue their anti-bias professional development. You should differentiate experiences to meet the needs of your staff. The following are familiar professional strategies in the ECCE field, but in this case, the content, specific approaches, and role of the program leader focus on supporting an anti-bias mission.

Using Scenarios and Case Studies as Practice Tools. Use mini-case studies or scenarios as a way for teachers to practice responding to anti-bias moments in the classroom. The scenarios can depict interactions with children and/or interactions with adults, families, or colleagues. In small groups of four, teachers read and consider the dynamics of and possible solutions to the scenario. They then debrief each scenario in the large group.

Directions: Read the scenario and discuss. Assign a note-taker for the share-out.

- What are the child's underlying observations and questions?
- What are the core anti-bias issues raised in this scenario?
- How might the child's developmental level and intersecting social identities affect your responses?
- How would you respond in the moment?
- Would you bring this issue to the entire classroom community? Why? How?
- What could you do in your classroom curriculum to address the issues in the long term?
- How could you work with families around this issue?
- How do you work through any conflict that may occur? (See Chapter 7 for the Third Space strategy.)

Scenario Examples: These scenarios can be adapted to your setting or changed to have more or less detail. When the scenario does not include specific identity information, the participants often make assumptions or consider different possibilities (e.g., Is this child BIPoC?) that can be discussed later.

- During a discussion on community helpers in a preschool classroom, one child says, "My mom said, 'The police are not our friends.'" Other children comment, "Yes they are! They keep us safe. That's what my dad says."
- On a neighborhood walk, Emily (a child) notices a person with dark skin who is houseless and says, "That woman's sleeping on the ground with garbage."
- Devlin is a 3-year-old child who expresses gender-fluid behavior. Devlin wears dresses to school, has long hair, and likes to play with dolls in the dramatic play area. Other children in the class are asking, "Is Devlin a boy

or girl?" Devlin says she is a girl. The parents are not sure what to do and look to the school for guidance on how to help their child. The teachers are also wondering how to respond in the classroom.

- Tian is three-and-a-half years old and just started your toddler/preschool program. When it is snack and lunchtime, the teachers notice she does not like to eat. When her parents pick her up after school, teachers mention that Tian has not been eating her lunch or snack. The parents ask, "Why don't you feed her? That's what we do at home."
- Martha and Lila are toddlers playing with the dollhouse. There are brown- skinned and white-skinned doll figures. The girls are fighting over the White doll figures. When you suggest, there are more dolls here, the girls push those dolls away and say "no."

Assigned Readings and Videos. You can give the staff a shared assignment to complete for a discussion group, meeting, or retreat. This may be an article, a video, a book (fiction or nonfiction), a blog entry or website, or a chapter from a book. Make sure that your selections match the literacy level of your staff members and can be completed in the time available. Some program leaders provide time during staff meetings to watch a video or read a written excerpt together (see Appendix A for a list of suggested resources at www.tcpress.com).

The purpose of the assignment is to provide a common knowledge base that everyone can then discuss in the whole group or small groups. You can use prompts such as: What did this mean to you? How does it apply to anti-bias work? What is your takeaway message from the assignment?

Workshops. Part- or full-day workshops with outside facilitators are useful as occasional activities. They can introduce new topics with which they have experience and that you may not feel ready to offer to staff by yourself. They also help staff see how the work at their center connects to a bigger context, allow you to be a learner along with the staff, and reinforce concepts and content that staff is exploring. An outside workshop facilitator may be a teacher or program leader from another center, an anti-bias educator at a nearby community college or university, a local diversity/social justice leader, or family and community members talking about values and childrearing practices from their cultural background. For example, during his second year as director, John invited Debbie to come to his program to lead an anti-bias training:

> As friends and colleagues, Debbie and I had already begun to develop relationships between our staffs. Teachers from her center had visited us, and vice versa. Some teachers from both centers had presented at a conference together, so there were personal and collegial connections. She wasn't simply an outsider. Second, I felt Debbie would not be confrontational. She makes folks feel comfortable, is very down-to-earth and concrete in her delivery, but still stretches folks' thinking. I wanted this to engage everyone in a joyful way and get their juices

running—to be excited about the work, not dreading it! Third, Debbie is a BIPoC woman and comfortable, open, and clear about her identities. I knew she would project this to staff. In many ways, inviting Debbie was an important turning point in engaging all the staff in a more concrete conversation about how to implement our anti-bias commitment in the classroom.

In Seattle, Directors Karina Rojas Rodriguez and Julie Bisson are part of a citywide consortium of centers where programs pool resources and dedicate a couple of days a year when they close the center and do daylong PD specifically on "undoing institutionalized racism" as part of their Anti-Bias/Anti-Racist (ABAR) work.

Keep in mind that while occasional workshops by outside experts are a useful part of an anti-bias professional development plan, they do not take the place of ongoing professional development facilitated by the program leader.

Hybrid Learning. Living through the pandemic of COVID-19 provided all of us with opportunities to develop new models for professional development. These models combine face- to-face meetings with virtual and online learning such as virtual (Zoom) staff meetings, and webinars. Since the murders of George Floyd and Breonna Taylor and the resurgence of the Black Lives Matter movement, there has been a dramatic increase in webinars on racial justice and equity. Organizations such as Embrace Race, https://www.embracerace.org/, provide multiple free, accessible, and high-quality webinars on these topics. Most webinars are recorded and can be viewed later. Program leaders have found that while virtual meetings have provided more flexibility and accessibility for many staff and families, there are always advantages and disadvantages. Communicating clearly and working through the emotion of conflict is particularly onerous in virtual spaces. It can easily lead to misunderstandings. Meeting in real time, whether in person or in a virtual space, is always preferable when complex issues are involved.

Staff Retreats. Staff retreats provide a concentrated time to focus on specific aspects of professional development and on community-building, away from the distractions of daily teaching. They differ from regular staff meetings, which usually occur after a long day with children, for 1–2 hours, and with many different agenda items to cover. Staff retreats are ideal for focusing on anti-bias work, as there is more time to really immerse in in-depth conversations. Some retreats begin with a guest speaker, and then small-group discussion and planning follow.

Attending Professional Conferences. Allocating release time and funds for educators to attend targeted conferences to learn about diversity and equity beyond their own classroom and program educates and reinforces their own efforts. When two or more teachers attend together, it allows for personal reflection and trust. It also creates a higher likelihood that learning from the conference will transfer to the rest of the staff. Encouraging educators to present their ideas at a conference is also an empowering experience. Doing this as a team, where you and teachers present together, is a good way to mentor them to gain the confidence and competencies they need to disseminate what they know and do. As mentioned in Chapter 5, adding interested family members to a conference presentation enhances their involvement in your anti-bias efforts. Let us now expand the discussion of professional development to focus on teacher–family interactions.

FACILITATING TEACHERS' WORK WITH FAMILIES

Trying to make different members of the community feel respected when their beliefs are in contradiction to my own or others' is difficult.

—*Teacher*

Program leaders also facilitate teachers effectively reaching out to and interacting with all families. This section describes several PD strategies for strengthening teachers' work with families on anti-bias issues, which build on those shared in Chapter 5.

Support Critical Self-Assessment

Assess how comfortable and familiar teachers are with families who come from different backgrounds and social identities, and then determine ways to help teachers stretch outside their comfort zones. In addition, facilitate their critical reflection and problem-solving about their conversations and interactions with families. Integrate professional development about families into ongoing anti-bias work with staff, including individual supervision meetings, staff meetings, and professional development workshops, as mentioned in the previous section of this chapter.

Anti-Bias Self-Study Guide. This tool, developed by Chen et al. (2009), is discussed in detail in Chapter 8 and provided in Appendix D, which is available online at www.tcpress.com. The guide has a section on "relationships with families and community" with questions that are a helpful starting place for teachers to self-assess how they feel about working with families. Based on how each staff member responds to these questions, you can identify individual professional goals and plan relevant professional development trainings.

Unpacking the Ghosts at the Table. Sarah Lawrence-Lightfoot (2003) studied parents' and teachers' perspectives on parent–teacher conferences and discusses how everyone brings previous histories with schooling into the present, whether those were positive or negative experiences. Lightfoot calls this the "ghosts" at the conference table. Parents and other caregivers' previous experiences influence their expectations for their children now. Teachers also need to be aware of their own baggage and how this may interfere with how they relate to families. One way to address this issue is to have teachers and families share their own personal schooling stories with each other.

Families come from a wide range of previous school experiences: urban, rural, private, traditional, schools where many languages are spoken, and so on. There will also be a range of responses, from happy memories where teachers or families remember the play-dough or special snack they had, to emotional stories about feeling abandoned and crying all day because "the center did not accept my tribal identity and allow me to sing in my language." The discussion may be about how it felt to be left at school, how the parent must have felt, and how the teacher handled the crying. You can then discuss how these memories influence how families handle separation with their own children or the strategies the teacher may use in the classroom.

Their history and expectations also influence how families look at the role of the teacher. For example, in some cultures home and school are seen as separate worlds:

- It is not the role of the family to come into the classroom and read a story or do a cooking project.
- The parent's role is at home or making a living.
- Family members are not trained or educated to be "a teacher" and should not be in the classroom.

Some teachers may not be aware of these cultural norms and assume that some families are not involved in school life because they are "not interested." Your task is to help teachers unpack the conversations and interactions, not make assumptions, in order to better support families.

Fears About Engaging Families. Teachers may feel uncomfortable and nervous about how to respond to questions or concerns parents have about anti-bias issues. As the leader, let teachers know that you are a resource and will back them up when needed. They need to know that it is okay to make a mistake or misspeak as part of their learning process. Their anxiety about specific topics often reflects the teachers' identity and personal experiences. But some topics, like sex and religion, are typically touchy subjects for any teacher because of views about the boundaries between parent and school responsibilities.

You should look for the balance between supporting teachers starting where they are comfortable and challenging them to take more risks with curriculum and conversation. When controversial conversations occur between children in the classroom, it is critical for the teacher to share this with families, either with the individual families of the children involved or with the whole class in a newsletter or meeting. The purpose is to let families know how the teacher is handling the challenging topic and the curriculum response being planned, and to allow families an opportunity to share questions or concerns. You can talk the teacher through this process of responding (by asking questions and offering suggestions and resources) or even by being present at a meeting. Debbie recalls her experience related to handling a challenging topic. In this case she offered to participate in a potentially challenging parent–teacher conference.

> One time during our supervision meeting, a teacher shared with me that she overheard a set of twins in her preschool classroom talking about their family using the words "surrogate, egg donor, two daddies." The teacher thought the language the children were using among themselves should be shared with their family. We discussed that it would be important to first meet with the two dads of the twins to find out what language they use at home. The teacher requested I also join the meeting, since this issue could feel intrusive. The teacher was worried that the two dads would think the school was challenging the choice of words they used at home with their children. In the end the teacher was comfortable leading the meeting, but my support to preview the situation with her and then just to be in the room provided her with additional confidence. The two dads appreciated the opportunity to share about their family, and the teacher and dads eventually drafted a letter (that I reviewed) that went out to all families about the language the children use.

Sharing Your Identities. An anti-bias approach requires staff members to build awareness of their social identities (see Chapter 4). This enables them to be more conscious of the impact of identity on perceptions of and interactions with families with whom they may share similarities or differences—or both. Sharing experiences relating to one's social identities with families can demonstrate a willingness to talk about and embrace differences. It can also enable educators to better connect and empathize with families in their program, particularly those feeling marginalized. Typically, traditional notions of professionalism give implicit permission for staff to share areas of identity that reflect mainstream values and culture, while often keeping other aspects less visible. For instance, a teacher who is heterosexual happily shares news of her upcoming wedding, while a teacher who is lesbian may feel pressure not to share similar news. A Muslim staff member decides not to share with families that they are fasting and taking time off to celebrate Ramadan, while families and staff freely talk about holiday plans for the "Christmas" break. A teacher who is stressed and late one morning because she can't afford to get her car fixed does not share her predicament with families, while a teacher who is jet-lagged from a vacation trip draws empathy from parents.

Healthy relationship-building between ECCE staff and families requires a comfortable and ongoing exchange about who they are in the world. Program leaders can model and show support for staff to share their identities with the school community in ways that respect confidentiality and agreed-upon professional boundaries. Setting these boundaries can be complex and entails dialogue and mindfulness about the values and goals of an anti-bias approach.

Further Skills for Interacting With Families

Staff members need coaching on effective skills for interacting with families in culturally responsive ways. You should both model these techniques as well as provide professional development opportunities for teachers to learn these skills.

What, How, and When to Ask. Given the multidimensional nature of working with diverse families, it is important for teachers to be open and to get as much information as they can about a child's background, beginning as soon as possible. As discussed in Chapter 5, teachers can undertake this process during the intake process, home visits, parent–teacher conferences, and ongoing conversations with families over time. The information can be gathered verbally or in writing. Open-ended as well as specific questions are helpful. Some examples include:

- Tell me about your child (temperament, personality, heritage, interests, abilities).
- What are your child's favorite activities?
- Are there any experiences your child avoids?
- Describe your child's sleeping schedule.
- Describe your child's eating patterns. What are their favorite foods?
- What languages does your child sign or speak at home? What languages does your child hear or see at home?
- What cultural, spiritual, and religious holidays, celebration, or traditions do you practice at home and in the community? Are there any that you would be willing to share with us at school?
- What are your expectations for your child?
- What are your aspirations, dreams, and hopes for your child?
- What do you view as your child's community/communities?
- Is there anything else you would like us to know about your child or family (traditions, cultural background, race, religion, home language, culture, and family structure)?

Cross-Cultural Communication. Ensure that the teachers understand cross-cultural communication. Communication between people from different backgrounds is very complex because of the inseparability of language and culture. We usually mean more than what we communicate though speaking or signing different languages. Nonverbal communication, such as eye contact, proximity, touch, facial expressions, body positions, and gestures, can mean different things for different social and cultural groups. Providing resources, such as *Developing Cross-Cultural Competence: A Guide for Working with Children and Their Families* (Lynch & Hanson,

2011) and *Look at Me When I Talk to You* (Helmer & Eddy, 2012), can help staff become aware of and understand these potential differences. At the same time, it is important to emphasize that each family may vary from the communication styles associated with a particular ethnicity or nationality. Through your ongoing supervision and professional development, staff can develop cross-cultural communication skills, including:

- Identifying their own communication code
- Taking time to listen more carefully
- Paying attention to details
- Suspending judgment and considering alternatives
- Developing empathy
- Feeling relaxed with families who may be different from themselves

Cultural Conflicts. When teachers and parents come from different cultural backgrounds, the risk exists that teachers will not recognize or understand the social values underlying children's behaviors and a family's childrearing styles. It is vital for teachers to be aware of potential areas of conflict or misunderstandings early on, so they can be proactive in supporting the children and family. Likewise, families may misunderstand program policies and teacher actions because of differences in cultural values (York, 2016). Common areas of cultural conflict include the following:

- Discipline and child guidance techniques
- Gender roles and expectations
- Age-related expectations of children
- Children's learning approaches
- Sleep and bedtime routines
- Mealtime behavior and diet
- Child's responsibilities at home
- Health and safety
- Attachment and separation
- Views about the role of teachers and schools
- The significance of children's play

It is your role to help identify the potential cultural conflicts and support teachers in resolving them. In Chapter 7, we address the topics of disequilibrium and conflict as part of an anti-bias program and suggest guidelines for managing disagreements and working together for solutions that take the needs of all parties into account.

Home Visits. Some programs use home visits as a strategy to get to know children and their families on their own turf. Your task is to make sure that teachers are clear about the purpose of a home visit and have the skills for talking with the range of families served by the program.

In an anti-bias approach, teachers also need to be aware that some families may not be OK with a home visit, especially at the beginning of the program year. Some families feel intimidated or anxious about a teacher coming to their home, often because social class and cultural issues come into play. A family may feel that the school is coming to the home to check up on them as parents. Some may worry that a home visit is about confirming their legal immigrant status. A family could feel obligated to prepare a huge meal for the teacher as a sign of respect.

Because of these and other reasons, families may prefer to meet at a more neutral setting, like a playground or community center. It may take a long time for families to develop enough trust and comfort with the program to accept a teacher visit at their home. Virtual home visits are discussed in Chapter 5 as another option for making the home–program connection.

Documentation can be a way to add a new component to home visits. During home visits, with the family's permission, a teacher could take a photo of the front door of each child's home. By focusing on the door, rather than the entire house or apartment, parents are likely to be more at ease with sharing this aspect of their lives. Back at the program, the teacher and/or children paste each door photo onto the lid of an individual small cardboard box ($5'' \times 7''$). The inside of each box is decorated with a photo of the family and a short description of who lives in the house. The collection of "family doors" is then posted on the wall of the classroom or used by children as props (little homes) in the block area. This activity connects the home and program and visually recognizes the range of homes and families in each classroom.

Family Panel. Opportunities for teachers to hear directly from families about their experiences are particularly effective PD experiences. One strategy is to create a family panel to share their diverse experiences in schools, their hopes and dreams, and their challenges and concern with all staff. When creating a family panel, you should intentionally invite parents who represent a range of perspectives on a specific topic and come from a diversity of backgrounds. Some parents may feel that they are not articulate or outgoing enough to be on a panel. You need to be encouraging by assuring the family member that he or she has much to offer the community and staff. Parents find that they learn how teachers and other families think by participating on the panel. After the session, you can acknowledge and show gratitude to the participants on the panel by listing their names in the newsletter and writing thank-you notes.

Curriculum Night. You set the expectation that teachers will inform families about how they integrate anti-bias education into their classrooms. Debbie suggests two approaches:

The first parent meeting of the year was the fall curriculum night where teachers provided a curriculum overview of the year and what families could expect. As director, I asked that teachers include anti-bias education on the agenda by sharing how the approach is part of the classroom curriculum. Another strategy we tried was for me to open the evening by presenting a 15-minute overview about anti-bias education to families from the whole school. Families then went to their individual classrooms to discuss what anti-bias looked like in their classrooms with the teachers. This strategy ensured that everyone heard the same message but provided small-group and age-specific examples in each classroom.

Use the strategies we suggest for fostering teachers' awareness, knowledge, and skills for working with families on DEI issues; adapt them to meet the strengths and needs of your specific group; or create new ones. In the end, expanding staff's capacity to work effectively with families of all backgrounds will greatly improve the quality of your program in general, and particularly your anti-bias work.

STAFF DEVELOPMENT THROUGHOUT THE YEAR

Scaffolding and supporting the anti-bias professional growth of the adults in your program throughout the year has its challenges—such as carving out the time and resources to do it. At the same time, it is the only way to build and sustain an anti-bias early childhood program. Staff members' growth brings great benefits—for them, and for the children and families your program serves. It will also bring rewards to you, as you watch educators' understanding of themselves and the world evolve, and they gain a greater sense of professional confidence, competence, and commitment.

Next, we turn to one of the dynamics of anti-bias work that may worry you, yet has within it the possibilities for furthering professional development and the quality of your program. In Chapter 7 we examine the issues and strategies for constructively using the inevitable conflict and disequilibrium that are part of anti-bias change.

Managing and Negotiating Disequilibrium and Conflict

Change means movement. Movement means friction. Only in the frictionless vacuum of a nonexistent abstract world can movement or change occur without that abrasive friction of conflict.

—Saul D. Alinsky (1971, p. 21)

Learning the value of divergence (differing opinions), of the construction of assent (agreement), of negotiation was a long, complex exercise which is not finished. But it allowed all the protagonists (parents, teachers, politicians, other citizens) to understand that the concept of participation is not only a fundamental change of politics; it is also a way of being, of thinking of oneself in relation to others and the world.

—Carlina Rinaldi (2021, p. 115)

Early childhood program leaders worry about the possibilities for conflict if they pursue an anti-bias approach. If they are already under way with their anti-bias efforts, leaders may view disagreements as disruptive, unwelcome, and something to avoid. How a program leader prepares for and responds to conflict situations influences their outcomes. When a leader backs away from conflict, this can stifle progress toward an anti-bias vision.

Anti-bias endeavors do generate disagreements and dissonance. These dynamics are inevitable as teachers, families, and administrators act on their deeply held and diverse values regarding childrearing and education. More broadly contested grounds in ECCE, such as whether children are ready to recognize and learn about bias or if schools should have a role in achieving social justice, also fuel these conflicts. Emotional and cognitive disequilibrium often occur in conflict situations, accompanied by a range of feelings such as anger, frustration, and discomfort.

From a social constructivist framework, conflict is a productive part of the learning process. The disequilibrium created by individual and social conflict can be a prelude to problem- solving and sharing information, creating opportunities for people to expand and shift their perspectives and behaviors. With this in mind, anti-bias education leaders embrace conflict as a potentially healthy dynamic in the pursuit of change.

We begin this chapter by defining conflict in anti-bias efforts. Then we discuss several strategies for managing conflict situations between various combinations of program stakeholders (e.g., leader, staff, and family members). We examine the procedure of finding the third space as a preferred way to generate discrete solutions to particular conflicts in specific situations. Last, we consider the issue of pushback and opposition to anti-bias work and ways to stay on course.

UNDERSTANDING CONFLICT

Given the focus on building caring relationships in early childhood, many educators focus most of their energy on avoiding conflict and keeping the peace. This avoidance can also be a way to maintain the status quo of privilege and inequity (DiAngelo, 2018; Oluo, 2018). Anti-bias leadership requires that early childhood professionals reframe how they view the nature and purpose of conflict, as well as the disequilibrium and emotions it evokes. In this section we look at the meaning and dynamics of conflict from this perspective.

Forms of Conflict

Conflicts in anti-bias endeavors occur when there is dissonance between two or more perspectives on a specific equity, diversity, or bias issue. We distinguish three possible forms of conflict among program stakeholders: (1) inner disequilibrium, (2) disagreements, and (3) opposition. Each type also brings different degrees of intensity and discomfort for those involved, as well as possibilities for finding a productive resolution. All may be part of the change process. In this section, we explore some key dynamics of conflict including the role of relationships, knowledge, identity, and emotions.

Inner Disequilibrium. Conflict may be an inner and very personal struggle. Because ABE shifts the status quo and challenges some people's values and practices, it is inevitable that stakeholders will experience some level of intellectual and emotional disequilibrium, including the leader. It can be an uncomfortable experience to have one's current thinking shaken up. Everyone needs time to consider new information and perspectives. People can then respond to disequilibrium by modifying and expanding their thinking or, conversely, rejecting the new ideas.

Debbie shares an example from her work as an ECCE director. The story involved a family's request for a meeting to share feedback with her just as they were leaving the program and transitioning to elementary school. Even though she experienced considerable disequilibrium, Debbie took the time to reflect and learn from the situation.

> I assumed they wanted to say good-bye and to thank me for their experiences at the school. While they did express appreciation, they also

had something else to say. They told me they had been uncomfortable with our curriculum about families that included books and posters of same-sex families. Specifically, they noted that their religion did not accept same-sex families.

Surprised they were giving me this feedback now, I replied that I wish they had come to me earlier. When one parent asked, "Would you have changed the curriculum?," I knew the answer was no. I explained that the curriculum represented and made visible the diversity of families in the world, and even more importantly, in our own community. An inclusive family curriculum was an expression of the school's anti-bias mission. I also thanked the parents for telling me their feelings. I want my office and school to be safe places for families to express their viewpoints and concerns, even if the outcome is to agree to disagree.

This conversation echoed in my mind long after it was over. It was not an issue of whether or not we should include same-sex families in our curriculum, but I pondered what more I might have done to prepare our community. I kept thinking about questions such as:

Could I have presented the idea of the family curriculum differently and found out more about how families felt?

Did I take into consideration all the family viewpoints?

How did my own assumptions and values filter my responses both in the decision to have an inclusive family curriculum and to the family when they spoke up?

I concluded that this was a disagreement for which I could not find a solution that made everyone happy. I have noticed that, over time, my emotional responses to such moments of disagreement and disequilibrium have changed. Many years ago, I would have felt criticized by the family and disappointed by my inability to please them. I would have wanted to "fix it" and make everyone happy. I may have felt impatient toward the family for being unable to understand the importance of supporting same-sex families.

Why did the family come to see me in the first place? By openly sharing with me, they might have been looking for some resolution to their disequilibrium from the tension between their beliefs and their belonging to our anti-bias community. Today, I am less judgmental in my thinking about people with whom I disagree. I try to understand what underlies their positions and empathize with the conflicts they feel. My goal is to try to find common ground, but I can also accept that sometimes that does not happen, and I am at peace with agreeing to disagree. My experience with this family helped me to see that sitting with discomfort and living with disagreements are inevitable facets of anti-bias work.

Program leaders can assume that teachers and families will also experience disequilibrium as they encounter change. Leaders have a responsibility to help create a culture in which staff and families are more comfortable with this disequilibrium around anti-bias issues by using intentional provocations. A provocation may be new information, asking questions, or offering experiences that challenge staff and families to think about an issue in new and unexpected ways. For example, Debbie described the following strategy she used at her program:

> I challenged staff and family members to become more aware of stereotyping in the media and the world around us. I asked everyone to bring in books, posters, or toys to share at staff and parent meetings and to display (with questions) in the school's entranceway. People brought in provocative items such as wooden block figures that depicted Black people as servants and maids, chopsticks labeled as "chimp sticks" with a monkey at the end, and books with stereotypical illustrations. One teacher shared a package of miniature figures labeled "fat people" purchased from a local toy store. To facilitate discussion, I asked and posted questions such as:
> - What is the message this object or image might give your child?
> - What is fair or unfair, inaccurate, or hurtful about the message?
> - Why or why not would you use this with young children?
> - How would you explain the stereotypical messages to your child?

Provocations that challenge or push thinking also arise spontaneously. For instance, in the next story, John talks about inviting an expert on dual-language learning to the center for a family–teacher workshop, to open up thinking on the topic:

> When the diversity task force met after the workshop, a couple of teachers commented that they had hoped the speaker would be more explicit about the importance of maintaining one's home language. I responded that I saw the presenter engaging in a dialogue with family members who had different kinds of language learning situations at home (e.g., only one parent speaks two languages, both parents speak different languages other than English). She provided information about dual-language learning, but also invited family members to problem-solve about what to do in their homes. Some teachers were in disequilibrium because I was challenging their assumption that we should only be advocating for one approach. I asked the teachers to step back and reflect on the evening as a dialogue between parents who know a great deal about the everyday reality of language learning and professionals who have learned about the importance of supporting home languages. My provocation led to an energizing conversation in which teachers moved out of "we can *teach* families something about this" to "can we create a more authentic *dialogue* in which ideas and experiences are shared?" This approach holds the potential for greater depth in learning and in relationships.

Stakeholder Disagreements. Each of the stakeholders in an early childhood program, including families, staff, and administrators, may have disagreements with the program's anti-bias mission or a specific topic. They may express their disagreement to the program leader, or to teachers, or to families. Stakeholders can also remain silent about disagreements, or, as in the story from Debbie earlier, wait until leaving the program or let much time pass before sharing their views and feelings. Both situations make it difficult for the program leader to respond in a collaborative and timely way. Other people may be more explicit and forthcoming with their objections, in which case the leader has an immediate opening for dialogue.

People's individual and cultural histories, as well as their commitment to and views about children's well-being, are usually the underlying causes of disagreements. Understanding the role of identity in disagreements is critical, making it possible to perceive that what appears at first to be a small issue may be rooted in a person's worldview. Essentially, an individual is saying, "My perspective is important to who I am in the world." When changes challenge cultural values, people's emotions come into play. For some teachers, a shift in the culture of a program—such as changing the holiday policy—may destabilize their sense of belonging. Or a teacher focused on encouraging children to ask questions may feel that their teaching skills are being doubted when a Latinx parent expresses concern that their child is showing disrespect to elders by questioning them.

Most likely, the conflict is a resolvable difference in perspective related to issues of equity and bias. It might be the result of a misunderstanding, a lack of information, or a communication breakdown between members of your community. For instance, a teacher who speaks only English reacts defensively to the program leader's proposal to encourage home languages. She thinks that this will interfere with children's literacy development. Given that the teacher has a professional objection based on misinformation, engaging staff in a workshop on up-to-date dual-language learning (i.e., providing information) is one route to building the teacher's buy-in.

Disagreements can also occur when there is a lack of preparation or miscommunication about a program's anti-bias intentions. For instance, an administrator and teacher at John's center decided to move forward with using persona dolls in a preschool classroom. Teachers use these dolls to tell stories and engage children in critical thinking and problem-solving about a range of cultural and bias issues (Whitney, 2002). Rather than first focusing on the teacher's own classroom, they invited all the center families to a workshop on making dolls and brainstorming ideas for doll identities. The families from the teacher's class had a relationship of trust with her and had already received information about the purpose and use of the dolls. However, families from other classrooms who attended did not understand the rationale for persona dolls and came to voice their concerns. The staff had to backpedal and first explain the purpose of a persona doll to the family members at the workshop—a very different goal than some of the families had in mind. While the workshop ended positively by addressing parent concerns, the teachers could have stirred opposition unnecessarily by focusing on the intended outcome and not enough on the steps to get there.

Families seek to keep their children safe by ensuring that childrearing choices abide by their cultural norms. A family's emotional commitment to these choices connects to their role as the child's ultimate protector. For some families, this includes keeping their children safe from experiencing bias–or even knowing it exists. For others, it can mean keeping them safe from having to talk about, or even experience, human differences. John saw these dynamics at play in the parents' varying reactions to the use of persona dolls, as seen in the previous story from his program. Some parents were worried that using the dolls would raise differences that they believe are, and should be, invisible to their children. From a different perspective, another parent was anxious that a doll wearing glasses might be too much like their own child and attract unwanted attention to this difference from peers in the classroom.

As representatives of a program undergoing change, teachers and administrators are often the targets of disagreements. It is important to realize that families can also be the ones pushing the change. Disagreements can occur when a parent wants the program to move faster in its anti-bias work than appears to be happening. For example, as John recounts, a Black parent at his center questioned why the program had been unsuccessful in hiring BIPoC teachers to reflect the increasing diversity in the families:

Although I agreed that we needed more teachers of color, my first response was to feel defensive. I wanted to justify the situation by explaining the challenges of recruitment in our geographic setting. I also wondered if the parent trusted my commitment. Instead, recognizing my defensiveness, I managed to push it aside, acknowledge that the situation was not satisfactory, and make a verbal commitment to think and act more creatively about ways to bring more ethnic, linguistic, and racial diversity into the adult community at the center. While we continued to be unsuccessful in diversifying the full-time staff, we were able to increase the gender and ethnic/racial diversity among our part-time teachers.

Opposition. When conflict is at the opposition level, the individual's intent is to disrupt anti-bias change and question leadership, not to seek a resolution. Staff and families can be very explicit and closed-minded in their objections to anti-bias policies and practices. The intensity of the opposition often indicates the gulf between a stakeholder's views and the anti-bias mission. Again, the personalities, histories, and social identities of those involved can also fuel emotions. If someone is simply arguing and not listening, and if emotions are raw and volatile, there is not going to be an exchange of viewpoints. This level of conflict can feel uncomfortable and even threatening to those involved, including the program leader.

Returning to the earlier dual-language example, if the underlying reason for the teacher's opposition was her political views regarding the importance of cultural assimilation and learning English only in order to be a bona fide "American" (rather than a lack of developmental information), she is unlikely to be open to a dialogue about the importance of including home and heritage languages in early learning. In cases such as this, conversations that help the teacher consider her professional responsibility to use what research considers best practices versus her personal views may lead to her becoming open to trying a dual-language approach. On the other hand, the leader may need to recognize that there are limits to change through dialogue and be clear with the teacher about the nonnegotiable values and mission of the program.

Sometimes, opposition to anti-bias values makes finding a solution that works for both parties simply too difficult. A staff member or a family may even decide to leave the program if this is a realistic option. When a staff member does not have the option to leave their job, there is still a responsibility to carry out the program's mission—even if they do not agree with it.

Chris Amirault, director of an ECCE program serving low-income families in Oklahoma, shared his organization's approach to handling microaggressions related to people's social identities within their employee progressive discipline policy. Spurred on in part by a book discussion focused on the Tulsa Race Massacre (Amirault et al., 2021) and the resulting shifts in the program's mission, Chris and other leaders found they had to find ways to work with a number of White staff members who were struggling with the agency's strengthened DEI expectations. Chris shared:

> Fortunately, several BIPoC staff felt empowered to notify me of inappropriate, offensive statements—often ones that they had written off in the past as "that's just how [they are]." This required that leadership approach these individuals directly if we truly were committed to the values we were espousing.
>
> We came up with what we hoped would be both a clear declaration of our explicit expectations and a supportive structure to aid individuals' change in behavior, framed as a discussion with the school director (me) and the head of Human Resources. This process included:
>
> 1. Clarifying that this was a confidential conversation.
> 2. Explicitly stating the agency expectations about microaggressions and biased language about individuals or groups of people.
> 3. Talking through the difference between "intent vs. impact."
> 4. Encouraging the staff member to ask themselves the question, "Does saying this out loud help?"
> 5. Offering an open door to talk at any time about related thoughts.
> 6. Reminding the staff member that "your apology is changing your behavior" and that approaching the person who raised the concern would be taken as retaliation.
> 7. Stating that if it happens again or they retaliate, we enter into the next stage of the formal HR disciplinary process.

We also expressed confidence that the person would be able to work through this. These conversations were powerful, fascinating discussions, always very tearful for the person we were engaging. They were generally horrified that others would perceive them as racist or offensive and thus truly grateful to be approached directly, and by all accounts they seemed to have been motivated to change so that their work identity would not be so damaging to others and their own sense of self. (Personal communication, 2022)

Similarly, most families will not have the option to leave the program because of their opposition to anti-bias values. Of course, the program leader stays open to making adjustments to the program that don't require abandoning the core mission. Unfortunately, there are times when the best you may be able to do for a family who remains opposed to ABE is to offer and expect a respectful relationship that supports their child. In John's program in New Hampshire, he made a point of continuing to reach out to and welcome a parent who had unsuccessfully tried to curtail the center's commitment to including LGBTQ+ families in the curriculum.

Opposition may also reflect external political and ideological agendas that reach beyond a program's stakeholders and daily operations. For instance, a political candidate campaigning against immigration reform could zero in on a program's support of dual-language learning and publicly attack the program. While most programs are never embroiled in this kind of public and hostile opposition to its anti-bias mission and work, leaders may still be fearful of the possibility that it will be. The intimidation from public political opposition can lead to considerable stress and creates a chilling effect, dampening or halting the drive for change. We return to this issue at the end of the chapter.

BUILDING THE FOUNDATION FOR PRODUCTIVE CONFLICT

As program leader, you have significant influence over the course of anti-bias conflict situations at your program and the potential for positive learning and behavioral outcomes. These efforts begin way before an angry parent or staff member storms into the office. The program climate you create affects what issues become a conflict, as well as the possibility for productive change through conflict. By *climate*, we mean the emotional tone and quality of interactions between children and adults, including physical proximity, language, and the range of feelings and responses (Bloom et al., 2016). Tashon McKeithan, the executive director of a multi-site ECCE program, begins building a climate for anti-bias education by helping staff and families to develop the emotional skills to engage in meaningful dialogue:

How do we not live in the land of nice? How do we start to engage with each other? That engagement has to come with this emotional intelligence. I'm comfortable sharing my emotions with someone else. And they're comfortable sharing their emotions with me. And now we have a platform in which we can dialogue about anything.

In Chapters 4, 5, and 6, we shared a variety of community-building activities intended to develop teacher and family participation in and commitment to anti-bias education. These activities also create a respectful and warm program climate that helps preempt or de-escalate some potential conflicts. In this section we build on these activities by considering other strategies and dynamics that are part of a proactive approach to conflict.

Perception and Reality

Uncovering and examining one's own fears about the potential for conflict is an important step. As part of being strategic, it is necessary to think realistically about the possible reactions to anti-bias change from the various stakeholders and broader community. At the same time, you do not want your own anxieties and fears about those reactions to rule what you do or do not do. Do a mental assessment and determine if your fears stem from a perceived or a real problem. In some cases, a leader's (or teacher's) fears about what *might* happen tap into an internal struggle around a particular issue of diversity and bias. A lack of knowledge or experience about a specific anti-bias issue can lead to feelings of uncertainty.

Consider the following examples of internal issues that, if left unaddressed, can get in the way of constructively handling conflict situations. A program leader sees the need to encourage teachers to be more effective in their inclusion of a child with cerebral palsy but is apprehensive about making such a request. She realizes that her own previous difficulties with inclusion as a teacher fuel her fears about how the staff might react. In another situation, a teacher observes that a family with Native tribal membership has ideas about toddler dietary needs that differ from their own. Upon reflection, the teacher becomes aware of their lack of information and experience about the family's cultural practices. The teacher's concern that the parents will be offended if they ask questions holds them back from doing anything. Finally, a leader and teachers have observed a White child who is exhibiting discriminatory behavior and language toward children with brown and black skin tones. The teachers are fearful of how families might respond if they raise the issue, and the leader helps them think through a way to approach the issue with tact and clarity.

In these kinds of situations, leaders may find that their fears about how others will respond to anti-bias issues are either unfounded or blown out of proportion. If they act with thoughtful intention and authenticity, leaders will often discover that staff and families are receptive and open to change, even if it takes time.

The Role of Institutional Policies in Managing Conflict

From an anti-bias perspective, policies should be the result of a thoughtful and inclusive process. The intention is to improve clarity and transparency.

While policy often has to be responsive to external requirements such as licensing and accreditation, a facilitative leader can still approach policy development with flexibility, an open mind, and a commitment to an anti-bias approach.

Policies developed with DEI in mind can be useful when conflicts arise by providing a starting point for thinking about a difference in perspective or even by providing a potential resolution. The leader can reference policies such as ones regarding the inclusion of children of all abilities, the provision of translation services, the program's approach to holidays, and expectations for civil adult behavior. Policy adaptations can also be the result of using the third-space strategy discussed later in this chapter.

A program's anti-bias mission statement also provides a reference point for discussing conflicts and searching for solutions. For instance, a family raises concerns about a teacher discussing neighborhood houselessness, which the children observed during a field trip or neighborhood walk. In response, the program leader can share how the anti-bias mission encourages teachers to be responsive to children's observations of and questions about differences.

Power Dynamics

While the ideal is for all parties in a conflict to enter a discussion as equals, program stakeholders hold different positions of power, formally and informally. As program leader, you hold the most status and power by virtue of your leadership position and responsibilities for supervision, admissions, and policy development. Informal power dynamics also influence relationships. A particular teacher or staff person may hold a higher status than others by virtue of skills, seniority, or ability to influence people. A family member may be able to exercise power by participating on the governing board and committees, by being a spokesperson for other families, or even just by making life unpleasant for staff. In ECCE programs, differences in the economic class and resulting power dynamics of staff and families often impact how a conflict plays out.

Finding solutions to conflicts can too easily become an issue of who has the power to make a decision. You have the task of leveling out power differences in discussions so that all participants are part of the problem-solving. At the same time, you protect what is nonnegotiable in the program's anti-bias mission; this includes responsibility for identifying what behaviors and practices are and are not acceptable at the center.

If a staff member is being explicitly discriminatory toward children, families, or colleagues, then it becomes a performance and supervision issue—not just a disagreement about practice. If a family's beliefs about diversity result in asking for the exclusion of a child, staff, or family member because of that person's identity, then it becomes a breach of the program mission. In those situations, the program leader takes action to reinforce the nonnegotiable values and beliefs of the program. We return to this issue later in the chapter.

TURNING CONFLICT INTO GROWTH

Conflict among stakeholders about anti-bias work is not, in principle, about winners and losers. Finding win–win solutions to specific conflicts is always the first strategy. However, reality is likely to be more complex. Managing conflict productively requires dealing with each situation in its real-life context. We have found that working from the concept of conflict maintenance (Olatunji, 1998) is particularly useful. From this perspective, you manage conflict in a way that moves the program forward to greater equity and inclusion, rather than simply seeking a quick end to the conflict.

Loretta Ross, a professor and racial justice activist, argues that "calling out" people with whom we disagree can be destructive of relationships and close down the possibility of change. Instead, she asks for "calling in" people, like colleagues and parents, to engage in dialogue. Ross advises: "I'm trying to create a culture shift within the human rights movement where we really focus on holding people accountable, but doing so with love and respect instead of anger, blaming, and shaming" (quoted in Stockwell, 2022, p. 60). Listen closely to stakeholders, support the respectful sharing of perspectives, and reflect on decisions in the context of multiple views. This requires perseverance and the ability to accept the uncertainty of not knowing the outcome immediately. It also calls on all involved to be open to changing their thinking and to trying out new ways of acting.

In the next section we explore different ways to approach and resolve stakeholder conflicts, including a process we call a third-space solution. We also consider the complexities of anti-bias problem-solving and the importance of being clear about the nonnegotiable values in this work.

Find the Third Space

We view the third space as a place where people in conflict, through a distinct process of communication, reach agreement that goes beyond their initial positions. A third-space solution is particularly desirable because it draws on the creativity and openness of both parties to arrive at a new alternative that does not favor either position. This is both an intellectual and emotional experience in which the participants create fresh understandings and solutions. Engaging in it requires that people are willing to enter into a mutual dialogue with respect for each other and a willingness to learn (Freire, 1970). Barrera et al. (2012) argue that a third-space strategy supports "choosing relationships over control" (p. 59). Their approach

> focuses on creatively reframing contradictions, which are exclusive, into paradoxes, which are inclusive. It invites practitioners to make a fundamental shift from dualistic perceptions of reality to a mindset that integrates the complimentary aspects of diverse values, behaviors, and beliefs into a new whole within which each contributes something. (p. 66)

When possible, the leader models this process in conflicts with stakeholders and facilitates these discussions between teachers and families. The following steps of *acknowledge, ask,* and *adapt* constitute one useful third-space strategy for responding to conflicts, particularly those involving differences in cultural perspectives (adapted from Derman-Sparks, 2013b).

Step 1: Acknowledge. You, as the leader (or a teacher), acknowledge to yourself that a cultural or values clash exists. You recognize the discomfort and other emotions the parties involved may be feeling and examine your own feelings. You clearly communicate (both verbally and nonverbally) your awareness that a problem exists and needs attending. In family conflicts, do not blame the child or family; the child is often caught in the middle. Perhaps most importantly, you avoid becoming defensive or rushing to judgment about what underlies the conflict. Reflect on any power dynamics that may be in play. For instance, a family or staff member with a heritage language other than English may be relying on you to provide translation services.

Step 2: Ask. You collect information that will contribute to a greater understanding of what underlies the conflict. You talk to the parties involved and to any others you think will provide additional information. Find out what the behavior means to the family (or staff member), what they would do in the situation, and what they have done in the past. What is the child's experience at home and at the program? Clarify the priorities in the dilemma and hasten slowly: Do not rush the "ask" step, but keep it timely, because decisions about changes in practice may be necessary. Julie Bisson, director of the Epiphany Early Learning Preschool in Seattle, drew on her extensive anti-bias experience to share this strategy for Step 2:

> I try to approach it from a learning place. What is this parent saying? What's important to them about this? Why are they reacting this way? What's something that I don't know about them? It's an opportunity for me to practice holding down my knee-jerk reaction to say, "Well, maybe the school isn't the right school for you."

You also engage in self-reflection, getting clear about your own values and position on the issue causing the conflict and asking, "Do I *want* to make this change?," and if so, "*Can* I make this change?" While a lack of resources, particularly in staffing, is a reality that leaders often have to consider, it can also be a convenient cover for avoiding the complex issues involved in anti-bias conflicts. It is critical to confront doubts and fears about change so that you are honest about your own (and the program's) limitations. Be open to the need for professional growth and expanding your knowledge base as keys to resolving the conflict.

Step 3: Adapt. You consider ways to adapt policies and practices in your program, while paying attention to the information gathered in the "acknowledge" and "ask" steps. Seek to find common ground among those involved and consider multiple alternatives. The underlying principle is to find the most effective way to support each child's (or staff member's) best growth, taking into account the cultural, diversity, and bias issues in the situation, as well as the needs of all the children (or staff) and the responsibilities of the program. The objective is to ensure greater responsiveness to cultural practices and alignment with your anti-bias mission. Referring to the third space as "Setting the Stage for Miracles," Barrera et al. (2012) affirm, "the intent is to move beyond what is known in order to allow something greater to emerge" (p. 74).

Adapting is indeed a balancing act. It is also critical to be honest and explicit about your nonnegotiable values—what you are and are not willing to change.

Prioritize and Affirm Nonnegotiable Values

Conflict discussions and the resulting outcomes highlight the complexity of anti-bias work. The four core goals of anti-bias education create a framework within which these discussions take place (Derman-Sparks et al., 2020). In a given situation, one or more anti-bias principles may clash. Since these are not abstract discussions, but attempts to reach behavioral decisions, one principle may have more weight than another in any given outcome. For instance, while you might seek to affirm all families' religious identities, you decide that this can't result in the program ignoring a child whose gender expression differs from traditional norms.

Strategic leadership requires you to step back from the fray in order to see what is going on. Both teachers and families can lock into their particular viewpoint about what is best for the child. At times, cultural practices will come into conflict with anti-bias values, and you will need to tread carefully, show sensitivity, and be understanding of how change can be difficult. You have to try to balance the several values of anti-bias education and create movement toward the program's mission. The hope is that ultimately groups in a conflict come together and create a workable solution. Nevertheless, while it is important not to be dogmatic and inflexible about goals, you also do not want to abandon the nonnegotiable values of the program's anti-bias mission. In our interviews with program leaders, Tashon McKeithan, executive director of the Child Educational Center in Southern California, talked about a situation at one of her programs in which a parent objected to their son wearing a dress during play at the center:

> We listen, it's important to do. But we also said, part of our job is to allow our children to explore, and this is the exploration he has chosen. And that we would not say "no" to that. We create an environment of "yes," we don't create an environment of "no." That's who we are, that's our values. Of course, what you tell your child at home—we can't fight that. But while he is here, this is what we will continue to let him explore. That was hard, because obviously we are in the service of families. But in some ways, very easy, because it focused on our values as educators in that space.

An anti-bias approach does not mean that all beliefs and values are acceptable. Sometimes respecting the wishes of a family or staff member, on the one hand, and practicing anti-bias education, on the other hand, may be in contradiction. Consider these possibilities: A parent tells the teacher that he does not want a Deaf child in his son's class because the child will take up too much of the teacher's time. Another parent informs the teacher she does not want her daughter sitting next to a child whose mother is incarcerated. She is afraid that the child will be a "bad influence" or hurt her own child. In these situations, the program leader is faced with not being able to fully honor the principle of respect for a family's beliefs. Finding a path through this clash of values involves you continuing to seek ways for the family to remain in your program while still staying true to your commitment to social justice. Your efforts could include the following communication:

> I understand that you are uncomfortable with your child learning about this aspect of diversity. Here at the center, we believe strongly that we have to be inclusive of every family—even those who are different from us. That makes it tough for us to resolve your concern. Tell me more about what is making you feel so strongly. What might make the situation more amenable for you and still maintain our community value of not discriminating against other children in our community?

Fortunately, most anti-bias conflict situations stemming from cultural differences in childrearing practices have reachable solutions. All parties usually have to accept some changes from what they had wanted. Sometimes the balance tips in favor of the family's needs, at other times in favor of the program. In some cases, you will need to make a final decision, especially when the issue concerns what happens at the program and affects a classroom community rather than a single family or staff member. If it is about a practice at the center, you may have to say, "Well, this is the best we can do," and the parent may respond, "Okay, we can live with that." If it is a practice in the home, ultimately the parents have the right to make that decision if it does not affect what happens in the program. While as much continuity as possible between home and school environments is desirable, children are capable of shifting between different rules in the different contexts.

You will also have times when you decide to let go of a desired outcome, at least for the time being, in order to build deeper relationships of trust in the program. We have found that even when a third-space outcome is not possible, staff, families, and administrators still learn from the exploration of the multiple perspectives about the specific conflict. Deeper and more authentic relationships often result.

Recognize Agreeable Solutions for Differing Conflicts

Each conflict solution is unique to the situation under consideration. While the third-space procedure of "acknowledge, ask, and adapt" works for many kinds of conflicts, there are no one-size-fits-all outcomes. The purpose of the "acknowledge, ask, and adapt" procedure is to help people generate a solution that best fits the context of their conflict.

Several types of other outcomes are possible and acceptable in conflicts with families, including the following:

1. The program leader or teacher understands and agrees to follow the solution preferred by the family member to maintain consistency with the family's childrearing beliefs.
2. The family and program leader and/or teacher agree to an action that is a modification of what each of them does.
3. The family, upon understanding why a program or teacher uses a particular practice, approves the practice or decides to live with it. (Derman-Sparks, 2013b)

Conflicts between the program leadership and a staff member or between members of the staff have similar possible outcomes, with some unique dynamics. For instance, program leaders supervise staff members and hold them responsible for following the mission and job expectations. In ECCE, teachers typically co-teach in the same classroom, making it essential to find workable solutions.

The following examples, adapted from our collective experiences, illustrate different conflict situations: between a family and the program; between staff members; between a staff member and the program leader. Our intention is to give you a sense of what they can look like, with the caveat that each process is unique.

Are They Old Enough? A White father complained to the child care director that his child's preschool teacher had sent an email home about an upcoming read-aloud, an award-winning picture book about Rosa Parks. When the director asked the dad about his concern, he said the children are too young to learn about the civil rights movement and how Black people were treated unfairly. "It will be scary and sad for my child. As a single parent, I want to make sure my child feels safe at school."

The director asked, "Have you shared your concern with the teacher?" The parent replied, "No. I'm worried that might upset my child's teacher. I wanted to talk to you first." In reply, the director suggested a meeting with everyone involved—the teacher, the parent, and the director.

At the meeting, the dad shared his concerns; the teacher and director listened carefully and acknowledged how important children's safety is to everyone. The teacher explained why they chose the book. "It is a beautiful and empowering story about a brave, smart woman who was part of a larger group of people working to make change." The director shared that children are not too young to learn about the civil rights movement. "The story is presented in a developmentally appropriate way. This is book is one of many stories the children are exploring about what is fair and unfair in their world—and how you can change things."

At the meeting, with the father's input, they shared ways to help children connect to the story in a meaningful and hopeful way. For instance: *When you notice things that are unfair, what can you do?* The dad appreciated that the teacher had sent an email home in advance of reading the book and that they had the opportunity to discuss how it would be used in the classroom. Finally, the teacher invited the dad to share what he hears from his child at home and to borrow some of the other picture books they have been using to raise issues like racism.

Who Diapers? A family brought to the program leader their concerns about a male caregiver diapering their daughter. Their unease reflected their cultural values and views about child development, which were in conflict with the program's ethical values concerning the importance and rights of men as caregivers. Indeed, the leader had been intentionally recruiting to specifically include teachers representing gender diversity in the youngest classrooms, which focused on caregiving.

Early conversations with the parents focused on assuring them that the staff had heard their concerns and viewed them as important. As the staff moved into the "ask" stage, it became apparent that many of the parents' concerns had a lot to do with their own process of coming to terms with developmental changes in their daughter as she moved out of toddlerhood. The teachers thoughtfully considered the various issues in the conflict.

Although wanting to respect cultural and family issues, the program leader realized that the rights of the male teacher were equally important to consider. There were several possible solutions, but none might be able to meet everyone's needs. How should the program adapt? Meeting the family's expressed needs meant assuring them that only female caregivers would do the diapering. However, the staff and program leader agreed that this solution violated their professional code of ethics opposing gender discrimination, and that their ethical responsibility to the male caregiver was paramount. Essentially, they said to the family, "We understand why you are uncomfortable, but we cannot exclude the male caregiver from this task. It would unfairly imply that he was not able to safely carry out a basic responsibility as a teacher of infants and toddlers."

At the same time, the program leader offered to develop a written policy about diapering of children. This policy addressed some of the parents' issues concerning safety and supervision, and applied to both male and female caregivers. The family was satisfied with this solution, so ultimately, the program was able to come to an agreeable third-space resolution and avoid moving into an oppositional response. The family learned about the importance of gender diversity of caregivers in infant/toddler classrooms; the program leader and staff gained a deeper appreciation of the gender issues families face negotiating in unfamiliar cultural terrain; and the program gained new and useful policies.

Is It Professional? In this example, two beliefs about being an effective teacher come into conflict. One is the premise that the professional role of the teacher requires a separation between one's personal (home) and professional (work) lives in order to maintain objectivity in relationships with children and families. The second is the anti-bias principle about the importance of being aware of your own social and cultural identities and sharing your understanding of them with colleagues and families.

Some teachers at the center were uncomfortable with the way that other colleagues talked about their social-class identity with families. Those who did share often identified as working-class and argued that it helped with making social class visible in the center, building authentic relationships, and supporting families with similar circumstances.

In response to the conflict, the program leader called a staff meeting on the topic and commented that while the program needs boundaries regarding what staff share about their personal lives with families, boundary rules also may keep some identity differences invisible. The staff then discussed the questions: Are there differences in sharing your personal identity with families (our clients) and teachers (our colleagues)? How can we talk about social class and still maintain our view of professionalism? The leader also referenced the issues raised by the *Code of Ethical Conduct and Statement of Commitment* (NAEYC, 2011), which advises against personal relationships with families that might be exploitative or weaken a teacher's effectiveness.

While the discussions did not create an end point in the conflict, they did serve to open up the issue to thoughtful reflection about identity and invisibility. The leader had to take responsibility for drawing some boundaries about sharing personal information, while also realizing that anti-bias conflicts have many gray areas that need to be revisited and grappled with over time.

How About You Just Come? Victor Bradley, a former early childhood teacher in Cambridge, Massachusetts, shared the following story in a webinar (Bradley & Reynoso, 2022). The events unfolded in response to a family's concern about his school's annual gay pride assembly.

[The] parents love the school and they enrolled their child in the school and they were all fine with all the other social justice work we were doing, but when it came to the gay pride assembly, they were like, "We're going to keep our family home." And I said, "Oh, why?" And so we talked about it and I said, "How about if you don't feel comfortable having your child, how about you just come? You come to the gay pride assembly, you and your partner." And they agreed. And so they came and then they were crying at the end. And said, "Why did we think that something was going to be wrong with this? Why did we not trust that you were going to be developmentally appropriate here for the whole school and for all the kids?" So, that was a win in that situation. I respected them. Their child stayed home with their grandparent and did not come because [the parents] were so uncomfortable. I wanted to meet them sort of halfway. And I'm so glad they were able to come and see the assembly. Sometimes that's not always the case, but I got lucky that time.

Victor also talked about the fundamental values behind his approach to negotiating conflict and finding a third-space solution (Bradley & Reynoso, 2022).

I keep bringing it back to have everybody feeling safe and back to kindness. That's really what it's about. And people so often think, "Oh, you're putting things in kids' heads or this is too radical or they don't understand," but it's really just about kindness. I'm treating everyone well and learning about other people and learning about people in their classroom who they're with every day, and families. When people are really upset and really confrontational, I just listen, just listen and listen and listen, and really hear what they're saying and try to sort of figure out where that hurt, where that pain is or where that confusion is. I think that's probably the most important thing. But what I've done is I've read books. I've had those conversations when they've come up and I've explained why I've had those conversations.

Maintain the Values Basis of Anti-Bias Education

Leaders need to be prepared for the misconception that anti-bias education means that all beliefs and actions are acceptable. This oppositional strategy can get very confusing for a leader who is also committed to creating a democratic and caring community. Parents or staff may use the argument, "We thought you appreciated all beliefs here," as a way to defend practices that clearly conflict with anti-bias values. Being able to see through insincere appeals to your inclusive values requires that you have clarity about your mission.

Practices that stereotype or discriminate against individuals because of their membership in particular groups are never acceptable in an anti-bias approach. Consider the following example: A teacher likes to call on children to share their ideas at group time, but rarely invites the children who have been identified as neurodiverse to contribute. When the program leader conveys what they observed, the teacher explains that they call on children who "speak and behave correctly" to ensure that the activity is "successful." The program leader reminds the teacher that every child deserves opportunities to share their thinking. This can be done in different modalities, not just orally. Responding inequitably to children is harmful to everyone's development. The teacher counters that the program is hypocritical about its anti-bias mission because the leader is not allowing them to practice their teaching beliefs.

Even in these kinds of conflicts, trying to use the "acknowledge, ask, and adapt" process is still the place to begin. The approach is, "Let's talk about what it means to be able to equitably include and serve *all* families in this program, while also affirming every child's identities." As mentioned previously, the leader needs to enter these conversations with clarity and confidence about nonnegotiable anti-bias values.

On occasions, it may become clear that the "acknowledge, ask, and adapt" process isn't proving useful in finding an amicable or third-space solution and that the conflict is really a case of opposition to anti-bias education.

RESPONDING TO PUSHBACK AND OPPOSITION

As long as people are open to finding solutions, including living with a contradiction between a personal belief and a professional anti-bias value, then a program moves forward. Sometimes, however, one or more program stakeholders push back against or oppose a part of or the entire anti-bias education approach. In these cases, the person (or group) usually does not want to enter into a dialogue, but rather to obstruct or end anti-bias efforts. A stakeholder who takes this oppositional stance may try to get other stakeholders and people or organizations outside the program to join in the stand against the program.

Be Strategic—Connect to Allies

When you think and act strategically in response to conflict of this kind, it is manageable, even if it is also unpleasant. On the other hand, a hasty reaction can undermine a program's work. It is essential to stay calm and not take these attacks personally. Opposition can be destructive to anti-bias education efforts if you are not self-aware or clear about goals or do not have a range of potential strategies in your repertoire.

If needed, you can intentionally deflect some of the emotional heat away from staff so they can continue their work in the classroom. Teachers are involved in a close relationship with parents—they are helping to care for and educate their children—which means there is a lot of emotional vulnerability for all involved. The program leader is in the best position to deal with the emotions that come with pushback and opposition. If the parent is annoyed with you, the conflict has less effect on the teacher's ability to work with the child and family.

In the following example, a parent came to John's office at the ECCE program he directed to criticize the quality of the children's books in a classroom.

As I listened carefully and tried to find out more about the specifics of what the parent did not like, it seemed that the "quality" issue was a screen for something else—opposition to the inclusion of children's books with gay and lesbian families. Rather than circling around the problem, I then tried to establish that we needed to be honest with each other if we were going to have a useful discussion. Naming the conflict explicitly, I tried to establish a third-space dialogue. The parent angrily denied this and began questioning my competency. In this situation it became clear to me that the goal of the parent was to obstruct movement toward the program's anti-bias mission, not to engage in dialogue and problem-solving. The parent later went to a meeting of the center's parent committee to question the anti-bias mission and the "out-of-date" children's literature. After a discussion, the committee, whose members had participated in learning about anti-bias education, backed the anti-bias mission and my commitment. Unable to stop the center's anti-bias mission, the parent unsuccessfully attempted to discredit my reputation by contacting colleagues in child care licensing and professional organizations. The parent even contacted a local radio personality known for opposing social justice efforts. Fortunately, the timing didn't fit with the radio program's agenda!

Early childhood program leaders can feel professionally vulnerable due to their complex responsibilities and accountability to licensing, accreditation, and numerous clients. Fortunately, John had proactively appraised the parent committee and his child care licensor of the situation in the story above. He was also an active member of local and state professional organizations and had built a network of allies in anti-bias work. Their emotional support and advice assured him that there were colleagues out there who supported his solutions if faced with similar opposition.

While John had to spend unwelcome time and energy dealing with this situation and lost some sleep, it ended without any negative impact on the program and its anti-bias work. The conflict also became an opportunity to affirm the program's commitment to anti-bias values and to be more visible about its efforts. Upon reflection, John realized that the groundwork done over the course of several years had resulted in critical support from families and his network of colleagues during this public visibility of anti-bias values.

External Opposition and Intimidation

Opposition and even attacks may come from political organizations external to the program that reject all forms of multicultural, anti-bias, and social justice education. They put forward moral, religious, and patriotic objections such as that affirming children's diversity of gender expression is child abuse and that discussing the history of violence toward Indigenous peoples is anti-American. These groups may also focus on other issues relevant to the ECCE field. This may include decrying the effect of children's rights on family authority and complaining that ECCE teachers are not competent in preparing children for later schooling.

Typically, these oppositional groups are not interested in dialogue or negotiation with the groups or individuals they attack. Instead, they attempt to stir up and exploit controversy around a program's anti-bias work for their political and social agenda. In most situations, external attacks on a particular ECCE program eventually go away and these groups move on to the next controversy that will draw media and supporter attention to their cause. Still, these situations have a chilling effect; they raise fears about what might happen and can cause leaders to pull back on their social justice advocacy. An ECCE teacher who had previously been mentored in ABE by their director experienced the vulnerability that can come when you take on a more activist and public role in your anti-bias journey. In this case, the teacher was presenting a workshop online about anti-bias education. Unknown to them, people from a group opposed to anti-bias values attended and recorded their workshop. Later, the video was excerpted by the group as part of their online streaming program that vented against "woke" teachers. In the group's narrative, the teacher was breaking state laws enacted to eliminate discussion with students in publicly funded programs about identity, bias, and privilege that might cause them to experience "discomfort" (Kim, 2021). The teacher wisely chose not to engage directly with this opposition and add fuel to the fire. Instead, the teacher turned to allies, including program families and those in supervisory roles, for reassurance that they had the teacher's back. The teacher felt supported and continued with their anti-bias advocacy work.

Another story comes from a case study of Head Start education managers (center directors) in a rural Oregon county (Agudelo, 2022). In the following story, the Head Start program was involved in an affordable housing project being constructed in the city that would serve Latinx migrant workers. The local residents were ". . . vociferously opposed. . . . Their protestations were abusive and demeaning to the would-be residents, the Head Start staff, and the construction workers doing their jobs" (p. 106). An employee of the local grocery store recognized Beatrix, a White education manager interviewed by Agudelo (2022), as being from Head Start and confronted her.

> The store clerk was angry at the [Mexican] migrants getting "free stuff" from the government and yelled at [the education manager] for encouraging such a thing. Beatrix recalled, "There were people going to meetings trying to protest, saying not to build our site there, not to build the housing. It was bad enough that at one point, I was just wearing my badge that had [town name] right on it. And, you know, I'm at the grocery store in [town name], and I'm just getting my groceries, and the cashier like sees my badge, and she's like, "How can you encourage those people [Mexican migrants]," like "How can you give free things to those people who aren't even citizens?" And I'm just like, "They pick your fruit." It's so frustrating to me. . . . (p. 106)

In this situation, the education manager did not believe she had the power to change what was happening. In her words, "there was nothing else to say because this person already had their mind made [up]" (p. 106). Because of the public setting, Beatrix did mention the abusive language to the manager of the grocery store but felt that it was unproductive to engage in a public argument with the employee. Ultimately, she felt that this a broader issue in which the community needed to experience the migrant workers as human beings who contribute to the community.

Here is an example of how another Head Start program dealt more strategically with hostile and public opposition from an outside group. Again, it is an issue of children's books depicting gay and lesbian families in the story and images.

A regional Head Start agency held a workshop for its staff about selecting children's books, which included displays of books for multicultural education. A parent from one of the agency's centers who attended the workshop became very upset by the inclusion of stories with gay and lesbian families and contacted a political advocacy group in which she participated. The group mounted a campaign against the regional agency that had presented the workshop, claiming that the entire national Head Start program was teaching children to be homosexual. The agency countered this attack by inviting the media to visit the area's Head Start centers to observe teachers working with children and to talk with staff about the purpose of including children's books depicting a range of people and families. In addition, agency staff disseminated information about national Head Start's commitment to diversity to the media, early childhood organizations, and community organizations in the agency's region. In the end, the larger community came to the program's support, and the campaign against them dissipated. More people were now aware of and better informed about Head Start's work.

When faced with opposition from an outside political group, it is essential that you take a deep breath, stay calm, and recognize that you need allies to help you deal with the situation. You must be clear and articulate about the rationale for anti-bias education and draw on the program's reputation and community support. It is also important to be wary of wasting time and resources trying to convince such groups about the value of anti-bias education or to try to come to a negotiated solution. In the end, you need to keep your focus on the stakeholders the program serves, especially the children. It is important to take time to consider whether the opposition, and the intimidation and anxiety you experienced, have caused you to get diverted from your commitment to social justice. And if so, what will it take for you to keep on going? These are ethical choices you make as an anti-bias educator.

THOUGHTFUL RISK-TAKING

The early childhood leader constantly assesses what needs to change, what can change, and how teachers and families will embrace and engage in making change that is lasting and significant. To use conflict productively as part of the change process, the leader takes a long-term view. This means being proactive instead of reactive, picking one's battles, and prioritizing where to invest energy and resources.

From a strategic point of view, a leader faced with difficult anti-bias conflicts sometimes needs to ask: "How willing am I to put myself on the line and put my position in jeopardy? Are there limits to the ways I would temper my anti-bias commitment?" These are very personal questions. To answer them, individuals bring their own complexities to deal with, including their identity, learning style, and life history. Each leader has a certain comfort level with disagreement and heated discussion, and both dispositions and vulnerabilities with regard to taking risks. Having a marginalized identity can make this risk-taking even more complex. As a woman of Asian descent, Debbie points out that she is sensitive to staff or families accusing her of advocating for an anti-bias agenda simply because she is Chinese American:

> I have had to figure out when to push and when to hold back because of these perceptions. I walk a fine line. I also did not want teachers to view me as the expert on Chinese New Year or Chinese culture. While I am

willing to share my knowledge, I risk having my cultural identity trivialized or pigeonholed. When a teacher suggested a schoolwide Chinese New Year celebration, I suggested we change it to a "New Year celebration" and explore diverse cultural ways that families in the school celebrated this holiday—Lunar New Year, Jewish New Year, Russian New Year, Greek New Year, and so on. This allowed children, families, and staff to compare and contrast the different rituals and traditions.

A leader moving into a new center has to be strategic about building support and allies before pushing too many buttons. That is sensible. Regardless of commitment and passion to an anti-bias approach, it simply is not wise for a leader to come in the first day and send out a newsletter that changes a long-held tradition even if it violates an anti-bias value. Becoming a lightning rod for everyone's fears and ignorance is not likely to serve a leader's long-term goals.

Whenever conflict about an anti-bias issue unexpectedly flares up, it is easy to feel stress because you do not know where the conflict is going to lead or how it will end. These realities underline the importance of understanding the role of conflict and disequilibrium in movement toward your anti-bias mission and the significance of thinking and acting proactively to create a positive role for conflict. Conflict is one indicator that movement is happening; the program culture is shifting toward greater equity and inclusion. When stakeholders are not questioning the way things are or having a disagreement over policy or practice around inclusion, you should wonder if the program is settling into a comfortable place, rather than moving forward on its anti-bias mission.

Someone else who is equally committed to anti-bias values might come to a different solution or decision than you would. You may even come to think of a better strategy in hindsight. There is no perfect solution for any given conflict situation, just one that makes the best sense in that specific context. Part of the trick is living with some ambiguity in these situations and being able to move forward with the knowledge that you are always learning.

In the next chapter we build on the process of reading your program discussed in Chapter 3 by turning to the program leader's ongoing work of documenting and assessing anti-bias change as the basis for setting future goals and strategy.

CHAPTER 8

Documenting and Assessing Anti-Bias Education Change

We are reflective, always asking ourselves: How would I analyze this situation, what am I doing with this situation? How can I move forward? And what is enabling me to get to that with this child?

—Karina Rojas Rodriguez, center director

Documenting our anti-bias work forced me to articulate my thoughts and questions and pushed me to reflect more deeply. It was also a way to share with the larger school community about what we were doing and get their feedback, too.

—Teacher

Documentation is the process of observing and recording to make change and growth more visible. Documenting changes in the anti-bias education work of a program is a necessary part of moving your anti-bias mission forward. It is also challenging, because, as we have emphasized throughout this book, anti-bias education change is a journey that goes through many phases, bumps, and sometimes temporary stops, rather than following a linear trajectory.

Documenting change throughout the year in a program's overall climate and culture, in the members of the program (children, staff, and leader), and in educational practices in the classroom guides the forward movement of anti-bias work. First, you can identify accomplishments and what more you need to do at the individual, classroom, and program levels. Second, you can identify transformations in beliefs, assumptions, and attitudes, and shifts in the relationships among community members. Both kinds of documentation are essential. The authenticity and effectiveness of an anti-bias program rests on a combination of change and growth in a staff's consciousness and thinking, in the quality of adult–child and adult–adult interactions and relationships, and in the curriculum, learning environment, and materials.

In addition, analysis of the data you have gathered through documentation activities is necessary. This includes your own reflections, conversations with individual teachers, and discussions with the entire staff. Some programs share documentation stories with families and invite their reflections on them as well. Engaging in the process of gathering and analyzing documentation data enables you to make sense of what is happening, to learn from it, to share it with others, and to determine next steps in your work. Krechevsky et al. (2010) view "documentation as a powerful tool for supporting three forms of accountability: (a) accountability to self, (b) accountability to each other, and (c) accountability to the larger community" (p. 65).

Documentation also captures the inevitable times when the program's anti-bias education seems to be in a holding pattern, or even regressing. This is also useful data for analysis. Are there other demands (like preparing for licensing) that are sapping energy? Have you intentionally decided to back off on challenging teachers because they feel stressed due to increased pressure from initiating changes in other areas of the curriculum or from external demands from new local or national regulations? Or is opposition to implementing an anti-bias approach from a few teachers, or families, or a community group, taking its toll on energy from the staff and you? It is important to understand the influences on the pace of your anti-bias efforts.

Last, your analysis of the information from the initial reading of the program (see Chapter 3) helps determine how and what to document in a particular setting. It is a baseline for documenting and reflecting on what is and what is not changing. For instance, knowing whether a program has a history of reflective practice or encouraging productive conflict will be important in later considering the depth of the teachers' dialogue about identity and bias.

While the process of documentation throughout the year informs ongoing anti-bias education work, program leaders also have the responsibility of assessing and evaluating teacher, staff, and program performance. This assessment is summative—giving you a snapshot of your program's and teachers' anti-bias efforts at a particular moment in time. Such assessment typically occurs at midyear and/or at the end of the school year. It can involve more formalized strategies that often rely on standardized criteria. Documentation data collected throughout the school year using the strategies described in this chapter should play an important role in informing these more formal assessments.

This chapter began with a discussion of the perspective that guides our thinking about documenting anti-bias education growth. Next, we share the reflections of a group of experienced ABE program leaders about doing documentation and assessment, which we hope also acts as prompts for your own thinking. Then we turn to indicators and tools for observing and noting change relevant to the work of program leaders and staff. These include markers for: (a) the leader's growth and efficacy; (b) teachers' growth in anti-bias classroom practice, awareness, and related dispositions and skills; (c) children's progress in meeting anti-bias goals; and (d) the shifts in the broader program culture, including families, policy, environments, and networks.

Finally, the last section of this chapter explores ways to strategically manage required external assessment protocols and learning standards in relation to anti-bias education. These expectations tend to focus on summative evaluation. However, as we discuss later in this section, it is also possible to creatively use documentation data about your program's anti-bias education to inform standardized and more formal assessment criteria.

REFLECTIONS ABOUT DOCUMENTATION IN AN ANTI-BIAS PROGRAM

Conversations with anti-bias education program leaders about documentation offer insights into how they think about these activities in relation to their roles of coach, mentor, and supervisor, and resolving the apparent contradiction of wanting to model the equity goals of the anti-bias approach with their role as the program leader.

All the program leaders engage in some form of documentation, using observation, conversations with individual teachers and families, and staff discussions as ways to learn about the state of anti-bias education in their programs. Their teachers keep track of their own efforts and also note the children's ideas, questions, and actions relevant to the anti-bias work in their classrooms. These documentation data serve several purposes. One is as an essential source of information for curriculum development—for individual children, for the class as a whole, and for the program as a community. As Julie Bisson, Director of Epiphany Early Learning Preschool in Seattle, explains,

> It's about teachers being researchers and watching children closely to learn what their questions are, what conversations they keep coming back to, what stories they make up in their games, what interactions they are having, what teachable moments arise, and then offering more opportunities for the children to go deeper. We then try to figure out how to build on children's interests and passion about a particular topic and help them look at it from multiple perspectives.

Miriam Zmiewski-Angelova, previously director of the Daybreak Star Preschool in Seattle, elaborates on using documentation for children's anti-bias learning experiences, to build relationships with the families, and to give teachers useful feedback on how to improve upon their activities. She explains that "I knew that some of the teachers just had a much better relationship [with families] or spoke their home language. So, I asked them to check in with so and so and ask them their ideas about an activity we had done or were planning to do." Teachers also regularly shared stories with families about what they were doing with the children, some with photos or sketches. Miriam continued, "They might write something like, 'Hey, we're talking about our favorite foods, so while you're signing in, just jot down the name of favorite food at home.'"

The program leaders also use documentation data for coaching teachers' professional growth, and for end-of-year assessment of each teacher's work. If required, they also use ongoing documentation to inform externally required formal program assessments (see the discussion further on in this chapter). Julie Bisson suggests that it might be helpful for leaders to think about putting together a portfolio documenting anti-bias education experiences over the school year, similar to the portfolios that teachers use to document children's learning encounters and developmental journeys.

The program leaders also talked about managing what they experience as a dilemma between modeling the equity goals of the anti-bias approach and their coaching, supervisory, and mentoring roles. As Rukia Rogers, director of The Highlander School in Atlanta, Georgia, puts it: "I think my biggest struggle as a director is figuring out how do we manage people yet not be oppressive. I want teachers to know that their voice matters and to build their confidence." As do some of the other program leaders, Rukia asks her teachers to document their anti-bias education work using daily diaries, and then partner with her to make sense of it. They also hold and record teacher discussions on a particular anti-bias education question for further reflection. Rukia also asks teachers to share documentation of their work with families and invites them to reflect together about the learning experiences.

Tashon McKeithan, executive director of the Child Educational Center in Southern California, adds to the approach described by Rukia, sharing:

> I always come from a place of curiosity. And I want teachers to know
> that I'm here to figure out the best way to support children and them as
> things come up. I always start with questions. I want to position myself
> as a learner as well as the program leader and hear the teacher's thinking
> first . . .

Lastly, Tashon also offers a caution about moving from documentation to action:

> Taking action based on the "snapshots" we document needs to be
> intentional and reflective of what we know about the entire context of a
> child or teacher, and their strengths and weaknesses. It also has to be done
> with a sense of care and love. If what we do doesn't work, it's okay. We
> tweak it, we figure out something else.

INDICATORS AND STRATEGIES FOR DOCUMENTING ANTI-BIAS CHANGE

We now turn to indicators for documenting and assessing your anti-bias work in the many parts of an ECCE program. Indicators include the following areas: (1) the leader's (your own) growth and efficacy; (2) teachers' growth in anti-bias classroom practice, awareness, and related dispositions and skills; (3) children's progress in meeting anti-bias goals; and (4) the changes in other significant parts of the program, including families, policy, work environment, and networks. The broad anti-bias goals for children and educators outlined in Chapter 1 are the primary source for our formulation of indicators. We also suggest strategies and tools for collecting and making sense of the data you collect. As you gain experience in implementing anti-bias education, you may want to develop some your own indicators and documentation tools that fit your program. Another resource we have found helpful in considering the programmatic, classroom, and teacher levels of ABE work is Allen et al.'s (2021) checklists for creating anti-racist early childhood spaces.

Indicators of Program Leader Growth and Efficacy

ECCE leaders tend to focus on everyone else but themselves. In anti-bias work, you start with yourself. Given all you must do, it can be a challenge to take time regularly to document and reflect on your own anti-bias education growth. But it is essential!

The first set of indicators for documenting and assessing your anti-bias leadership focus on the foundational concepts of social identity and the dynamics of oppression and activism. The second set of indicators emphasizes a range of useful skills and dispositions. Dispositions are enduring habits of mind that affect how children and adults approach and respond to everyday interactions and tasks (Carter et al., 2021; Casio, 2010). It is also useful to refer to your baseline reading of readiness for anti-bias work (see Chapter 3).

Self-Awareness and Knowledge. Are you:

- Developing your awareness and understanding of, and ability to share, your multiple intersecting social identities?
- Demonstrating awareness of how the institutional power of "isms" advantages some social identity groups economically, legally, culturally, and politically, and, on the other hand, marginalizes or disadvantages others?
- Examining and sharing the values and ideas you have learned about human differences and similarities, including the stereotypes and prejudices you hold about yourself or others that reinforce the institutional isms?
- Exploring your ideas, feelings, and experiences of social justice activism?

Leadership Skills and Dispositions. Are you:

- Integrating anti-bias change into all aspects of your role as a leader and the workings of the program, rather than seeing it as a separate and disconnected focus?
- Feeling more at ease with and valuing disequilibrium and conflict as part of your anti-bias efforts?
- Balancing your immediate daily actions with taking a long-term and strategic view of your anti-bias efforts?
- Becoming clearer in communicating the purpose and rationale for your anti-bias mission in your interaction with others? For instance, you decide to share an overview of the anti-bias mission during your admissions tours with families.

- Demonstrating clarity and awareness of your ethical boundaries regarding anti-bias work (your nonnegotiables)? For instance, when a staff member raises objections to having a poster of a Muslim family (the mother wearing a hijab) on the hallway wall, you calmly explain the importance of ensuring all families feel included in the community, and all children knowing about and respecting how people are different and alike.
- Developing your ability to recognize and be at ease with the gray areas (complexity and ambiguity) in anti-bias work?
- Becoming more comfortable and strategic in communicating with and negotiating a third space in resolving conflicts with the various program stakeholders (see Chapter 7)?
- Making efforts to share and advocate for your anti-bias approach more visibly in your community and professional work outside of the program?

Tools for Documenting Leader Growth and Efficacy

You are likely to be your best and worst critic. At times, you will be overly hard on yourself and find little to celebrate. At other times, you will be unaware of the missteps you have taken or the opportunities you have missed. Documenting your ongoing work will help you keep your anti-bias education journey in perspective.

Tracking Your Internal Process. Take the time to document your thoughts, feelings, and actions through regular journaling in whatever ways work for you (e.g., writing in a book or on a computer, recording your self-reflections orally into a digital recorder on your phone, making and keeping notes you make during the day in a portfolio). Having a written or aural record enables you to revisit your journey over time.

You can also engage in a more systematic approach by using a formal self-assessment tool such as the Self-Study Guide (Chen et al., 2009; Appendix D) described in the section on teacher change indicators. Although John and his co-authors designed this tool for classroom teachers, the sections on "raising self-awareness" and "relationships with families and community" dovetail with our indicators of leader change noted above.

Turning to Colleagues. Leaders also need to reach outside of themselves to assess their growth and effectiveness. Sharing your experiences, thinking, concerns, and successes with trusted colleagues and allies on a regular basis (e.g., by email, online conversations, or at support meetings) provides you with a significant window into how you are doing. Visiting colleagues' programs is another way to become more aware of your own work. For example, John notes:

I observed the way in which Debbie's program had effectively supported the full inclusion of children with disabilities. After talking with her, I realized the need to be more proactive in using my budget creatively to ensure teachers had the capacity and resources to support all children.

Feedback from Teachers and Families. Reaching out to a program's primary stakeholders for specific feedback about one's anti-bias leadership is also vital. Families and teachers see your work from quite different perspectives than do colleagues and allies—or supervisors.

Surveys with specific questions can be an effective way of getting feedback from staff and families. You can tailor them to the needs of specific groups. Individuals who need or prefer to can complete a survey orally. For example, the director of a program serving immigrant families uses an annual survey to learn from families how they think their culture, language, values, and anti-bias practices were made visible and embedded in the program. Surveys provide a broad take on how teachers, staff, and families view the program's anti-bias commitment and the leader's effectiveness. They also provide anonymity. They may reveal a continuum of feedback, from avid supporters to folks who misunderstand and/or even strongly disagree.

Another strategy for getting useful feedback about anti-bias efforts is to use small focus groups, such as a staff anti-bias or diversity task force or family advisory group. This approach can provide you with more specific and detailed information from program stakeholders who share your commitment to the ABE mission.

However, gathering feedback from teachers and families, while essential, carries a noteworthy limitation. The leader holds a position of power over them, so the degree of trust, openness, and collaboration that exists in a program will influence the authenticity of the feedback. Debbie found this strategy to yield helpful information when framed by an open and collegial dialogue with her lead teachers. She posed the questions: "What does a leader need to do to create an anti-bias education atmosphere?" and "What do you, as teachers, need from the program leader?"

Indicators of Change in Teachers' Growth and Efficacy

Teachers carry out anti-bias education with the most important program stakeholders—the children. Thus, teachers' growth in their understanding, practices, and commitment to anti-bias goals is central to a program's efforts. Indicators consider teachers' classroom practice and skills, *and* their awareness and dispositions. We also offer some strategies and tools for documenting the changes suggested by the indicators.

Teacher Awareness and Dispositions. Dispositions, although less tangible than teachers' practices, are critical to the depth and authenticity of anti-bias education. The picture you get of each teacher generally suggests where each teacher is on their anti-bias journey at various points in relation to the adult developmental stages presented in Chapter 1 (i.e., *Before the Journey Begins,* etc.) and corresponding teacher stages in Chapter 3 (i.e., *Averse, Beginner*, etc.). This information is also useful for making decisions about the overall direction and pace of your anti-bias education work, as well as about professional development work with the staff as a whole.

Do teachers:

- Demonstrate movement beyond their comfort zones by taking thoughtful risks in the classroom with new anti-bias education activities; increased willingness to ask questions about anti-bias education; communicating anti-bias values, information, and intention to families and colleagues; and integrating an anti-bias perspective throughout the curriculum and in their work with families? For instance, a teacher shares the developmental rationale for ABE goals for children as part of a parent–teacher conference.
- Seek out the program leader and collegial support in thinking through and finding solutions to anti-bias issues, and show greater open-mindedness and willingness to change their thinking because of new information, and expanded perspectives? Examples might be (a) admitting to not knowing how to deal with a situation (e.g., a child refuses to sit next to another child because they "talk funny"—meaning speaking a language other than English); (b) demonstrating awareness of the complexity of anti-bias issues such as resolving a conflict between valuing a family's belief and the school's bottom-line philosophy about a specific issue (e.g., a family does not want their son to participate in cleaning up because it isn't a male role versus the school philosophy that everyone helps to clean up after their activities); and (c) acknowledging the emotional disequilibrium caused by one's desire to celebrate a holiday such as Christmas with the children and the anti-bias strategy to teach children about one another's holidays because not all children celebrate the same ones.
- Take the initiative to engage in anti-bias self-reflection and learning? For instance, a teacher shares that they watched the film adaptation of Ta-Nehisi Coates's book *Between the World and Me* online (Forbes, 2020) to deepen their understanding of the lives of some of her families and proposes that all the teachers watch and discuss it. Another example is a teacher planning with colleagues about attending workshops about anti-bias education at their state ECCE conference.
- Show awareness of the influence of their social identities and beliefs on their feelings and behaviors? For example, a teacher whose strong convictions about sexism are part of her gender identity has difficulty talking with a family that insists on traditional binary gender roles for their child. The teacher asks for help in attending to how their perspective might negatively affect their interactions with the family.

- Show growth in their ability to work through third-space solutions with families and colleagues in anti-bias conflicts (see Chapter 7)?
- Take a leadership role in anti-bias initiatives at the center? For instance, a teacher introduces the program leader to the director of a nearby Latinx cultural center and proposes they hold the staff retreat there.

Teachers' awareness and dispositions will show both times of forward progress and times of backward movement. Noticing when and about what issues teachers may deny or push back against, feel frustration or discomfort, or show a lack of skill or knowledge is as necessary as paying attention to their growth. Documentation also helps you name and tease out the dynamics of teachers who stay silent or peripheral participants in anti-bias work. Is this a reflection of personal style, or comfort level, or trust? You need to pay attention to what you do not hear, as well as what you do.

Classroom Practice and Skills. This section puts the spotlight on what teachers do in their classrooms to implement the four anti-bias education goals with the children. Documenting these behaviors throughout the year informs your decisions about how to scaffold each teacher's growth and to provide appropriate professional development opportunities. Observe the overall learning environment and what materials teachers make available, as well as the specific activities and teachers' handling of teachable/learnable moments that spontaneously arise as children interact with one another and with learning materials. Equally important, observe how teachers interact with the children. Pay attention to how culturally responsive and sustaining teachers are—listening to and encouraging children's ideas without interrupting by correcting how they are speaking and making efforts to have more than one language spoken by all teachers in the classroom). Are they equitable in response (e.g., encouraging girls to talk as much as boys) and intervening in inappropriate behavior regardless of a child's social identities? Also document examples of classroom climate—such as teacher's warmth and encouragement (e.g., who gets hugged, whose style of learning is honored).

Do teachers:

- Regularly initiate activities that foster children's awareness and appreciation of all aspects of their personal and social identities?
- Create a classroom environment that reflects the families and community in authentic ways and implement a curriculum that draws from the social identities, culture, and contexts of the children and families?
- Provide children opportunities to explore personal and social identities and their family's cultural differences and similarities throughout all the curriculum themes or investigations (e.g., learning about myself) and areas of learning (e.g., art, science)?

- Regularly notice and actively pick up on teachable/learnable moments when children's conversation and play reflect their curiosity, ideas, and attitudes about themselves and about human differences and similarities? Do teachers respond at once and in follow-up activities? For instance, when a child makes a comment about a Native American dad's long hair braid, the teacher affirms the observation and later implements learning experiences to explore diversity in men's hairstyles using picture books and photographs.
- Model clear and appropriate language for talking about difference, similarity, bias, and equity?
- Intervene whenever a child makes prejudiced or discriminatory actions toward or comments about another child, make it clear that such behavior is not acceptable, and help children work through the situation? (See Derman-Sparks & Edwards, 2020; Ramsey, 2015.)
- Guide children in engaging in actions for fairness in their school and community in meaningful ways? (See Derman-Sparks & Edwards, 2020; Pelo & Davidson, 2000.) In the film *Reflecting on Anti-bias Education in Action: The Early Years* (LeeKeenan, Nimmo, & McKinney, 2021), preschool children respond to the murder of George Floyd and the ensuing racial justice protests in their community. They create their own statement and signs of support for Black Lives Matter that they share with their school community.

Strategies and Tools for Documenting Teacher Change

Documentation of teacher change occurs in three key contexts: (1) the leader's ongoing observation and documentation of teachers' work as the basis for scaffolding their growth; (2) the leader's supervision and assessment of teacher performance; and (3) the teacher's self-study process. The two core purposes for documentation—growth and performance evaluation—can support each other. For instance, regular observation and documentation of growth and a teacher's self-study during the year may be included as part of the annual performance assessment. More recently, we have begun to see the development of more formalized tools to support the observation and assessment of early childhood teachers and their classrooms with a clear focus on equity. These include the Assessing Classroom Sociocultural Equity Scale (ACSES; Curenton et al., 2020), intended for supervisors, classroom coaches, and researchers.

Ongoing Observation. As we previously said, much of the program leader's documentation about teachers' anti-bias education growth comes from what they observe in the process of coaching, mentoring, and supervising them. Observations take place in the classroom, in informal conversations, in individual and group meetings, and in professional development sessions. Documentation may be in written forms (e.g., anecdotal observations or checklists) and visual/auditory forms (e.g., photographic, video, audio recordings). Making effective use of the various documentation opportunities takes being alert, organized, and intentional.

Teacher Self-Study Tool. The *Self-Study Guide for Reflecting on Anti-Bias Curriculum Planning and Implementation* (Chen et al., 2009) helps teachers systematically and intentionally document and reflect on their anti-bias development and practice. (See Appendix D online at www.tcpress.com). Program leaders can also use it with teachers to reflect together on growth and to set new goals.

The *Self-Study Guide* enables teachers to record at regular intervals examples of their growth and challenges in four key domains. Each domain includes a set of prompt questions for teacher reflection. The four domains are:

A. Raising self-awareness (e.g., "Am I aware of my own cultural identity and history?")
B. Physical environment (e.g., "Do all children have equal opportunity to participate in activities?")
C. Pedagogical environment (e.g., "Are my verbal and nonverbal messages free of stereotypes and hidden biases?")
D. Relationships with families and community (e.g., "Do I have enough knowledge of the local community to extend children's learning beyond the classroom walls?"). (Excerpted from Chen et al., 2009, pp. 105–106)

"[The] goal was to create a tool that invited a personal and introspective level of reflection, educated the user, and encouraged incremental changes in practice over time" (Chen et al., 2009, p. 104). John and his co-authors structured it to capture a range of responses about teacher's views of their growth—from "This is new territory for me" to "I do this with ease." They also hoped to get responses that showed internal processes and public practice.

The self-study tool was designed for collaborative self-assessment, reflection, and coaching between the program leader and a teacher who is new to anti-bias education. And a caution: while the *Self-Study Guide* is very useful as a tool for ongoing reflection and learning, we do not suggest it as a format for external assessment. "Using the tool is a necessarily subjective process in which one's responses will undoubtedly be impacted by what one knows about oneself (self-awareness), how honest one is prepared to be, and one's internalized values regarding diversity" (Chen et al., 2009, p. 104).

The following response to a self-study guide question by a teacher at the center John directed is an example of the kind of valuable evidence of growth that emerges from use of the tool. It also highlights how an activity with children may spark critical self-reflection. The teacher telling the story has been actively involved for some years in an anti-bias journey. Her story reveals a willingness to honestly scrutinize her own reactions publicly, which is likely not possible for a teacher new to anti-bias education.

I had chosen a book to read [to the children] at meeting [that] talks about the change in seasons and which tied in perfectly to the curriculum in the classroom and the observations children were having. It seemed benign, but as soon as I began to read it in the context of my classroom, I felt this awful pit in my stomach [as the story talks about the brown landscape]. Then it hit me; depending on how this is read or interpreted, children could think that brown is bad. At that moment, a child in my room proudly shouted, "Hey [Teacher]! I have brown skin!" I thought to myself, "You have got to take this on . . . how do I react. The . . . [child] is watching. My reaction to this book and the child's statement will speak volumes." And then I spoke: "You are right. You have beautiful brown skin. And do you know what? When I see the brown grass and the brown soil, I get excited [because] I know that means that the snow has melted, and that spring is on its way." We had a team meeting [of all the class staff] the next day, and I revealed the second-guessing, the embarrassment, and struggles I felt. All the things I felt inside were unnoticeable by the adults around me. . . . I think part of my reason for sharing it was to talk myself through what had happened but also because it was a teachable moment for me, my team, and our students. Diversity work is never finished for me—it is an ongoing, self-reflective journey.

Annual Performance Assessment (Summative). While the program leader's role in tracking teacher anti-bias education change over the school year is critical to both the teachers and the program's success, summative performance assessments are often required and can also be useful. These draw on the program leader's regular observation, documentation, and dialogue with teachers. (See Chapter 6 for more details.)

The annual assessment process starts at the beginning of the school year, with the program leader's up-front communication to teachers about the program expectations of anti-bias teaching practices, skills, and dispositions. This overview provides the context for teachers to individually set initial annual goals for their performance and professional development, with at least one anti-bias goal. As teachers meet their initial annual goals, they work with the program leader to revise and name new goals. Goals should build on each teacher's existing skills and knowledge.

While teachers primarily conceptualize their goals, there are times when it is necessary for the program leader to step in to identify specific areas that need attention but that the teacher does not recognize. And, as with any area of teacher performance, the program leader holds teachers accountable to at least meet a basic level of competency in anti-bias skills and knowledge.

Indicators of Children's Learning and Development

Classroom teachers have the primary responsibility for documenting children's growth on anti-bias education goals, and to use these data to make decisions about their work. Teachers also include anti-bias goals in their progress reports and conferences with families. The program leader's responsibilities include setting expectations for documenting and planning for children's anti-bias learning, suggesting documentation strategies, providing professional development, and supervising teachers' work. Ultimately, a program's impact on children's development and learning is one important window into the leader's efficacy.

The following broad indicators of children's change are organized according to the four anti-bias education goals (Derman-Sparks & Edwards, 2020). It may be necessary to adjust the indicators to make them appropriate to the age group and cultural backgrounds of the children you serve. The examples we offer are there to give you a sense of what to look for—but not to be used literally. In another words, we are not suggesting that you listen for those specific examples. Every child will demonstrate their ideas and behaviors in relation to the four anti-bias education goals in diverse ways. Program leaders and teachers must be alert enough to "hear" them." Finally, the anti-bias education goals for children fall under several learning and growth domains, including social studies, social–emotional, and cognitive development. Looking for indicators of children's growth on the four core anti-bias education goals in multiple domains of learning is a vital source for identifying the impact of anti-bias education on the children. Documenting these data is also valuable if a program must use standardized assessments tools—an issue we discuss at the end of this chapter.

Goal 1. Each child will demonstrate self-awareness, confidence, family pride, and positive social identities.

Does child:
- Identify own physical characteristics (e.g., skin color, has black hair, wears braces on legs)
- Use home languages at school?
- Eagerly talk about home and community life at school?
- Use approximately accurate crayon and paint colors to show their own skin color in self or family portrait drawings and painting?
- Recognize similarity with images of children and families in children's books and other materials?

Goal 2. Each child will express comfort and joy with human diversity; accurate language for human differences; and deep, caring human connections.

Does child:
- Matter-of-factly describe differences? For instance, a child comments, "Marsha has two mommies, Isoline has a mommy and daddy and I have a grandma and grandpa."
- Comfortably notice and show interest about similarities and differences in peers? For instance, a child comments, "We all talk, but not the same way." Or "Why does Mohamed talk with his hands? Can I do it too?"
- Play with and choose to sit next to children with different social identities (i.e., religion, languages, gender expression)?

- Demonstrate empathy to classmates with diverse social identities, as well as to classmates similar to themselves?
- Open to and enjoy learning words and phrases in languages different from their own?
- Sometimes choose learning materials (books, puzzles, play people) that depict differences from themself?
- Recognize strengths and challenges of each person? For instance, a child comments, "We all have things we are good at, and we all have things that are hard to do"; or "Jinan is deaf; he can read and use sign language, but it hard for him to hear us talk."

Goal 3. Each child will increasingly recognize unfairness, have language to describe unfairness, and understand that unfairness hurts.

Does child:
- Recognize exclusion of another child because of their identities? For instance, a child says to the teacher, "I want Miriam to play firefighters with us. Mary is not being fair; she said Miriam can't play because she doesn't speak like us," or "It hurts Luka's feelings to tease him because he uses a wheelchair."
- Reject stereotypes for themself? For example, draws a picture of themself as a surgeon in a gown and tiara.

Goal 4. Each child will demonstrate empowerment and the skills to act, with others or alone, against prejudice and/or discriminatory actions.

Does child:
- Stand up for themself and others when he notices something is unfair? For instance, a child comments, "It isn't fair to say Abraham [who uses a leg brace] can't play ball with us because he cannot run as fast as the other kids."
- Recognize examples of unfair (stereotypical) images in the program environment? For instance, during story-reading times, a kindergarten teacher hears the children make comments such as: "This book is not fair to Native Americans because the bear dresses up as if it was a Navajo person"; "Our books are not fair! I don't see anyone wearing a hijab like me."
- Recognize examples of fairness? For instance, the teacher in the previous example also noted children's comments such as "I like this book because the children help an old person fix her garden after someone messes it up."
- Contribute to finding a solution to an unfair situation? For instance, a small group of children find a way to change their musical game of Hokey Pokey so that a friend using a wheelchair can take part.

Strategies and Tools for Documenting Children's Anti-Bias Growth

Teachers (and program leaders) use observation protocols and checklists, as well as ongoing curriculum documentation strategies (such as audio-recording children's conversations and photography), to reflect on what children are learning in all domains. The following specific strategies are useful for observing anti-bias indicators:

- Record group discussions with the children that teachers plan as learning experiences about anti-bias concepts and behaviors. This includes learning experiences to evoke children's thinking and questions about the various aspects of differences and similarities among themselves, discussion about children's books and persona doll stories, responses to guest speakers, and problem-solving around conflicts between children that include negative comments about identity.
- Identify times in the day and areas in the classroom likely to involve examples of children's inclusion and exclusion of other children. What language, nonverbal behaviors, and gestures do children use? Who is excluded or included in the play?
- Listen for key words that children use in their attempts to understand difference, bias, and equity. Pay attention to the range, including inaccurate terms and words generally considered to be slurs or putdowns.
- Pay attention to children's understanding of and interest in diversity, including their "theories" and ideas that reflect misunderstanding, stereotypes, or lack of information.
- Listen for comments and questions that express a sense of empathy and fairness regarding human differences.
- Further explore potential indicators of change in children's growth on the core anti-bias education goals. Use the list of ECCE learning objectives in Stacey York's (2016) book *Roots and Wings: Affirming Culture and Preventing Bias in Early Childhood.* For teachers working with primary-age children, Learning for Justice, a project of the Southern Poverty Law Center, developed an anti-bias framework for children in Grades K–12 (Scharf, 2013). Its social justice standards and outcomes for identity, diversity, justice, and action are not directly applicable to preschool children, but may spark your ideas for creating indicators that are developmentally appropriate.

Indicators of Change in the Program Culture

In addition to documenting the primary stakeholders/players in an early childhood education program—the children's teachers and program leader—the program leader also keeps a finger on the pulse of the program culture in relation to anti-bias change. (Please review how we think of "program culture" and "climate" in Chapters 3 and 4.)

Given all the demands on the program leader, it is a challenge to be systematic in documenting shifts in the overall culture of your program, so you need to create a way to do this that works for you. Experienced leaders develop a gut-level sense of what is happening. While intuition sometimes offers a warning about specific issues that need attention, it is not a substitute for systematic documentation. Remember that the initial reading of the program at the beginning of the school year provides a baseline for assessing overall changes (see Chapter 3).

We describe indicators of change in the program culture in three broad areas: (1) evidence of welcoming and including all families and staff as members of the community, (2) changes in the structural elements of the program, such as mission, policies, budgeting, and approach to regulations, and (3) the visibility of the program's anti-bias approach.

Creating Community With Families, Teachers, and Non-Teaching Staff

Does the program:

- Accurately make visible, welcome, and include all families and staff in its visual and material environment? Does the program have signs in different languages, images of the many ways families and staff are diverse, images and home languages in the family handbook, and posters that show the program's support of inclusion and equity?
- Support children, families, and staff using their home/heritage languages at the center? Work to hire bilingual teachers and staff? Make translation assistance available when requested by a family? Invite families to share words in their home languages that ECCE programs use often and then integrate the words into daily classroom communication?
- Hire staff who reflect the diversity of the families and surrounding neighborhood? It sometimes takes creativity and persistence to meet this indicator. There is always a way.
- Furthermore, hiring is not sufficient. Diversification also requires making the program more inclusive of all, so that everyone can use their voices, and no one feels tokenized or marginalized.
- Intentionally seek to ensure that families and staff whose backgrounds differ from the dominant culture are visible at program events and participate in a range of leadership opportunities?
- Constructively work with individual staff and families from dominant cultural groups who assert that they feel left out when there is more equitable diversity in who is visible and active in the program's community? The leader's role is to help families and staff understand their responses to shifts in the culture of the program.

Establishing Structural Elements to Support Diversity and Equity

Does the program:
- Show evidence of an anti-bias lens, with anti-bias values and goals helping to shape decision-making about all aspects of the program?
- Have a clear statement of its anti-bias mission that all staff and families see and discuss each year?
- Revise or add policies in response to the diverse and changing needs of the community, rather than insisting on tradition ("this is the way we do things")?
- Create budgets that automatically prioritize resources for anti-bias efforts, including ones for inclusion of differing abilities, diversification of children's books and materials, translation services, and resources for families and for staff professional development?
- Make provisions for teachers to regularly have built-in time to reflect on and assess their anti-bias efforts with one another?
- Demonstrate creative alternatives for constructively dealing with challenges to diversity caused by external regulations and standards? For instance, a program was told by fire inspectors that they had to remove the wall display of photos and artwork they had created to reflect their diverse community. In response, the families and staff decided to use an entry space to create a 3D display that included cultural artifacts of importance to community members and still met licensing requirements for access.

Communication of the Program's Anti-Bias Values, Mission, and Practice in the Broader Community

Does the program:
- Have increasingly diverse network relationships with community organizations that support its anti-bias work?
- Promote its anti-bias education and advocacy in the broader community? This could be through stories in the local press, sharing curriculum documentation on the program website, a display at a community fair, or taking part in activism for children and families in the neighborhood. One word of caution: While dissemination in the broader community can be a great support to your work, broader visibility can also bring with it the possibility of misunderstanding or political opposition (see Chapter 7).

Strategies and Tools for Documenting Change in the Program Culture

Many of the strategies and activities detailed in Chapters 4, 5, and 6 about working with teachers and families also include numerous opportunities to document examples of desired changes in the program culture. Here are some additional tools and strategies designed for documenting these changes.

Revisiting Program-Wide Goals. Periodically reviewing program-wide goals that were first decided by the program leader and staff (and families in some cases) at the beginning of each school year reveals desired progress in integrating anti-bias education into the program and thereby making changes in the program culture. This revisiting occurs preferably at midyear and again prior to the development of new annual goals. John offers this description of his procedure for goal review:

> Before our annual spring retreat, attended by the entire staff, I asked individual staff members and classroom teams to submit specific examples of progress toward our annual program-wide goals. At the retreat, I formed cross-team small groups to discuss and share actions they and the center had taken to meet a specific goal. Soon after the retreat, I pooled and organized the feedback and distributed it to the staff and the parent advisory committee so they could reflect on what we had accomplished together.

Annual Family Survey. The annual family survey is an opportunity for families to offer anonymous feedback about the entire program—both as an organization and a community. Including questions specific to your anti-bias efforts in the survey yields another way to assess your work and make plans. John chose to formulate broad questions that family members could interpret in many ways. He hoped responses would provide both a read on the families' understanding of diversity and equity in an ECCE program and a sense of the range of views about this work. Examples of John's questions are:

Our center is seeking to be more effective in providing a program that respects diversity and promotes equity in all that it does.

- How effective are we?
- What feedback do you have regarding this goal?

John also took a further step and shared the results of the family survey with all stakeholders. Depending on the responses collected, the leader might share the raw data (with personal or inappropriate material removed) or create a more manageable summary of the responses. John explains:

> Over the years, there were specific ideas and feedback that alerted us to both changes we needed to make and varying perceptions of our work. For instance, parents had asked us to work on gender inclusion on the playground, the need for greater diversity among our teachers, and being more proactive about informing parents about events in the community. On the other side, I had also read comments that showed some parents saw "diversity" as focusing on countries and cultures around the world, a few who viewed it as "biased," and others who simply had not thought about the

issue. When a parent wrote, "The question is so broad I have no idea how to reply!," I realized it was time to be more explicit about our use of the term "anti-bias" and include specific questions focused on current initiatives.

Debbie chose to have a separate anti-bias education section in her program's family survey because of the school's long history with this work. She also used more specific questions:

- What have you learned as a member of an anti-bias education community?
- What have your children learned as members of an anti-bias education community?
- What has been challenging for your family?
- What have been the benefits for your family?

School Community Dialogue Prompts. In contrast to the individuality and anonymity of surveys, the program leader can invent more interactive strategies to collect feedback from members of the school community. For instance, Debbie described how her program used a prompt question to get feedback:

At the end of the program year, we posted a prompt question on the school's entranceway bulletin board. It read, "What have I learned about being a member of an anti-bias community?" and displayed responses the teachers had written on cardboard circles during an earlier staff meeting. Similar empty cardboard circles and markers were available for family members to also add comments. This kind of public documentation not only provides a source of interactive feedback but also shows the program's transparency and accountability to its anti-bias education mission.

Anti-Bias Education Forum and Exhibit. The following series of events illustrates how an early childhood program with experience doing ABE chose to disseminate its anti-bias work to a broader community. These activities were also a way for Debbie's program to take stock of where it was in its anti-bias journey, and to take further steps. Debbie explains:

The exhibit centered on a 2-year program-wide inquiry into anti-bias education that included classroom curriculum and teacher professional development. Families were also engaged in the inquiry through their individual classrooms and program-wide groups. During the second year of the inquiry, we disseminated our work and invited feedback by using a program newsletter and a community forum. The exhibit and gallery were the grand ending of the 2-year project.

The exhibit and gallery walk were available daily over the course of 2 weeks and included (1) an opening celebration at which the program leader gave a talk and invited outside guests to provide commentary on the exhibit; (2) documentation panels on each classroom's curriculum, which had focused on a different area of social identity; and (3) a community feedback activity—a wall or table is covered with a long sheet of paper, where people can write responses to the prompt: "In what ways does anti-bias work build and challenge a school community?" and make connections with others' ideas by drawing lines between them.

Community Network Mapping. With this tool, program leaders can map and assess their network of community supporters on an annual basis. By supporters, we mean individuals and organizations who may supply funding and grants, PD experiences for staff, guest speakers, materials for classrooms, or donations of their expertise on a specific project and other resources.

Here are some questions to guide this mapping process:

- Who are our current individual and organizational supporters?
- What ABE resources does each organization/individual offer?
- How have we used these resources in the past year?
- In what ways have we been able to provide support to the organizations/individuals?
- What other community organizations/individuals could we access and add to this network to support our ABE efforts?

STRATEGICALLY MANAGING EXTERNAL STANDARDS REQUIREMENTS AND ASSESSMENT TOOLS

State and federal early childhood education standards and standardized assessment instruments exist across the nation. Government-funded ECCE programs must use them, and many private and nonprofit programs also choose to do so. Programs in many states navigate through Quality Rating Improvement Systems (QRIS), which are often tied to state and federal government mandates for assessing program quality, as well as to receiving funding. Indeed, as early as 2002 a joint position statement of the National Association for the Education of Young Children (NAEYC) and the National Association of Early Childhood Specialists in State Departments of Education (NAECS/SDE) concluded that "early childhood education has become part of a standards-based environment . . . This movement presents both opportunities and challenges for early childhood education" (p. 1).

There are two types of assessment: (1) what a program is doing, and (2) children's learning. Unlike the documentation process, which focuses on children's ongoing learning over the course of the school year and tracks a program's anti-bias education evolution, required assessments typically evaluate a program's effectiveness and individual children's learning at predetermined points in time (usually at the end of the year). Assessment criteria are standardized, so that programs or children are measured with the same criteria. Documentation indicators are more open, with flexibility in the range of behavioral examples that illustrate them. Standardized assessment tools are meant to provide accountability to families, administration, and policymakers, rather than to guide ongoing educational decisions about individual children and a program.

Anti-bias capacities are not generally acknowledged as part of development and learning in the plethora of externally developed learning standards and assessment instruments used by various states. Some assessment tools include no mention of diversity, equity, and inclusion as components of quality ECCE, some include limited criteria on diversity, and a handful have criteria specifically addressing social identity development and anti-bias learning.

ECCE teachers and leaders who embrace anti-bias education believe that it is possible to positively manage the challenges of mandated state or federal standards and assessment requirements so that that they do not interfere with anti-bias education work. The key to doing this is to forge a proactive strategy that is relevant to your program. In another words, take a lemon and turn it into lemonade. Here is an example of a strategic approach from Karina Rojas Rodriguez, the director of Southwest Early Learning Bilingual Preschool in Seattle, an early childhood program serving children of immigrant families:

> Our program is 100% city funded. We have a lot of gatekeepers and stakeholders. When it comes to assessing the work we're doing, we must input observations into standardized assessment tools. We have ECERS [Early Childhood Environments Rating Scale], we have CLASS [Classroom Assessment Scoring System], we have our Early Achievers school coach who assesses program quality for the State of Washington. So we need to know what we're doing and be able to explain it articulately. At the same time, we also need to be able to regularly assess the work we're doing to make sure that we are going down the right path.

Program leaders must avoid the trap of "treating external standards and standardized assessments as defining the boundaries of a program's teaching. We must treat the standards as the Floor, not the Ceiling!" (C. Goins, 2014, personal communication). Goins further explains,

> My position is that standards only are the minimum requirements of what we must do. No rating scale can capture everything, nor does simply teaching to the assessment tool carry out our professional responsibilities to children and families. If we treat them as a limit or our only goals, it is unlikely that we will have culturally responsive and anti-bias education. Nothing stops you from doing anti-bias education if you know it well.

Creating and implementing an ongoing documentation process for your program is fundamental to managing mandated external assessment productively. Creatively applied to items in external standards and assessments, your documentation data become evidence to advocate for the program's anti-bias education mission as an integral party of your program's quality. Here are some additional strategies for managing mandated standardized assessments without weakening your anti-bias education work.

Be Well-Grounded in the Current ECCE Knowledge Base

Knowing current research about child development and best practices for quality early childhood education, which includes the influences of cultural diversity and societal inequity, is essential to managing mandated standards and assessment tools. If the required external standards your program works with reflect awareness of this knowledge base, then you can use them to support aspects of anti-bias work. In several states, early childhood educators were members of the committees that created standards and were able to include criteria the field accepts as best practices. Peter Mangione, who directed California's development of ECCE's state foundations, described an example of how his committee did this:

> We had enough research to understand that children belong to and take part in numerous groups, and their various group identities influence diverse kinds of experiences with others. This allowed us to not just focus on the individual self when we looked at foundations for self-awareness and self-concept. (Personal communication, May, 2013)

Luis Hernandez, who has worked with and trained Head Start staff for many years, advocates that standards with a focus on the individualization of learning and development open the door to looking at children in the context of their family, home life, community, gender, and class. From this perspective, there is room to address diversity by individualizing teaching and learning. Programs can use anti-bias goals in conjunction with external learning standards that name family engagement, positive self-concept development, social-emotional development, cooperative social interaction skills, and social science curriculum.

Find Connections Between Anti-Bias Goals and Standards/Assessment Criteria and Language

This strategy relies on being grounded in anti-bias education. The program leader carefully uses an anti-bias lens to search through the standards and assessment criteria to identify where specific items and language can intersect with anti-bias goals and curriculum. As we mentioned previously, standards such as individualization, family engagement, positive self-concept development, learning cooperative social-interaction skills, and social science curriculum can be linked with anti-bias education goals.

Some state program standards and assessment tools, as well as national Head Start requirements (Office of Head Start, 2015), also include explicit items about diversity issues such as family culture, home language, and inclusiveness.

Although these indicators are usually insufficient from an anti-bias perspective, they can serve as a bridge to anti-bias goals and objectives.

While the program leader carries the primary responsibility to find connections between external required standards and assessment and the program's anti-bias education, including staff in the process strengthens the staff's ability to implement the connections in practice. In sum, with grounding in anti-bias education and ECCE best practices, and developing skills to expand external standards and assessment tools to include anti-bias education goals, the program leader and staff can go a long way to ensure that mandated requirements are the floor and not the ceiling of a program's work.

Be Able to Explain Your Anti-Bias Work to Outside Evaluators, Regulators, and Other Stakeholders

The overall goal is to persuade external evaluators and program stakeholders such as your school's board, city/state administrators, and program funders (e.g., foundations and donors) that an anti-bias education approach empowers a program to implement required standards more fairly and fully for all children. You have the material you need to articulate, explain and advocate for your program's anti-bias education work if you (a) regularly collect internal documentation, (b) keep up on the early childhood education knowledge base (e.g. NAEYC's positions statements on advancing equity in early childhood education [2019b] and developmentally appropriate practices [2020]), and (c) figure out how your anti-bias education mission, goals, and curriculum activities relate to specific standards and assessment items.

Connect With Like-Minded Colleagues to Act Beyond Your Program

In the short term, program leaders and staff must thoughtfully and creatively manage mandated standards and assessment tools as well as they can. To change the landscape of standards and assessments beyond one's own program, working collaboratively with other early childhood professionals, families, and interested people in general is necessary. As an anti-bias leader, you have a role in advocating for change beyond your program.

For the long term, it is still unclear what role standards and related assessment play in meaningfully defining and improving the quality of early childhood programs. And we are doubtful that it is possible or even desirable for one-size-fits-all standards and assessment tools to incorporate the diverse cultural contexts of development and the multiple ways young children develop and learn. Both are critical question for the field of early childhood education—and for our nation. The increasing role of corporate business in producing and selling for-profit, one-size-fits-all curriculum and assessment materials is worrisome. These materials promise high assessment scores while often ignoring what the ECCE field views as best practices based on research about development. Furthermore, the push for one-size-fits-all standards and assessment tools seems to formalize and heighten existing contested issues (Karp, 2013–2014).

There are several ways to join with other ECCE colleagues beyond your own program who want to address the challenges of these critical standards and assessment issues. Your local director's network is one place to look; state and professional conference workshops are another. Work with college ECCE faculty in your local community to teach their students to make connections between external standards and assessment and anti-bias education goals. This strategy can build a pool of new teachers who have grounding in implementing anti-bias education in the climate of required standards.

Work with state departments responsible for early learning standards (e.g., Education or Health and Human Services) by serving on task forces and giving feedback on draft standards during the public comment period. John describes his experience working with the state early learning standards task force in New Hampshire:

> This work gave me the opportunity to influence the development of the standards with anti-bias values in mind and to develop a network of allies. I advocated successfully for the inclusion of clear language about dual-language learners and made sure those examples and expectations were appreciative of differences in culture and ability. Along with colleagues on the taskforces, I worked to ensure that appropriate language regarding children's social identity development and even anti-bias capacities were included. While there is still a long way to go toward truly reflecting all the anti-bias goals in the standards, we made a start and engaged in an important dialogue with stakeholders from across the state.

Negotiating required learning and program standards and assessments with anti-bias education adds more tasks to program leaders' already very full plates. However, our experience tells us that while it is challenging to find ways—and time—to work beyond our classrooms, doing so helps to sustain ourselves over the long haul of building anti-bias early childhood programs.

DOCUMENTATION AND EMPOWERMENT

Change is a long-term undertaking, and we do not see all the fruits of our commitment to an anti-bias mission in the short run. Rather, we—leaders, teachers, and staff alike—take vital steps toward it. Documenting anti-bias changes in ourselves, in our program, and in the various members of our ECCE community helps sustain us to keep moving forward. It enables us to know where we have been, where we are now, and where we want to go in the anti-bias education journey. As a tool to track your documentation efforts, we have compiled a worksheet of indicators from this chapter in Appendix E at www.tcpress.com.

On a more personal level, we see documentation as providing valuable opportunities for program leaders to celebrate their own and their ECCE community's efforts and successes along the way. And keeping track of how anti-bias education change is happening in our programs also helps us to communicate and collaborate with families, community allies, and other ECCE colleagues to advocate for anti-bias education to advance building equitable care and education programs for all children.

Epilogue
Sustaining the Anti-Bias Vision

Don't feel afraid to push back hard on things that you really believe in; be persistent, speak up. Like John Lewis, I like the trouble. We need to advocate for what is needed and keep the vision. It's worth it. It's worth it to try.

—Miriam Zmiewski-Angelova, center director

We must accept finite disappointment, but we must never lose infinite hope.

—Martin Luther King Jr. (in C. S. King, 1983, p. 25)

How do people who lead anti-bias education programs keep up their commitment over time? What sustains us as we pursue a vision of social justice? In this Epilogue, we share several themes drawn from our many years of experience in directing early childhood centers and in facilitating anti-bias education efforts around the United States and internationally. We also include the insights of the other experienced and diverse ECCE program leaders from whom you have heard throughout this book.

MOTIVATION COMES FROM OUR INNER CORE

We all agree that doing anti-bias work is inseparable from who we are. Here are our diverse ways of describing this essential aspect of being an anti-bias educator.

Debbie: I always felt on the outside, growing up Chinese American in predominantly White communities. My firsthand experiences of feeling different, being ostracized and the target of bias and racism, resulted in my becoming an activist. There was a period when I felt like I did not belong anywhere. These feelings motivated me to create communities that celebrate differences and are safe and inclusive places for all children and families. At the same time, I also wanted to build a community that was safe for my own growing multiracial family.

John: Taking on anti-bias leadership is a natural extension of my core values of respect for others and a love of diversity in the human experience. To me, diversity of experience and the willingness to step outside of your comfort zone are essential to learning and growth. As a White, upper-middle-class cisgender male, I believe that I am particularly aware of the importance of anti-bias goals to children who are growing up with access to unearned power in this society.

Julie: I always noticed unfairness as an elementary school kid. And then I got really invested in women's studies issues when I was doing my undergraduate program and got involved in antiwar efforts . . . When I was an ECE director for the first time, I realized that I had no training about how to be an effective leader for families of color. That took me to a college teaching about anti-bias education with young children. Now I can't imagine anti-bias values not being a part of what I do. There isn't really another option.

Karina: The sphere of biculturalism plays a crucial role in the anti-bias work we do. This is something my dad and my mom have always said: "We live in this country, we want you to be bicultural, we want you to be bilingual, we want you to be who you are. And we want who we are to be visible." I'm not going to stop being Mexican at home, I'm not going to stop being Mexican here. I'm Mexican American, and I'm going to share who I am with you. And that's what we want from the families.

Louise: In a sense, my desire to do anti-bias education work came with my mother's milk, since my parents were social justice activists their whole lives. When I chose to be an early childhood educator, it became very clear to me that there is no "quality" in early childhood care and education programs unless "equality" also exists. So doing anti-bias education seemed integral to my professional commitment, which included nurturing all children's development and learning—and to do no harm in the process. As simple and as complex as that.

Miriam: My lived experience is being multiracial; my family's Black, Native, and Ashkenazi. And I grew up in Taiwan, speaking Taiwanese. I was a multilingual child growing up in a culture that wasn't my family's culture. I was of many people, in many places, and yet, I was not of any specific person or place, and I wasn't of one person or place. And so I experienced constant code-switching and figuring out, where do I fit in. I'm really thankful for all those along the way who taught me little kernels of knowledge about inclusion, empathy, and humility and staying curious.

Rukia: For me, it's definitely a spiritual tradition of love and community and yearning. Our journey has also been reclaiming our African values, our indigenous values that have been stolen from us, and what does it mean to be in community in a collective way.

Tashon: I grew up in New York with my grandparents. My grandfather was functionally illiterate, and my grandmother had some schooling and could read and write on a basic level. But in my house, I was taught that education is a gift, one which wasn't available to them. I carry my grandparents' experience on my teaching journey, and it motivates me to do anti-bias education on my work with children and adults. When

I look back on history, I want to make sure that what happened to my people [African Americans] never happens to anyone again.

"MAN MAN LAI": SLOWLY IT WILL COME

Who we are fuels our vision of a more just future, but as leaders, we also bring intention, patience, and strategic thinking to our actions.

"Man man lai" is a traditional Chinese maxim that literally means "slowly, slowly it will come." We take that to mean, "appreciate the small steps that lead to bigger movement." This is one of the most important principles underpinning anti-bias work and leadership. But practicing *man man lai* is not easy. As John explains, "I feel uneasy that we are not doing enough to move anti-bias work forward. I have to remind myself that anti-bias change is often both one step at a time *and* long range." And Debbie adds,

> It helps to pay attention to the "small changes" and to keep reminding ourselves that our work is a step-by-step process. When the work gets really complicated or frustrating, I break down the problem, just focus on one aspect for today, and not worry about all the other pieces until another day. In other words, it is useful to take one day at a time—sometimes even one hour at a time. And to remember, it is one step in front of the other and to keep walking.

Along with the principle of *man man lai*, change work calls on us to draw on vision, dreams, and hopes, plus analysis and strategy. Our dreams and vision give us motivation, energy, direction, and persistence. As Rukia asserts:

> Invite your families, your teachers, your whole community to reimagine this world, starting with the lives of young children. When you invite people to the bigger visions of what you're hoping for and explain how the anti-bias goals *are* strategies—a means to get there—then they will take it up with you.

At the same time, experience teaches us that change also requires strategic decision-making based on thoughtful analysis. "In the end," as John affirms, "what matters most is balancing urgency with impatience and vision with analysis. We honor the call to dream and act, and the patience and strategy to be in it for the long haul."

FOSTERING A COMMUNITY FOR CHANGE

Anti-bias change requires both leadership and grass-roots investment. Both Debbie and John—and the other program directors with whom we spoke—work from the principle that anti-bias change is an ongoing, dynamic interaction between the program leader and its stakeholders. As John explains:

> I focus my efforts on creating a grassroots commitment to anti-bias values, rather than simply using my authority to require change. When a teacher suggests a book for the staff to read together, or a group of parents undertakes facilitating a diversity dialogue, or a teacher challenges the equity of a decision, their acts of initiative fuel my commitment.

> I worked hard to find the right balance between directing (Do it this way), challenging (How could you do it differently?), and affirmation (You took the risk to do something new in your practice!). I also thought a great deal about the parents and staff members who are silent about anti-bias change. What are they thinking and feeling? How could we engage in a dialogue? I try to be aware of and reach out to community members who may seem to be on the sidelines of anti-bias changes. Maybe they are going through their own process of disequilibrium and change.

Debbie adds:

> The concept of grassroots investment means sharing some power with your staff. When I first came to my center in Massachusetts, I found that the previous director had planned and led the monthly staff meetings. I began shifting this model by instituting a staff survey on what topics they were interested in learning about in the upcoming year. Eventually we moved to having each classroom team be responsible for leading a staff meeting. The biggest outcome was the investment of staff in the staff meetings; they now felt ownership for the success of the staff meetings.

Rukia Rogers emphasizes building a beloved community:

> We can center ourselves in a place of love, openness, and fluidity—that it's truly a journey. And a place of deep courage, to be emotionally prepared for the work from a place of love. It's complicated. Dealing with humans is complicated. We must model the anti-bias goals for ourselves and for adults—how do we see the identities of the teachers and their families and who they are and their beliefs that they hold? How do we find joy in diverse perspectives? How do we build a curriculum that centers the community for both children and adults?

Tashon McKeithan adds practicing empathy and offering space for each person's anti-bias journey:

> I had a board member who didn't understand anti-bias education. He said, "I need a foundational understanding of this." I realized we needed

to carry him through this and not make him feel bad. Calling people in and bringing them into the conversation and holding their hand when it becomes uncomfortable is going to be critical to how we move as a community.

And finally, Miriam Zmiewski-Angelova reminds us of the importance of building trust and respect in an ECCE community.

It's going to take time. We have to start from the beginning, and we have to build up slowly. We can't assume that relationships are going to be [built] fast. We can't be asking for feedback right away. [Families and staff] need to feel that their wants and needs, questions and concerns, and their hopes and dreams are being [seen].

STAYING OVER THE LONG HAUL

Changing the culture, climate, policies, and daily curriculum of an early childhood program is complex. It is both personal and systemic, and requires a range of strategies and many steps. Change involves the people, the policies, the relationships, and the infrastructures of an early childhood program. And the process of change takes many forms, subtle or obvious, slow or abrupt, easy or difficult. Because an ECCE program is grounded in a system of relationships, the multiple layers of change for the leader, children, families, teachers, and program are interrelated.

At the same time, change can and does happen! Learning to read the many indicators of anti-bias education change, and to use them to scaffold what to do next, enables you to facilitate your program's change journey more effectively. Leading change successfully also means committing to keep carrying on—to stay in the work for the long haul.

Being thoughtful and paying attention to where the individuals you lead are in their own anti-bias journeys takes discipline and energy. And every so often you need to recoup. Reminding yourself why you decided to do anti-bias education helps. Revisiting your vision and hopes for a better world can keep you going over the long haul. Acknowledging the anti-bias steps that have been taken and the growth that has occurred is equally necessary. It is too easy to beat yourself up about what you did not do, or did not do well, or what you wished you had achieved.

It is important to take care of yourself, whatever that may mean to you. Most especially, having a group of supportive colleagues helps keep you going. As longtime colleagues, we have become close friends over the years. No matter where any of us were, we felt we could pick up the phone or drop a text any time we wanted, and our colleagues would be there for us. At conferences and professional meetings, our meals and conversations with trusted colleagues outside our programs and projects were as important as the conference sessions and meeting topics. They sustained and nurtured us.

Julie Bisson responds to what keeps her going:

> I would say that one of the most important dispositions that allows me to
> keep going forward is humility. That I can actually stop and say, "Okay,
> what can I learn from this [situation]? And how can this make me be better
> at and make us be better at who we are and who we say that we are?" But
> if you don't have that element of humility, if you're not willing to say, "Oh,
> wait," and approach this as a learning moment, as an opportunity to learn
> more but just to reaffirm you know what you're already doing, then you
> don't have an opportunity for growth.

Debbie shares that many of the strengths she developed to lead anti-bias work
took time:

> As I got older, I also became more experienced, and, hopefully, wiser. My
> biggest challenge was learning to embrace conflict and disequilibrium as
> possibilities for growth. At first, it was very hard when everyone did not
> agree. I wanted to be open to different viewpoints, yet also hold to the core
> anti-bias values. It was difficult when I felt like I let someone down, or some
> people were not pleased with how it went, or people felt misunderstood
> when we disagreed, or I felt misunderstood. I took disappointment that we
> could not reach consensus as a personal rejection.
>
> There were times when I could not let it go and brought the work home,
> waking up in the middle of the night upset with these feelings. I got tired.
> Eventually, I stopped seeing everything as right or wrong, and accepted
> that most things are more complicated and nuanced than that. I learned to
> identify and accept people where they are and to feel good about helping
> them move along. I do believe in and have bottom lines, but I can also
> agree to disagree and let some things go. Over the years I have found
> more balance—no longer expecting a transformation to happen overnight,
> appreciating the small steps of change and movement. I was able to handle
> the long haul with optimism.

John reflects on other challenges:

> As a leader, you are in a vulnerable position because it is part of your job
> to stand by the teachers, families, and anti-bias values. This public role has
> made me feel vulnerable, especially when someone's objections to anti-bias
> change becomes emotional and personal. Part of my challenge is not to let
> my fears about what might happen when I take on difficult issues hold me
> back. Over the years, I have often been surprised, delighted, and humbled
> by the willingness of families and teachers to embrace change and to share
> their stories of dealing with bias.

Taking stock of the movement for change, Louise offers:

> Early childhood anti-bias educators sow seeds. Sometimes we see these seeds grow before us; other times they come to fruition after we can no longer see them. One dynamic that gives me hope is there are now many anti-bias seed planters and growers in the USA and in many countries around the world. We keep carrying it on.

Ultimately, as leaders, we come back to our fundamental commitment to young children, as Karina shares:

> At the end of the year, we really want the children to leave our program with a powerful sense of identity, of language and their abilities, and for them to really act on any biases and injustices or anything that they see not happening. And I think that that really sets them up for the future. And that keeps me going.

And Tashon adds her own sense of urgency:

> We are creating a better world. We are creating it for our children and our grandchildren and the children that we will never meet. Because we can see White supremacy starting to creep up——like the attack on education. But, if we stay the course, we will create a better everything. So that's why I do what I do. That's why I stay in it even when it's hard.

CARRY ON THE MOVEMENT FOR CHANGE

Anti-bias endeavors are part of a proud educational tradition—one that continues to seek to make the dream of justice and equality for all a reality. It happens day by day, and calls on our best teaching, relationship, and leadership skills. It also takes being part of a network of supportive colleagues with whom we can be totally honest, share both failures and successes, and grow personally and professionally. And it takes being part of the larger movement for social justice and equity for all in our country and throughout the world.

While children are at the heart of ECCE work, they are not the only critical factors that profoundly affect what we do. The adults who teach and parent them, the infrastructures and canon of early childhood education, and the larger economic and social-political dynamics in a society all contribute to what we can do, as well as what we need to do. While the ECCE field has its own unique role to play, its practitioners also must connect to larger social justice movements. This includes joining with colleagues to improve the working conditions, benefits, and salaries of early childhood practitioners and to include regular time for reflection and planning. It also involves advocating at the local, state, and national levels to modernize the ECCE body of knowledge, so that it incorporates culturally sustaining and anti-bias perspectives, policies, and infrastructure. As Julie stresses,

> It is a multipronged approach. There is essential work we do with children to undo misinformation and empower children to stand up for things that are unfair. But it's also essential that we work on our own adult issues and on systemic issues that are bigger than what we do in the classroom. We have to help make things fairer on the world stage, at the same time that we're doing the work with children. We can choose what aspect of larger social justice work we invest in. However, we always have the professional responsibility to be part of ongoing change.

We conclude our Epilogue with the following words to you: We yearn for the time when every child will grow up nurtured and able to be fully who they are, with no barriers of poverty, systemic discrimination, undemocratic governance, or war. We hold a vision of the time when equity and diversity are inherent in the quality of ECCE programs. Until that day comes, we must keep carrying on with faith in our dreams, our vision, and the possibility of positive change—in ourselves, in others, in our programs, and in our larger society.

References

Aboud, F. E., Tredoux, C., Tropp, L. R., Brown, C. S., Niens, U., & Noor, N. M. (2012). Interventions to reduce prejudice and enhance inclusion and respect for ethnic differences in early childhood: A systematic review. *Developmental Review, 32,* 307–336.

Agudelo, C. P. (2022). *Critical awareness, reflection, and action in Head Start leadership: A Critical consciousness case study of Head Start leaders* [Doctoral dissertation, Portland State University].

Alinsky, S. D. (1971). *Rules for radicals: A pragmatic primer for realistic radicals.* Random House.

Al-Jubeh, D., & Vitsou, M. (2021). Empowering refugee children with the use of persona doll. *International Journal of Progressive Education, 17*(2), 210–227. https://doi.org/10.29329/ijpe.2021.332.13

Allen, R., Shapland, D. L., Neitzel, J., & Iruka, I. U. (2021). Creating anti-racist early childhood spaces. In I. Alanis, I. U. Iruka, B. Willer, & S. Friedman (Eds), *Advancing equity in early childhood education* (pp. 114–119). National Association for the Education of Young Children.

Amirault, C., Benish, M., Bowers, M., Harris, P., Knight, T., Tate, N., & Williams, J. (2021). Journeying together: How our program addresses race and anti-bias education. *Young Children, 76*(2). https://www.naeyc.org/resources/pubs/yc/summer2021/journeying-together

Anderson, M. L. (2006). Race, gender, and class stereotypes: New perspectives on ideology and inequality. *Norteamérica, 1*(1), 69–91.

Arao, B., & Clemens, K. (2013). From safe spaces to brave spaces: A new way to frame dialogue around diversity and social justice. In L. M. Landreman (Ed.), *The art of effective facilitation: Reflections from social justice educators* (pp. 135–150). Stylus Publishing.

Barrera, I., Kramer, L. & Macpherson, T. D. (2012). *Skilled dialogue: Strategies for responding to cultural diversity in early childhood* (2nd ed.). Paul Brookes.

Beneke, M. R. (2021). Investigating young children's conceptualizations of disability and race: An intersectional, multiplane critique. *Educational Researcher, 50*(2), 97–104.

Blackson, E. A., Gerdes, M., Segan, E., Anokam, C., & Johnson, T. J. (2022). Racial bias toward children in the early childhood education setting. *Journal of Early Childhood Research, 20*(3), 277–292.

Bloom, P. J., Hentschel, A., & Bella, J. (2016). *A great place to work: Creating a healthy organizational climate* (2nd ed.). New Horizons.

Bonilla-Silva, E. (2017). *Racism without racists: Color-blind racism and the persistence of racial inequality in America.* Rowman & Littlefield.

Bowman, B. (1997). New directions in higher education. In S. Kagan & B. Bowman (Eds.), *Leadership in early care and education* (pp. 107–114). National Association for the Education of Young Children.

Bradley, V., & Reynoso, V. (2022, July 13). *Teaching and learning about race: Fantastic practice in early childhood* [Webinar]. Embrace Race. https://www.embracerace.org/resources/teaching-and-learning-about-race-fantastic-practice-in-early-childhood

Brown, B. (2008). *Equality in action: A way forward with persona dolls*. Trentham Books.

Brown, N., & Manning, J. (2000). Core knowledge for directors. In M. Culkin (Ed.), *Managing quality in young children's programs: The leader's role* (pp. 78–96). Teachers College Press.

Carter, M., Casio, L. M., & Curtis, D. (2021). *The visionary director: A handbook for dreaming, organizing, and improvising in your center* (3rd ed.). Redleaf Press.

Casio, L. (2010). Cultivating dispositions for cultural democracy. *Exchange, 32*(6), 58–60.

Chen, D. W., Nimmo, J., & Fraser, H. (2009). Becoming a culturally responsive early childhood educator: A tool to support reflection by teachers embarking on the anti-bias journey. *Multicultural Perspectives, 11*(2), 101–106.

Child Study and Development Center. (2005). *Diversity commitment.* Child Study and Development Center, University of New Hampshire, Durham. https://chhs.unh.edu/child-study-development-center/about-us

Child Study and Development Center. (2011). *Family handbook* [Unpublished manuscript]. Child Study and Development Center, University of New Hampshire, Durham.

Clark, K. B. (1963). *Prejudice and your child* (2nd ed.). Beacon Press.

Clark, K. B., & Clark, M. P. (1947). Racial identification and preference in Negro children. In T. M. Newcomb & E. L. Hartley (Eds.), *Readings in social psychology* (pp. 169–178). Free Press.

Clifford, R. (1997). Commentary. In S. Kagan & B. Bowman (Eds.), *Leadership in early care and education* (pp. 103–104). National Association for the Education of Young Children.

Crenshaw, K. (1991). Mapping the margins: Intersectionality, identity, and violence against women of color. *Stanford Law Review, 43*(6), 1241–1300

Cross, W. E. Jr. (1991). *Shades of black: Diversity in African-American identity*. Temple University Press.

Cui, J., & Natzke, L. (2021). *Early childhood program participation: 2019* (NCES 2020-075REV). National Center for Education Statistics, Institute of Education Sciences, U.S. Department of Education. http://nces.ed.gov/pubsearch/pubsinfo.asp?pubid=2020075REV.

Curenton, S. M., Iruka, I. U., Humphries, M., Jensen, B., Durden, T., Rochester, S. E., Sims, J., Whittaker, J. V., & Kinzie, M. B. (2020). Validity for the Assessing Classroom Sociocultural Equity Scale (ACSES). *Early Education and Development, 31*(2), 269–288.

Derman-Sparks, L. (2011, May 20). *Putting visions into practice: Reflections from an anti-bias educator*. Keynote presentation for Building Peaceable Communities: The Power of Early Childhood, The Global Learning Initiative on Children and Ethnic Diversity Conference, Amsterdam, The Netherlands.

Derman-Sparks, L. (2013a, January 10). *A guide for selecting anti-bias children's books* (updated). Teaching for Change. https://www.teachingforchange.org/selecting-anti-bias-books=

Derman-Sparks, L. (2013b). Developing culturally responsive caregiving practices: Acknowledge, ask, and adapt. In E. A. Virmani & P. L. Mangione (Eds.), *Infant/toddler caregiving: A guide to culturally sensitive care* (2nd ed., pp. 68–94). California Department of Education.

Derman-Sparks, L., & The Anti-Bias Taskforce. (1989). *Anti-bias curriculum: Tools for empowering young children*. National Association for the Education of Young Children.

Derman-Sparks, L., & Edwards, J. O. (2010). *Anti-bias education for young children and ourselves*. National Association for the Education of Young Children.

Derman-Sparks, L., Edwards, J. O., & Goins, C. (2020). *Anti-bias education for young children and ourselves* (2nd ed.). National Association for the Education of Young Children.

Derman-Sparks, L., & Phillips, C. B. (1997). *Teaching/learning anti-racism: A developmental approach*. Teachers College Press.

Derman-Sparks, L., & Ramsey, P. G. (with Edwards, J. O.). (2011). *What if all the kids are white? Anti-bias/multicultural education for young children and families* (2nd ed.). Teachers College Press.

DiAngelo, R. (2018). *White fragility: Why it is so hard for White people to talk about racism?* Beacon Press.

Dunst, C. J., & Trivette, C. M. (2012). Moderators of the effectiveness of adult learning method practices. *Journal of Social Sciences, 8*, 143–148.

Durden, T. R., & Curenton, S. M. (2021). Recognizing shortcomings of a traditional professional knowledge base. In I. Alanis, I. U. Iruka, B. Willer, & S. Friedman (Eds), *Advancing equity in early childhood education* (pp. 41–47). National Association for the Education of Young Children.

Eliot–Pearson Children's School. (n.d.). *FAQs about anti-bias education at the Eliot Pearson Children's School* [Unpublished manuscript]. Author.

Escayg, K. (2018). The missing links: Enhancing anti-bias education with anti-racist education. *Journal of Curriculum, Teaching, Learning and Leadership in Education, 3*(1), 15–20.

Espinosa, L. (1997). Personal dimensions of leadership. In S. Kagan & B. Bowman (Eds.), *Leadership in early care and education* (pp. 97–104). National Association for the Education of Young Children.

Flores, B. B., Herrera, S., & Flores, J. B. (2021). Early childhood teacher educators' critical role: Preparing culturally efficacious early childhood teachers. In I. Alanis, I. U. Iruka, B. Willer, & S. Friedman (Eds.), *Advancing equity in early childhood education* (pp. 120–126). National Association for the Education of Young Children.

Forbes, K. (Director). (2020). *Between the world and me* [Film]. HBO.

Forester, J. (2013). *Planning in the face of conflict: The surprising possibilities of facilitative leadership*. Routledge.

Foubert, J. M. (2022). *Reckoning with racism in family-school partnerships: Centering Black parents' school engagement*. Teachers College Press.

Freire, P. (1970). *Pedagogy of the oppressed*. Seabury Press.

Freire, P. (1985). Reading the world and reading the word: An interview with Paulo Freire. *Language Arts, 62*(1), 15–21.

Fu, D., Hadjioannou, X., & Zhou, X. (2019). *Translanguaging for emergent bilinguals: Inclusive teaching in the linguistically diverse classroom*. Teachers College Press.

Gay, G. (2018). *Culturally responsive teaching: Theory, research, and practice* (3rd ed.). Teachers College Press.

Gilliam, W. S., Maupin, A. N., Reyes, C. R., Accavitti, M., & Shic, F. (2016, September 28). *Do early educators' implicit biases regarding sex and race relate to behavior expectations and recommendations of preschool expulsions and suspensions?* [A Research Study Brief]. Yale University Child Study Center. https://medicine.yale.edu/childstudy/policy-and-social-innovation/zigler/publications/preschool%20implicit%20bias%20policy%20brief_final_9_26_276766_54643_v1.pdf

Goleman, D. (2005). *Emotional intelligence: Why it can matter more than IQ* (10th ed.). Random House.

González, N., Moll, L., & Amanti, C. (2005). *Funds of knowledge: Theorizing practices in households, communities, and classrooms*. Lawrence Erlbaum Associates.

Gonzalez-Mena, J. (2012). *Child, family, and community: Family-centered early care and educa-tion* (6th ed.). Pearson.

Goodman, M. E. (1952). *Race awareness in young children*. Addison-Wesley.

Greene, E., Rashid, R. M., & Young, J. C. (2022). Preparing teachers to deal with race, cul-ture, and hegemony. In M. Sykes & K. Ostendorf (Eds.), *Child care justice: Transforming the system of care for young children* (pp. 102–123). Teachers College Press.

Hard, L., Press, F., & Gibson, M. (2013). 'Doing' social justice in early childhood: The po-tential of leadership. *Contemporary Issues in Early Childhood, 14*(4), 324–334.

Helmer, S., & Eddy, C. (2012). *Look at me when I talk to you: ESL learners in non-ESL class-rooms*. Pippin Publishing.

Helms, J. E. (1993). *Black and white racial identity*. Praeger.

Helms, J. E. (1995). An update of Helms' white and people of color racial identity models. In J. Ponterotto, J. Casas, C. Suzuki, & C. Alexander (Eds.), *Handbook of multicultural counseling* (pp. 189–198). Sage.

Hirschfeld, L. A. (2012). Seven myths of race and the young child. *Du Bois Review Social Science Research on Race, 9*(1), 17–39.

Hollins, C. D. (2023). *Inside out: The equity leader's guide to undoing institutional racism*. New Society Publishers.

hooks, b. (2004). *Teaching community: A pedagogy of hope*. Routledge.

Iruka, I. U., Curenton, S. M., Durden, T. R., & Escayg, K. (2020). *Don't look away: Embrac-ing anti-bias classrooms*. Gryphon House.

Iruka, I.U., Durden, T.R., Escayg, K., & Curenton, S.M. (2023). *We are the change we seek: Advancing racial justice in early care and education*. Teachers College Press.

Isik-Ercan, Z. (2021). Developing the three Cs of reciprocity. In I. Alanis, I. U. Iruka, B. Willer, & S. Friedman (Eds), *Advancing equity in early childhood education* (pp. 61–64). National Association for the Education of Young Children.

Jaboneta, N. (2019). *You can't celebrate that! Navigating the deep waters of social justice*. Ex-change Press.

Jacobson, T. (2003). *Confronting our discomforts: Clearing the way for anti-bias in early child-hood*. Heinemann.

Jemal, A., & Bussey, S. R. (2022). Liberatory education: We are the ones we've been wait-ing for. In M. Sykes & K. Ostendorf (Eds.), *Child care justice: Transforming the system of care for young children* (pp. 20–47). Teachers College Press.

Jones, E., & Nimmo, J. (1994). *Emergent curriculum*. National Association for the Educa-tion of Young Children.

Kagan, S., & Neuman, M. (1997). Conceptual leadership. In S. Kagan & B. Bowman (Eds.), *Leadership in early care and education* (pp. 59–64). National Association for the Education of Young Children.

Karp, S. (2013–2014, Winter). The problems with the Common Core. *Rethinking Schools, 28*(2), 1–10.

Katz, P. A. (1976). The acquisition of racial attitudes in children. In P. A. Katz (Ed.), *Towards the elimination of racism* (pp. 125–154). Pergamon.

Kaufman, E. A., & Wiese, D. L. (2012). Skin-tone preferences and self-representation in Hispanic children. *Early Child Development and Care, 182*, 277–290.

Khalifa, M. (2018). *Culturally responsive school leadership*. Harvard Education Press.

Kim, R. (2021). What critical race theory is and what it means for teachers. *Learning for Justice*. https://www.learningforjustice.org/magazine/what-critical-race-theory-is -and-what-it-means-for-teachers

Kissinger, K. (2017). *Anti-bias education in the early childhood classroom: Hand in hand, step by step*. Routledge.

King, C. S. (Ed.). (1983). *The words of Martin Luther King Jr.: Selected by Coretta Scott King*. Newmarket Press.

Krechevsky, M., Rivard, M., & Burton, F. R. (2010). Accountability in three realms: Making learning visible inside and outside the classroom. *Theory Into Practice, 49*(1), 64–71.

Kuh, L., Beneke, M., LeeKeenan, D., & Given, H. (2016). Moving beyond anti-bias activities: Supporting the development of anti-bias practice. *Young Children, 71*(1), 58–65.

Kurusa, M. (2008). *The streets are free*. Annick Press.

Lawrence-Lightfoot, S. (2003). *The essential conversation: What parents and teachers can learn from each other*. Ballantine Books.

LeeKeenan, D., & Nimmo, J. (2021). *Reflecting on anti-bias education in practice: The early years. Viewer and facilitator guidebook*. Authors. https://www.antibiasleadersece.com/guidebook/.

LeeKeenan, D., & Nimmo, J. (Producers), & McKinney, F. E. (Director). (2021). *Reflecting on anti-bias education in practice: The early years* [Film]. Brave Sprout Productions.

LeeKeenan, D., & Ponte, I C. (2018). *From survive to thrive: A director's guide for leading an early childhood program*. National Association for the Education of Young Children.

Long, S., Souto-Manning, M., & Vasquez, V. M. (2015). Courageous leaders: No empty platitudes. In S. Long, M. Souto-Manning, & V. M. Vasquez (Eds.), *Courageous leadership in early childhood education: Taking a stand for social* justice (pp. 7–18). Teachers College Press.

Lynch, E., & Hanson, M. (Eds.). (2011). *Developing cross-cultural competence* (4th ed.). Brookes.

Mac Naughton, G., & Davis, K. (2009). *"Race" and early childhood education: An international approach to identity, politics, and pedagogy*. Palgrave Macmillan.

McKnight, J., & Block, P. (2012). *The abundant community: Awakening the power of families and neighborhoods*. Berrett-Koelher Publishers.

Matias, C. E. (2016). "Why do you make me hate myself?": Re-teaching Whiteness, abuse, and love in urban teacher education. *Teaching Education, 27*(2), 1–18. http://dx.doi.org/10.1080/10476210.2015.1068749

Meek, S., Iruka, I. U., Allen, R., Yazzie, D., Fernandez, V., Catherine, E., McIntosh, K., Gordon, L., Gilliam, W., Hemmeter, M. L., Blevins, D., & Powell, T. (2020). *Fourteen priorities to dismantle systemic racism in early care and education*. The Children's Equity Project. https://childandfamilysuccess.asu.edu/cep

Morgan, C. W., Cheatham, G. A., & Park, K. K. (2022). Follow their lead: A conversation about person-first and identity-first language in early childhood settings. *Young Exceptional Children, 25*(4), 221–225.

Morgan, G. (2000). The director as a key to quality. In M. Culkin (Ed.), *Managing quality in young children's programs: The leader's role* (pp. 40–58). Teachers College Press.

Morgan, H. (2008). A director's lot is not a happy one. In B. Neugebauer & R. Neugebauer (Eds.), *The art of leadership: Managing early childhood organizations* (pp. 41–43). Exchange Press.

Morris, A. (1993). *Bread, bread, bread*. HarperCollins.

Murray, C., & Urban, M. (2012). *Diversity and equity in early childhood: An Irish perspective*. Gill & Macmillan.

Nash, K., Howard, J., Miller, E., Boutte, G., Johnson, G., & Reid, L. (2018). Critical racial literacy in homes, schools, and communities: Propositions for early childhood contexts. *Contemporary Issues in Early Childhood, 19*(3), 256–273.

National Association for the Education of Young Children. (n.d.). TORCH (The Online Resources Center Headquarters). In *NAEYC Accreditation*. www.naeyc.org/academy/primary/torch

National Association for the Education of Young Children. (2011). *Code of ethical conduct and statement of commitment: A position statement of the National Association for the Education of Young Children* (rev. ed.). https://www.naeyc.org/sites/default/files/globally-shared /downloads/PDFs/resources/position-statements/Ethics%20Position%20State- ment2011_09202013update.pdf

National Association for the Education of Young Children. (2019a). *Early learning program accreditation standards and assessment items.* https://www.naeyc.org/sites/default /files/globally-shared/downloads/PDFs/accreditation/early-learning/standards _assessment_2019.pdf

National Association for the Education of Young Children. (2019b). *Advancing equity in early childhood education position statement.* https://www.naeyc.org/sites/default/files /globally-shared/downloads/PDFs/resources/position-statements/advancingequitypo sitionstatement.pdf

National Association for the Education of Young Children. (2020). *Developmentally appropriate practice (DAP) position statement.* https://www.naeyc.org/resources/position -statements/dap/contents

National Association for the Education of Young Children. (2022). *Developmentally appropriate practice in early childhood programs serving children from birth through age 8* (4th ed.). Author.

National Association for the Education of Young Children (NAEYC) & National Association of Early Childhood Specialists in State Departments of Education (NAECS/ SDE). (2002). *Early learning standards: Creating the conditions for success: A joint position statement.*

Neugebauer, R. (2000). What is management ability? In M. Culkin (Ed.), *Managing quality in young children's programs: The leader's role* (pp. 97–111). Teachers College Press.

Nieto, L., Boyer, M. F., Goodwin, L., Johnson, G. R., & Smith, L. C. (2010). *Beyond inclusion, beyond empowerment: A developmental strategy to liberate everyone.* Cuetzpalin.

Nimmo, J. (2008). Young children's access to real life: An examination of the growing boundaries between children in child care and adults in the community. *Contemporary Issues in Early Childhood 9*(1), 3–13.

Nimmo. J., LeeKeenan, D., & Derman-Sparks, L. (2021). Being an equity leader. *Young Children, 76*(3), 21–27.

Office of Head Start. (2015). *The Head Start early learning outcomes framework.* https://eclkc .ohs.acf.hhs.gov/sites/default/files/pdf/elof-ohs-framework.pdf

Olatunji, C. (1998). Toward a model of cross-cultural group process and development. In S. Cronin, L. Derman-Sparks, S. Henry, C. Olatunji, & S. York (Eds.), *Future vision, present work: Learning from the culturally relevant anti-bias leadership project* (pp. 92–109). Redleaf Press.

Oluo, I. (2018). *So you want to talk about race.* Seal Press.

O'Neill, C., & Brinkerhoff, M. (2018). *Five elements of collective leadership for early childhood professionals.* Redleaf Press.

Palmer, P. J. (1997). *The courage to teach.* Jossey-Bass.

Paris, D., & Alim, H. S. (2017). *Culturally sustaining pedagogies: Teaching and learning for justice in a changing world.* Teachers College Press.

Park, C. (2011). Young children making sense of racial and ethnic differences: A sociocultural approach. *American Educational Research Journal, 48*(2), 387–420.

Park, C., LeeKeenan, D., & Given, H. (2014). A family, a fire, and a framework: Emotions in an anti-bias school community. In S. Madrid, D. Fernie, & R. Kantor (Eds.), *Reframing the emotional worlds of the early childhood classroom* (pp. 19–35). Routledge Press.

Paschall, K., Madill, R., & Halle, T. (2020). Demographic characteristics of the early care and education workforce: Comparisons with child and community characteristics

[OPRE Report #2020-108]. Office of Planning, Research, and Evaluation, Administration for Children and Families, U.S. Department of Health and Human Services.

Pelo, A., & Davidson, F. (2000). *That's not fair: A teacher's guide to activism with young children.* Redleaf Press.

Perry, I. (2019). *Breathe: A letter to my sons.* Beacon Press.

Peters, L. (2020). Activism in their own right: Children's participation in social justice movements. In S. A. Kessler & B. B. Swadener (Eds.), *Educating for social justice in early childhood* (pp. 87–99). Routledge.

Phillips, C.B. (1995). Culture: A process that empowers. In P. Mangione (Ed.), *A guide to culturally sensitive care* (pp. 2–9). WestEd and California Department of Education.

Polson, B., & Byrne-Jiménez, M. (2016). Developing a wealth mindset and a critical stance: Collaborative inquiry as a path to social justice. In S. Long, M. Souto-Manning, & V. M. Vasquez (Ed.), *Courageous leadership in early childhood education: Taking a stand for social justice* (pp. 69–79). Teachers College Press.

Raabe, T., & Beelmann, A. (2011). Development of ethnic, racial, and national prejudice in childhood and adolescence: A multinational meta-analysis of age differences. *Child Development, 82*(6), 1715–1737.

Ramsey, P. (2015). *Teaching and learning in a diverse world* (4th ed.). Teachers College Press.

Reid, J. L., & Kagan, S. L. (2022). Reaching for consensus about preschool curricula. *Phi Delta Kappan, 104*(2), 50–55.

Rideaux, K. S., & Salazar Pérez, M. (2020). Countering color-blindness in early childhood education: Elevating the embodied experiences, perspectives and voices of Black women educators. In S. A. Kessler & B. B. Swadener (Eds.), *Educating for social justice in early childhood* (pp. 20–33). Routledge.

Rinaldi, C. (2021). *In dialogue with Reggio Emilia: Listening, researching and learning* (2nd ed.). Routledge.

San Pedro, T. (2021). *Protecting the promise: Indigenous education between mothers and their children.* Teachers College Press.

Scharf, A. (2013). *Critical practices for anti-bias education.* Learning for Justice/Teaching Tolerance. https://www.learningforjustice.org/sites/default/files/2021-11/LFJ-2111-Critical-Practices-for-Anti-bias-Ed-November-2021-11172021.pdf

School Reform Initiative (SRI). (2014a). *Diversity rounds.* https://schoolreforminitiative.org/doc/diversity_rounds.pdf

School Reform Initiative (SRI). (2014b). *Four "A"s text protocol.* https://schoolreforminitiative.org/doc/4_a_text.pdf

Schwartz, R. (2016). *The skilled facilitator: A comprehensive resource for consultants, coaches and trainers* (3rd ed.). Jossey-Bass.

Shapiro, I. (2002). *Training for racial equity and inclusion: A guide to selected programs.* Aspen Institute.

Souto-Manning, M. (2013). *Multicultural teaching in the early childhood classroom: Approaches, strategies, and tools, preschool–2nd grade.* Teachers College Press.

Souto-Manning, M., Buffalo, G., & Rabadi-Raol, A. (2020). Early childhood teacher certification as a site for the re-production of racial and cultural injustice. In S. A. Kessler & B. B. Swadener (Eds.), *Educating for social justice in early childhood* (pp. 46–57). Routledge.

Stewart, F. (2019). *Building together: Collaborative leadership in early childhood systems.* Redleaf Press.

Stockwell, N. (2022). 'Holding people accountable, with love and respect': An interview with activist Loretta Ross. *The Progressive, 86*(3), 58–60.

Sullivan, D. R. (2023). *Learning to lead: Effective leadership skills for teachers of young children* (3rd ed.). Redleaf Press.

Sykes, M. (2014). *Doing the right thing for children: Eight qualities of leadership.* Redleaf Press.

Tatum, B. D. (1992). Talking about race, learning about racism: The application of racial identity development theory in the classroom. *Harvard Educational Review, 62*(1), 1–24.

Tatum, B. D. (2017). *"Why are all the black kids sitting together in the cafeteria?": And other conversations about race* (rev. ed.). Basic Books.

Terrell, A. M. (2018). *Graceful leadership in early childhood education.* Redleaf Press.

Tuhiwai Smith, L., Tuck, E., & Yang, K. W. (Eds.). (2019). *Indigenous and decolonizing studies in education: Mapping the long view.* Routledge.

Ukpokodu, O. N. (2016). *You can't teach us if you don't know us and care about us: Becoming an Ubuntu, responsive and responsible urban teacher.* Peter Lang.

UNICEF. (1990). *Fact sheet: A summary of the rights under the Convention on the Rights of the Child.* UN General Assembly. Retrieved from www.unicef.org/crc/files/Rights_overview.pdf

Van Keulen, A. (Ed.). (2004). *Young children aren't biased, are they?!: How to handle diversity in early childhood education and school.* SWP.

Vandenbroeck, M. (2007). Beyond anti-bias education: Changing conceptions of diversity and equity in European early childhood education. *European Early Childhood Education Research Journal, 15*(1), 21–35. https://doi.org/10.1080/13502930601046604

VanderVen, K. (2000). Capturing the breadth and depth of the job: The administrator as influential leader in a complex world. In M. Culkin (Ed.), *Managing quality in young children's programs: The leader's role* (pp. 112–128). Teachers College Press.

Vasquez, V. M., Long, S., & Souto-Manning, M. (2016). *The courage to lead: Strategies for action.* In S. Long, M. Souto-Manning, & V. M. Vasquez (Ed.), *Courageous leadership in early childhood education: Taking a stand for social justice* (pp. 175–185). Teachers College Press.

Virmani, E. A., & Mangione, P. L. (Eds.). (2013). *Infant/toddler caregiving: A guide to culturally sensitive care* (2nd ed.). California Department of Education.

Washington, V. (1997). Commentary on Kagan and Neuman. In S. Kagan & B. Bowman (Eds.), *Leadership in early care and education* (pp. 65–66). National Association for the Education of Young Children.

White, A., & Wanless, S. B. (2019) P.R.I.D.E.: Positive racial identity development in early education. *Journal of Curriculum, Teaching, Learning and Leadership in Education, 4*(2), 73–84.

Whitney, T. (2002). *Kids like us: Using persona dolls in the classroom.* Redleaf Press.

Wijeyesinghe, C., & Jackson, B. III. (2012). *New perspectives on racial identity development: Integrating emerging frameworks* (2nd ed.). New York University Press.

Williams, A., & Steele, J. (2019). Examining children's implicit racial attitudes using exemplar and category based measures. *Child Development, 90*(3), e322–e338.

Wong, A. (2022). *Year of the tiger: An activist life.* Vintage.

Wright, B., & Counsell, S. L. (2018). *The brilliance of Black boys: Cultivating school success in the early grades.* Teachers College Press.

Yu, H. M. (2020). Understanding race and racism among immigrant children: Insights into anti-bias education for all students. *Early Childhood Education Journal, 48*(5), 537–548. https://doi.org/10.1007/s10643-020-01021-z

York, S. (2016). *Roots and wings: Affirming culture and preventing bias in early childhood programs* (3rd ed.). Redleaf Press.

Yosso, T. (2005). Whose culture has capital? A critical race theory discussion of commu-
    nity cultural wealth. *Race Ethnicity and Education, 8*(1), 69–91.

Zeece, P. D. (2008). Power lines: The use and abuse of power in child care programming.
    In B. Neugebauer & R. Neugebauer (Eds.), *The art of leadership: Managing early child-
    hood organizations* (pp. 25–29). Exchange Press.

Index

About the Authors

Louise Derman-Sparks has worked for over 60 years on issues of diversity and equity as a preschool teacher at the Perry Preschool Project, child care center director, human development faculty member at Pacific Oaks College, and activist. She is author and co-author of several books, including *Anti-Bias Education for Young Children and Ourselves, What If All the Kids Are White? Anti-Bias/Multicultural Education for Young Children and Families*, and of numerous articles. Louise has presented keynote speeches, workshops, and consultations throughout the United States and internationally. Now retired as a professor emerita, Louise continues to write, conduct webinars, consult, and network with anti-bias educators around the world.

Debbie LeeKeenan is a lecturer, consultant, and author and has been in the field of early education for over 50 years. She is a former preschool, special education, and elementary school teacher. Debbie was director of the Eliot-Pearson Children's School at Tufts University from 1996 to 2013. She has been a member of the early childhood faculty at Tufts University, Lesley University, and the University of Massachusetts Amherst. Debbie is a producer (with John Nimmo) of the award-winning film *Reflecting on Anti-Bias Education in Action: The Early Years*, released in April 2021. Her co-authored books include *From Survive to Thrive: A Director's Guide for Leading an Early Childhood Program* and *Leading Anti-Bias Early Childhood Programs: A Guide for Change*. In addition, Debbie has published numerous chapters and articles including in *Young Children* and *Exchange*. She holds a M.Ed. from the University of New Mexico.

John Nimmo is a professor of Early Childhood Inclusive Education at Portland State University, Oregon. From 2003 to 2013, he was executive director of the Child Study and Development Center and an associate professor of Family Studies at the University of New Hampshire. In addition to presenting nationally and internationally for 40 years, he has been a visiting scholar at universities in Ghana and Australia. Formerly, he was core faculty at Pacific Oaks College Northwest in Seattle. John's co-authored books include *Emergent Curriculum* (with Elizabeth Jones) and *Loris Malaguzzi and the Teachers* (with Carolyn Edwards and Lella Gandini), as well as many chapters and articles. John's films include *The Voices of Children* and *Reflecting on Anti-Bias Education: The Early Years* (with Debbie LeeKeenan). He holds a doctorate from the University of Massachusetts Amherst and was previously an early childhood and elementary teacher in his first home of Australia and in the United States.